The English-speaking World

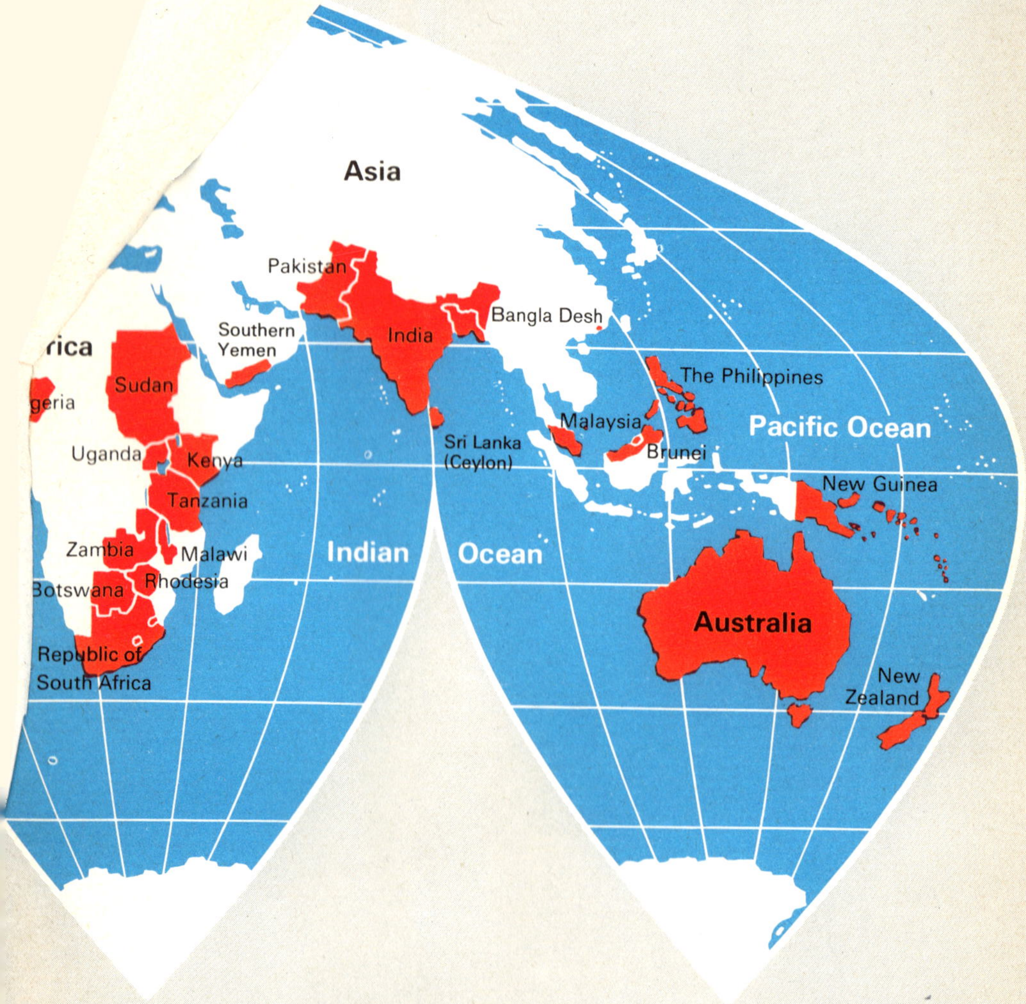

Learning English N 5/6

America Britain and the Commonwealth

an advanced language course

edited by Wilhelm Thielke in collaboration with

Siegfried Müller and Alfred Meyse

Ernst Klett Stuttgart

Learning English,
Ausgabe N

Bearbeitet von
Wilhelm Thielke, Regierungsdirektor in Lüneburg;
Alfred Meyse, Schulrat in Kiel;
Siegfried Müller, Realschuldirektor in Essen.

Das Bearbeitergremium dankt den Herren Studiendirektor Willy Piert und Oberstudiendirektor Karl Beilhardt, sowie Mr. Kenneth L. Warner für die Gestaltung der Lesestücke und die kritische Durchsicht des gesamten Manuskriptes.

Bildquellen-Nachweis: British Features, Bonn, S. 7, 27 (2—3), 28 (4), 28 (6), 59, 67, 75 (1—3), 76 (5—6); Radio Times Hulton Picture Library, London, S. 11; Paul Popper Ltd., London, S. 15, 19, 27 (1), 28 (5), 39, 76 (4); © Punch, S, 30; U.S.I.S. (Amerikadienst Stuttgart), S. 32, 35, 52 (1—3), 53 (4—6), 83, 87, 91, 93; Ford Corporation, Köln, S. 43; Australian News & Information Bureau, London, S. 56; Ullstein, Berlin, S. 80.
Illustrationen: Hans Köhler, Stuttgart

3. Auflage 3[9] 8 7 6 | 1976 75 74 73

Alle Drucke einer Auflage können im Unterricht nebeneinander benutzt werden. Die letzte Zahl bezeichnet das Jahr dieses Druckes.
© Ernst Klett Verlag, Stuttgart 1966. Nach dem Urheberrechtsgesetz vom 9. September 1965 i. d. F. vom 10. November 1972 ist die Vervielfältigung oder Übertragung urheberrechtlich geschützter Werke, also auch der Texte, Illustrationen und Graphiken dieses Buches — mit Ausnahme der in den §§ 53, 54 URG ausdrücklich genannten Sonderfälle — nicht gestattet. Dieses Verbot erstreckt sich auch auf die Vervielfältigung für Zwecke der Unterrichtsgestaltung, wenn nicht die Einwilligung des Verlages vorher eingeholt wurde. Im Einzelfall muß über die Zahlung einer Gebühr für die Nutzung fremden geistigen Eigentums entschieden werden. Als Vervielfältigung gelten alle Verfahren einschließlich der Fotokopie, der Übertragung auf Matrizen, der Speicherung auf Bändern, Platten, Transparenten oder anderen Medien.
Einbandgestaltung: H. Lämmle, Stuttgart
Druck: Ernst Klett, 7000 Stuttgart, Rotebühlstraße 77. Printed in Germany.
ISBN 3-12-095500-0

Inhalt

Alle Abschnitte, deren Ziffern in Winkelklammern < > stehen, sind unverbindlich.
(* = Gedicht)

II. The United States

III. The Commonwealth

Literary Texts contained in the lessons of this book

British Authors

American Authors

I. The British Isles

1 A. Magna Carta — The First Step to Freedom

1. Nobody had a good word to say for King John, neither his people nor his family. Before he had become king, he had tried to steal the crown from his brother, King Richard the Lionheart, who was on a crusade at that time. Now that John was king, things had become even worse.

Fearing for his crown, he murdered his young nephew, a fifteen-year-old boy.

He made the barons angry, taking their land away and forcing them to pay large sums of money to him.

Queen Elizabeth II at the opening of Parliament in London. Magna Carta laid the foundation for England's Parliament, which is the oldest in the world.

He made the townspeople and merchants angry, seizing their goods and hindering their business.

He made everybody else angry, throwing men into prison without any trial. Many lost their lives in jail.

At last some of the great barons wanted to put an end to it all. Together with the Archbishop of Canterbury they drew up a long list of what the King should not do in future. It was so long that they called it 'Magna Carta' or the Great Charter. They sent it to John and threatened to seize his castles if he did not agree to it.

John listened, frowning while the sentences were read. He heard that he had to promise not to ask for money without the consent of the lords and bishops. He had to promise not to put free men into prison without a fair trial. He had to promise to let the merchants travel in peace.

When John had heard the contents of the Charter, his face changed colour. "Why don't they make me a slave?" he cried. "Why don't they take all my kingdom?" In a rage he threw himself on the floor, shouting that he would promise nothing.

2. The date was June 15th, 1215. Barons, bishops and wealthy merchants together with a great number of soldiers had left London early in the morning. They all had a common aim. They were on their way to Runnymede, a field on the River Thames. After some hours they could see the royal banner on a large tent. The King was already at Runnymede. The lords had only one thought: Would John sign the Charter? And if he did, would he keep his promises? Could anybody trust him?

King John was sitting in his tent. When the barons arrived, his face did not show any anger. He even managed to smile, although inwardly he was boiling with fury.

The Archbishop of Canterbury unrolled the parchment on the table.

"Would your Majesty fix the seal to the Charter, please?" he asked. John sat there looking round. The men in the field were his enemies. Each of them was heavily armed. What could he do? "They can ask me anything," he thought. "I'll just have to do it. But my time will come."

And he put his seal to Magna Carta.

3. From that moment onwards, John's only thought was of revenge. As many had expected, he did not keep the promises he had given in the Great Charter. He got money and help from abroad. Soon the news spread that he was gathering a large army to punish every lord who had been at Runnymede. Like a whirlwind he swept down the Thames valley with his soldiers. Any resistance he met was broken immediately.

His campaign was making good progress when death struck him down. He died suddenly after a meal, and many believed he had been poisoned.

His son, Henry III, upon the advice of the Archbishop of Canterbury, confirmed the Charter, which has remained a living document of English liberty until today. It is to be seen at the British Museum in London.

<B. London Through the Ages>

London was already a town in the days of the Romans, but in the first ten centuries of our time it remained a small south-eastern port on the Thames. The royal residence of the Anglo-Saxon kings was Winchester. Yet at the time when the Great Charter was signed, London had already become England's largest city.

In the 16th century the capital was one of the most important cities in Europe. More than 100,000 people lived within its walls flanked by the mighty Tower.

Not very far away to the south-west, also on the River Thames, was another city, much smaller in comparison, the royal city of Westminster, where Parliament used to meet. It contained Westminster Abbey and its famous school, the royal Palace of Whitehall, government offices and the houses of courtiers. All English kings and queens since William the Conqueror have been crowned in Westminster Abbey. The walk from Westminster to London along the Thames led through green fields past the village of Charing Cross, where one could stop to have a drink.

Today Charing Cross is one of the busiest parts of the huge ant-hill called Greater London, which has a population of 12 million and is not only the capital of Great Britain but also the centre of the Commonwealth. Its ancient heart, the City, has become the business centre with a day population of 440,000 and a night population of only 5,000.

London is also the biggest industrial town in England and the largest port. 23 per cent of Britain's exports are sent from the Port of London; its docks stretch 36 miles along the River Thames.

Millions of Londoners spend hours daily in suburban trains, buses and the Underground, taking them from the suburbs into town and back again. They lunch in crowded restaurants, in canteens, eat their sandwiches in city offices, or, in fine weather, in the open air, in parks and even on the steps of St. Paul's Cathedral.

Though everyone wants to get home as quickly as possible in the evening, the discipline of the people in the traffic rush is one of London's most striking features.

<**Anecdotes**>

1. Politeness. On a narrow country road two cars approached each other from opposite directions. The road was not wide enough for them to pass, so both cars stopped. Neither of the drivers would give way to the other. Neither of them said a word.

After a few minutes' silence one driver took a newspaper from his pocket and began to read. Half an hour later, with the silence still unbroken, the other driver put his head out of the car window and said: "When you've finished—perhaps you'd be kind enough to lend me your paper."

2. A Difficult Choice.

1st Voter: Did you see the candidates?

2nd Voter: Yes.

1st Voter: And what did you think of them?

2nd Voter: Well—I thought what a blessing it is that only one of them can get into the House of Commons!

3. A Question of Conscience. A man appeared in court, charged with selling his vote to both the Conservative and Labour candidates.

"Do you admit having received five pounds from the Conservative candidate?" asked the judge.

"Yes, my Lord."

"And do you also admit having received five pounds from the Labour candidate?"

"Yes, my Lord."

"But how on earth did you vote, then?" asked the astonished judge.

"According to my conscience, my Lord."

4. A Compromise. Once upon a time there were three diplomats, one of whom was British. They were disputing the possession of a recently discovered island. At the end the Englishman took one of his two colleagues aside.

"Let's make a compromise," he said. "You say that the island is mine and I will say that it doesn't belong to him."

5. The Dismissal. The head of a store noticed a boy whistling. "How much a week do you get?" he asked. "£2," replied the boy.—"Here's a week's money—now clear out."

The boy went. "When did we hire that boy?" the boss asked a departmental manager. "Never," answered the manager. "He was waiting for a reply to a message."

A turning-point in the history of the railway. George Stephenson's 'Rocket' wins the locomotive race at Rainhill, Lancashire, in 1829.

2 A. The Railway Story

1. "If anything is ridiculous," wrote a reporter in the 'Quarterly Review' in 1825, "it is the idea that locomotives are to travel twice as fast as horse coaches. We think that Parliament will fix the speed at eight miles an hour, which is considered to be the safety limit. There are enough good horses in England to take us through the country safely and quickly."

Four years later, at Rainhill in Lancashire, directors and engineers of the new Liverpool and Manchester Railway watched anxiously as three locomotives raced side by side in their attempt to win the £ 500 prize offered by the company for the best engine.

The winner, brightly painted in black, white and yellow, had a tall stove-pipe funnel. Her name was the 'Rocket'. Her fastest speed had been twenty miles per hour.

A week later her builder, George Stephenson, was appointed chief engineer of the Liverpool and Manchester Railway.

A year later Stephenson had a newer and better engine built, the 'Planet'. She did the journey from Manchester to Liverpool at an average speed of 31 m.p.h.

2. But the public still remained suspicious of the railway until in 1842 Queen Victoria decided to have a ride in a train. There was an immediate outcry: "Don't let the Queen risk her life!" "Britons! Don't be indifferent to the danger our Queen is in!" "We have got to protect our Queen!" But the Queen did travel by train.

"The journey was very pleasant," she said as she returned to Paddington Station. The nation at once changed its attitude towards the railways. The railway fever began. Railway companies shot up overnight and began covering the country with rails, sometimes laying them side by side along the same routes. When the fever died down, the smaller companies disappeared and thousands who had taken the railways for gold mines were ruined.

Finally, only a few great companies remained, dividing up the country into regions. That is why every great London station is a terminus. They belonged to different companies, for example Victoria Station to the Southern Railway, Paddington to the Great Western. Even today a traveller coming from the Continent has to cross London by Underground, bus or taxi to reach another station if he wants to go to the north, east or west of England.

The race for the fastest train was to develop between those companies. The three lines which ran between London and Edinburgh were bitter rivals. Month after month they had the speed improved with the result that the journey which had taken more than nine hours was in 1888 reduced to seven hours and thirty-two minutes.

3. The magic hundred miles an hour was not achieved until 1904 when an engine thundered through Somerset at the world speed record of 102·3 m.p.h. That record was to remain safe until 126 m.p.h. were reached in 1938.

Then the Diesel locomotives took over. The Germans seized the record when a Diesel train ran at over 133 m.p.h. between Hamburg and Berlin in 1938. The war broke out. When peace came France needed to rebuild and modernize her railways. She had powerful new electric locomotives built, and one of these broke the existing world record with a speed of 151 m.p.h. A year later two more French engines reached the speed of 205 m.p.h., and in 1965 a Japanese locomotive set up a new record with 207 m.p.h. Will any other locomotive ever go faster?

Now Britain, too, is joining the ranks of countries which have electrified their main lines. The rivalry of the different railway companies, however, does not exist any more. After World War II they were nationalized by the Government under the banner of 'British Railways'. But new rivals have appeared in the field of transportation: motor-cars of all kinds and the aeroplanes. They are mighty competitors to the railways both in England and the rest of the world.

B. Conversation: Going by Train

1st traveller: Excuse me, is this anybody's seat?

2nd traveller: I'm afraid so, but the corner seat is vacant.

1st traveller: Thank you, I nearly missed the train. I took a taxi at Victoria, and there was a traffic jam at Hyde Park Corner.

2nd traveller: I caught it in the nick of time myself. It's due to start any moment.

1st traveller: We are off. The train is bound for Birmingham, isn't it?

2nd traveller: Yes, it is a non-stop train.

1st traveller: A non-stop train? But I want to get off at Leamington Spa. I must change at Leamington for Stratford-on-Avon.

2nd traveller: You'll have to travel back from Birmingham to Leamington by another train.

1st traveller: Is there a good connection from Birmingham?

2nd traveller: You may look at my time-table if you like.

1st traveller: Oh, thank you *(consults the time-table)*. There is an express train from Birmingham at 11 a.m. I'll have an hour's wait at Leamington to get the connection to Stratford.

2nd traveller: Are you going to see a play of Shakespeare's?

1st traveller: Yes, I've booked a seat for the matinée at the Royal Theatre. I'm going back to London tonight. The train is due back at Paddington at 10.25 p.m.

2nd traveller: Do you mind if I open the window? The air is rather stuffy in this compartment.

1st traveller: Yes, it is quite close in here. Do you know if the dining-car is in the front or in the rear?

2nd traveller: It's in the rear. I'm afraid you are not allowed to smoke in here. This is a non-smoker, and the penalty is nearly as heavy as if you pulled the communication cord.

1st traveller: Thank you for drawing my attention to it. I think I'll look for a smoker.

<Stephenson and his Opponents>

Many members of Parliament tried to prove that Stephenson's railway plans were foolish and dangerous. At a meeting one of them asked Stephenson:

"Suppose now, one of these engines was going along at nine or ten miles an hour and a cow strayed on the line. Would that not be awkward?"

"Yes," replied Stephenson, "very awkward—for the cow!"

<**Night Mail** — an extract>

This is the night mail crossing the border,
Bringing the cheque and the postal order,
Letters for the rich, letters for the poor,
The shop at the corner and the girl next door.
Pulling up Beattock, a steady climb—
The gradient's against her, but she's on time.

Dawn freshens, the climb is done.
Down toward Glasgow she descends
Towards the steam tugs yelping down the glade of cranes,
Towards the fields of apparatus, the furnaces
Set on the dark plain like gigantic chessmen.
All Scotland waits for her:
In the dark glens, beside the pale-green lochs
Men long for news.

Letters of thanks, letters from banks,
Letters of joy from girl and boy,
Receipted bills and invitations
To inspect new stock or visit relations,
And applications for situations
And timid lovers' declarations,
And gossip, gossip from all the nations,
News circumstantial, news financial,
Letters from uncles, cousins, and aunts,
Letters to Scotland from the South of France,
Written on paper of every hue,
The pink, the violet, the white and the blue,
Clever, stupid, short and long,
The typed and the printed and the spelt all wrong.

Thousands are still asleep,
Asleep in working Glasgow, asleep in well-set Edinburgh,
Asleep in granite Aberdeen,
They continue their dreams,
But shall wake soon and long for letters,
And none will hear the postman's knock
Without a quickening of heart;—
For who can hear and feel himself forgotten?

Wystan Hugh Auden

Blackpool is the main seaside resort for the great industrial cities of Lancashire. Every year more than 7,000,000 people spend their holidays there.

3 A. From the Cradle to the Grave

1. Six o'clock in the morning. The hooting of the factory sirens wakes up the people of Oldham, Lancashire. Lights begin to show in the dark windows of the small houses. John and Nancy Robinson jump out of bed. John is a fitter, Nancy a packer in the same factory. They have two sons, Derek, aged sixteen, and Kevin, his fifteen-year-old brother.

Sixteen-year-old Derek will have to sit for his school-leaving examination this summer in order to get his General Certificate of Education at Ordinary Level (GCE 'O' Level). He wants to become a scientific assistant at Harwell, the Atomic Energy Centre of Great Britain.

"How are things at school, Derek?" asks his father at breakfast.

"Pretty grim, Dad."

"Will you be able to make it? You could if you wanted to."

"You know I want to. I shan't be allowed to enter Harwell if I haven't got my GCE in at least four subjects, and two of them must be English and mathematics."

"You ought to make it," says his mother. "You're good at mathematics."

"I should be all right in maths," says Derek. "It's English that worries me."

Both Derek and Kevin attend the secondary technical school. There are no school fees, and their books do not cost them anything, and school dinners cost 10p.

2. Five mornings a week Mr. and Mrs. Robinson drive to the factory in their new car, which like their TV set, refrigerator and washing-machine, they have bought by hire-purchase. Sometimes they go to the cinema, and John is a regular customer at the 'Red Lion'.

Once a year Oldham's factories shut for a fortnight in the summer, and the 150,000 inhabitants—including the Robinsons—will go to Blackpool where they hope to enjoy the sun for two weeks on its sandy beach.

"We might have more luck with the weather next year," Mrs. Robinson will say every time they leave Blackpool and return home in the rain, but they all agree that they couldn't have a better holiday anywhere else.

"After all we mustn't forget that it may even rain in Spain," says Kevin, for whom the slot-machines on the pier are the chief attraction of Blackpool.

3. Can the Robinsons afford to live that way? Of course they can. John and Nancy earn together about £45 a week. They don't have to save for illness or unemployment. They pay the State about £16 a week in income tax and contributions to National Health Service and National Insurance. This is rather a big sum, but it means social security for the whole family.

A few weeks ago the teacher sent Kevin home. He hadn't been well for days, and suddenly during lessons he felt sick. When his parents came home at half past five, they found him lying in bed. In the evening the doctor came and diagnosed pneumonia. Kevin was taken to hospital the same night. A week later he was at home again. Thanks to the National Health Service the Robinsons did not have to pay anything for the doctor's visits, the medicine, the hospital treatment and accommodation.

4. State help begins at birth, which need not cost the parents a penny. The State puts £22 in the cradle of each new-born baby. Family allowances are also paid for all children after the first.

Should people save for old age? They are not obliged to. Even if people haven't been able or didn't want to save, they won't have to starve when they are old. Nancy at the age of 60, and John at the age of 65 will each receive a pension of at least £5 a week.

And when the death bell rings for a member of the family, the State will pay part of the funeral costs. So from the cradle to the grave the Welfare State looks after the whole family.

<B. A Sunday in Harlech>

Harlech in North Wales has been a town since the 13th century. To the west it faces the Irish Sea, to the north the blue mountains of Snowdonia. It is a very small town of about 1,100 souls. Yet it has seven churches for seven different religious communities, the largest being the Anglicans with 300 members.

It is Sunday morning. The inhabitants leave their grey stone houses and walk in different directions. Some go to the Anglican church whose bell is calling insistently. Opposite, on the other side of High Street, the Baptist church has its door wide open. A little further down to the right the Methodist minister welcomes the members of his congregation in front of the steps leading to his church. No further than two hundred yards along the street the Congregationalists have their church, and the last in the row is the white St. David's chapel of the Roman Catholics. The Presbyterian church is a little down the hill, while the Scottish Baptists have formed a community of their own, which meets in a small church above the town.

The Anglican church reminds one very much in decoration of a Roman Catholic church. It has coloured glass windows depicting scenes from the Bible, the eternal light burns above the altar, the font dates from the 15th century, a time when all Britain was Roman Catholic. The other churches in Harlech, except the Catholic church, are very plain. No decoration, no cross, no statue, no pictures on the walls, no coloured glass windows. There is no altar either. Just a platform for the minister, a table with the Bible on it, an organ. Music and community singing play an important part in the services of the 'Free Churches'. The Methodist Hymn Book contains more than a thousand hymns.

Religious activity in Harlech is typical of the diversity of Christian worship all over Britain.

<The Case for the Defence>

A man called Adams has been arrested for the murder of an old woman. Mrs. Salmon, who saw Adams leaving the old woman's house, is giving evidence at the trial.

The counsel for the Crown brought the story gently out. Mrs. Salmon spoke very firmly. Yes, she said, and then she had gone downstairs and rung up the police station.

"And do you see the man here in court?"

She looked straight across at the big man in the dock.

"Yes," she said, "there he is."

"You are quite certain?"

She said simply, "I couldn't be mistaken, sir."

"Thank you, Mrs. Salmon."

Counsel for the defence rose to cross-examine.

"Now, Mrs. Salmon, you must remember that a man's life may depend on your evidence."

"I do remember it, sir."

"Is your eyesight good?"

"I have never had to wear spectacles, sir."

"You are a woman of fifty-five?"—"Fifty-six, sir."

"And the man you saw was on the other side of the road?"—"Yes, sir."

"And it was two o'clock in the morning. You must have remarkable eyes."

"No, sir. There was moonlight, and when the man looked up, he had the lamplight on his face."

"And you have no doubt whatever that the man you saw is the prisoner?"

"None whatever, sir. It isn't a face one forgets."

Counsel took a look round the court for a moment. Then he said: "Do you mind, Mrs. Salmon, examining again the people in court? No, not the prisoner. Stand up, please, Mr. Adams," and there at the back of the court was the exact image of the man in the dock. He was even dressed the same.

"Now think very carefully, Mrs. Salmon. Can you still swear that the man you saw drop the hammer in Mrs. Parker's garden was the prisoner—and not this man, who is his twin brother?"

Of course she couldn't. She looked from one to the other and didn't say a word.

What we saw then was the end of the case. There wasn't a witness prepared to swear that it was the prisoner he'd seen. And the brother? He had his alibi, too; he was with his wife.

And so the man was acquitted for lack of evidence. But whether—if he did the murder and not his brother—he was punished or not, I don't know. That extraordinary day had an extraordinary end. I followed Mrs. Salmon out of the court and we got wedged in the crowd who were waiting, of course, for the twins. The police tried to get the twins to leave by a back way, but they wouldn't. One of them—no one knew which—said, "I've been acquitted, haven't I?" and they walked out of the front entrance. Then the crowd moved and somehow one of the twins got pushed on to the road right in front of a bus.

He gave a squeal like a rabbit and that was all; he was dead. Divine vengeance? I wish I knew. There was the other Adams getting on his feet from beside the body and looking straight over at Mrs. Salmon. He was crying, but whether he was the murderer or the innocent man, nobody will ever be able to tell. But if you were Mrs. Salmon, could you sleep at night?

Graham Greene (abridged)

A model of the proposed Channel tunnel between England and France. It is really two tunnels, each with four lanes of traffic and a railway at the side.

4 A. The Tunnel Project

In the school magazine of St. John's School, Folkestone, the following article appeared in June 1972:

"The school discussion group met last month. The subject for discussion: *'That the tunnel planned between Folkestone and Calais will bring progress and prosperity to this country.'* A number of Folkestone residents were present.

Robert Foster of the Sixth Form introduced the subject.

"For 168 years, engineers and statesmen have dreamt of building a tunnel under the English Channel. Today that dream is about to become reality. If everything goes according to plan, travellers will be able to go by train under the Channel as easily as they go now by Underground under the Thames. No longer, when a thick fog covers southern England, will London newspapers announce, "Continent Isolated!" No longer shall we spend six unhappy hours on a crossing which should have lasted two hours. No longer shall we be seasick when a storm rages on the sea.

Electric trains will take people from England to France in 30 minutes. Motor-cars and lorries will be carried on double-deck trains, each with room for three hundred vehicles. The trains will run every five minutes. Tunnel fares for motor-cars will be 30 per cent cheaper than the present ones."

"Would it not be more practical if a motorway were built instead of a railway?" asked Colin Brown, of the Fifth.

"I expected this question," replied Robert Foster. "The proposed tunnel between Folkestone and Calais will be the longest transportation tunnel in the world; 23 of its 32 miles will be under water. 7,200 cars an hour will be transported. If all those cars were to drive through, the exhaust fumes would make a much more expensive ventilation system necessary. Already the whole project will cost about £300 million. But the money will be well invested. The economic advantage will be enormous. Freight costs will be 50 per cent less than they are today. Our goods to the Continent will be cheaper and our imports from the other European Common Market countries less expensive. Folkestone will no longer be a quiet seaside resort. It will become the gateway to the Continent."

Alan Winter of the Fifth stood up. "I'm absolutely against this tunnel project," he began. "What will become of our harbour and our Channel ferries? Furthermore, what's the use of a tunnel which would be destroyed in the case of war? You'll admit that if the tunnel had been built before the Second World War, it would have been blown up, probably by ourselves to prevent the enemy from using it. What a waste of time and money."

"May I tell you, sir," interrupted Colonel Walker, a retired army officer and resident of Folkestone, "that the First World War would have been two years shorter if we could have sent our supplies through a Channel tunnel."

"The situation today is quite different, sir," replied Winter. "If the supplies for our troops were to be sent through the tunnel, modern rockets would easily reach Folkestone and destroy the whole town. That would be the fate of our peaceful seaside resort."

"If we were to follow such pessimistic ideas," objected James Smith of the Fourth, "we might as well give up the idea of any larger enterprise. Why build skyscrapers, bridges, motorways? Progress would come to a standstill."

"Even without a war," continued Winter, "the tunnel project is a risky project. As you all know, there was a time when Britain was not an island, when the Thames was a tributary of the Rhine, and the North Sea dry land. The Channel came into being by earthquakes. Remember the last earthquake we had in October 1963 on the coast near Portsmouth? A tunnel wouldn't have stood it. The ground near our south coast is still unstable. The cracks in the tunnel will let the water through and a catastrophe will be the result. Let Folkestone remain a peaceful seaside resort for retired people who enjoy

our seaside air, the sun, and a sea-journey to France; let Britain remain an island."

The discussion that followed was as lively as any in Parliament. Unfortunately there is not enough space for a further report on this interesting question. However, it may be said that the majority of those present were in favour of the tunnel. No doubt, after this the tunnel shares will rise on the Stock Exchange."

<B. Some English Traits>

1. Self-control. The Englishman has been trained not to show his feelings. This is called self-control. That is what English boys and girls are taught at school, that is what many of them will try to practise in later life.

The true story of how two British explorers met in Africa nearly a hundred years ago is still told today as a typical example of English self-control. The missionary and explorer David Livingstone had disappeared in the interior of Africa, and everybody believed that he was dead. Another explorer, H. M. Stanley, went to Africa to find him. After months of great hardship he at last stood face to face with the missing missionary.

Did the two men fall on each other's necks when they met? Nothing of the kind. "Dr. Livingstone, I presume?" said Stanley as if addressing him at an English garden-party.

2. A Nation of Sport Fans. Self-control also plays an important part in sport. This attitude towards sport began in the public schools and has been maintained on school playing-fields ever since. To win or to lose is considered less important than 'playing the game', that is playing fair according to the rules, and it is praise when someone is spoken of as 'a good loser'.

Sport is the Englishman's pastime and his passion. A famous scientist or artist can never become as popular as professional footballers, boxers, jockeys, or cricketers. Two famous sportsmen, Sir Gordon Richards, the jockey, and Sir Stanley Matthews, the footballer, have been knighted by the Queen.

Sport is one of the contributions that England has made to the other countries of the world.

3. Love of Animals. There is scarcely a home in England without at least one kind of animal, dogs and cats being the most popular. The best place in front of the fire or the best arm-chair in the room is not considered too good for 'Fluffy', the dog, or 'Whisky', the cat. They are members of the family. There is a dogs' cemetery in Kensington Gardens, and the London Zoo's special darlings are

given names which are familiar to everyone. "When I read that that poor little monkey was sent up into space in a rocket," wrote a lady to a newspaper, "I wept bitterly and I was not ashamed of it."

Although the English like to hide their feelings, they often show great affection for animals.

<**A Prospect of the Sea**>

It was high summer, and the boy was lying in the corn. He was happy because he had no work to do and the weather was hot. He heard the corn sway from side to side above him, and the noise of the birds who whistled from the branches of the trees that hid the house. Lying flat on his back, he stared up into the unbrokenly blue sky falling over the edge of the corn. The wind, after the warm rain before noon, smelt of rabbits and cattle. He stretched himself like a cat, and put his arms behind his head. Now he was riding on the sea, swimming through the golden corn waves, gliding along the heavens like a bird; in seven-league boots he was leaping over the fields; he was building a nest in the sixth of the seven trees that waved their hands from a bright, green hill. Now he was a boy with tousled hair, rising lazily to his feet, wandering out of the corn to the strip of river by the hillside. He put his fingers in the water, making a mock seawave to roll the stones over and shake the weeds; his fingers stood up like ten tower pillars in the magnifying water, and a fish with a wise head and a lashing tail swam in and out of the tower gates. He made up a story as the fish swam through the gates into the pebbles and the moving bed. There was a drowned princess from a Christmas book, with her shoulders broken and her two red pigtails stretched like the strings of a fiddle over her broken throat; she was caught in a fisherman's net, and the fish plucked her hair. He forgot how the story ended, if ever there were an end to a story that had no beginning. Did the princess live again, rising like a mermaid from the net, or did a prince from another story tauten the pigtails of her hair and bend her shoulder-bone into a harp and pluck the dead, black tunes for ever in the courts of the royal country? The boy sent a stone skidding over the green water. He saw a rabbit scuttle, and threw a stone at its tail. A fish leaped at the gnats, and a lark darted out of the green earth. This was the best summer since the first seasons of the world. There were no chimneys on the hills in the distance, only the trees which stood like women and men enjoying the sun. He could think of no words to say how wonderful the summer was, or the noise of the wood-pigeons. There were no words for the sky and the sun and the summer country: the birds were nice, and the corn was nice.

Dylan Thomas

<Britain and the British>

The Face of Britain

When people speak of Britain, they often use different expressions to mean the same thing. Sometimes they say 'The British Isles' or 'The United Kingdom'; sometimes they say 'Great Britain'; and sometimes, quite wrongly, they speak of the whole group of islands as 'England'. Let us first see what all these different expressions really mean.

1. The British Isles consist of two large islands—Great Britain and Ireland—and a large number of smaller islands. Together they cover an area of 121,000 sq. miles with a population of about 55 million. Between 1801 and 1921 they were all united in one state, but today Southern Ireland, under the name of Eire, is an independent republic.

2. The United Kingdom consists of Great Britain and Northern Ireland—that is all the countries of the British Isles which recognize Elizabeth II as their queen. Her official title is: 'Elizabeth the Second, by the Grace of God of the United Kingdom of Great Britain and Northern Ireland and of Her other Realms and Territories Queen, Head of the Commonwealth'. The United Kingdom is often simply called Britain.

3. Great Britain is the largest of the British Isles. It includes Scotland, Wales and England.

4. England is the south-eastern part of Great Britain. With an area of 50,000 sq. miles and a population of 45 million it is the largest and most densely populated part of the United Kingdom. From the earliest times England has always been the most powerful country of the British Isles. That is why many foreigners still speak of 'England' when they really mean Great Britain or the United Kingdom.

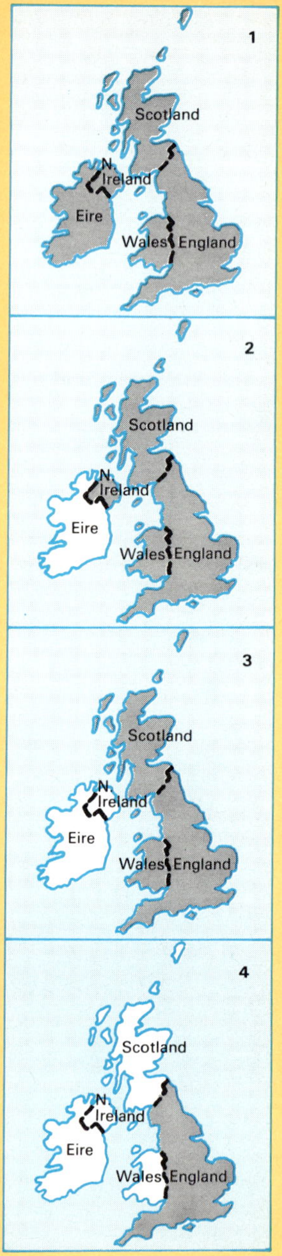

The Britons

A seafaring nation. The British Isles are separated from the mainland of Europe by the English Channel. From the cliffs near Dover, on a clear day, one can see the coast of France across this narrow stretch of water which has played such an important part in the history of the islands. For nearly a thousand years, since the Normans conquered the country in 1066, the Channel has often saved the country from invasion.

The British are islanders. They speak of their country as 'our island home', and, indeed, no place in Great Britain is more than 70 miles from the coast. The sea is never far from Englishmen's thoughts. It has always been a favourite subject of their poets and musicians, and many of the most famous figures in British history, men like Drake, Captain Cook and Nelson, have been seamen. It was sea-power that enabled Britain to found a huge empire overseas, and it was sea-power that held the Empire together and kept its trade routes open. For 450 years the British have been a seafaring nation, and this has had a deep influence on their history and their way of life.

A nation of town-dwellers. Among the countries of the world Britain is seventy-fifth in size, but in population she is eleventh, with 55 million people. 80% of these live in towns, and most of the remaining 20%, who live in the country, work in towns. Only 4% of the whole population work in agriculture.

During the 19th century the industrialization of Britain drew more and more people from the country into the growing factory towns, and today 40% of the whole population live in eight industrial centres. The largest of these is Greater London, an area within forty miles of central London, with a population of 12 million. The other seven centres are Birmingham, Manchester, Leeds, Newcastle-on-Tyne, Glasgow, Belfast and Cardiff.

Although in Wales and Scotland there are large areas with almost no inhabitants, the average density of Britain's population is one of the highest in the world—587 per square mile.

An industrial nation. Britain is first and foremost an industrial country, and her chief industrial areas are mainly centred on her rich iron and coal-fields. The great metal works of Birmingham and the Black Country produce everything from needles to locomotives. Manchester and Leeds are the centres of the cotton and wool industries, and in the London area there are countless factories, which mass-produce articles of every kind, large and small.

Shipbuilding is still a very important British industry, and Glasgow, Newcastle and Belfast are its main centres. Some industries are nationalized. They include coal-mining, gas and electricity production and railways.

Population and Industry

Persons per square mile

- Less than 100
- 100—500
- 500—1100 and over

Main industrial centres

1 London: miscellaneous
2 Birmingham and the Black Country: iron, steel
3 Manchester: cotton
4 Leeds: wool
5 Newcastle: coal, ships
6 Glasgow: coal, ships
7 Belfast: ships
8 Cardiff: coal, iron, steel

The quick development of industry during the 19th century meant that agriculture was neglected for many years. The bad effects of that are still felt today. Before World War II Britain produced only a third of the food she needed. During the war great efforts were made to make the country more self-supporting, and today 70% of the land is farmed. In spite of this, however, Britain can still only produce enough food for half the population. The rest must be imported and paid for by exports of manufactured goods.

Politics and the State

The oldest Parliament. The British system of parliamentary government has developed gradually during the past 700 years and has had a deep influence on parliamentary institutions in other countries, especially in those which belong to the Commonwealth.

Parliament today consists of two Houses—the House of Lords and the House of Commons. The main parliamentary power is centred in the House of Commons, whose 630 members represent the people. They are elected at a general election, which is normally held every five years. The members of the House of Lords are not elected, but they sit there by right of birth or nomination.

There are three parties: the Conservative Party, the Labour Party and the Liberal Party, which is very small. The party which wins the majority of seats at a general election forms the Government, and its leader becomes Prime Minister, who then chooses his cabinet ministers. The largest minority party becomes 'Her Majesty's Opposition'.

The most important official of the House of Commons is the Speaker, whose task is to see that all members obey the rules during a debate. In spite of his title he rarely speaks himself except to call a member to order or to explain a rule of the House. He is elected by the other members and is usually a man with long experience of Parliament and a great reputation for fairness.

The British Monarchy. The Monarchy is Britain's oldest institution, and the British sovereign can trace his descent back to the 9th century.

For many centuries the Monarch held supreme power, but, with the growth of Parliament, this power gradually decreased. Today the Crown plays no active part in politics. The sovereign reigns, but he does not govern. All political decisions are taken in his name, but the responsibility for them lies with the Government.

The sovereign has no power but a great personal influence on the whole life of the nation. Queen Elizabeth II, Britain's present monarch, symbolizes not only the unity of the United Kingdom but of the whole Commonwealth.

Important People

Five hundred years ago Britain was of little importance in the world. Yet in the next 450 years that small country built up the greatest empire the world had ever seen. At the height of its power, the British Government ruled over more than a quarter of the world's surface and controlled the fates of 600 million people.

Today the British Empire belongs to the past. In its place we have the Commonwealth, a free association of independent countries, no longer as powerful as the Empire of the past, yet still with an important voice in the affairs of the world.

The British people look back with pride on their past and on the many famous figures who made their contribution to British history.

1 *Queen Elizabeth I* (1533—1603) During the reign of Elizabeth I the English became a strong and united nation. The famous 'Sea Dogs', such men as Drake and Raleigh, challenged the power of Spain at sea. Although Elizabeth strove to avoid war she was fearless in an emergency. When the Spanish invasion threatened, she called the country to arms with the famous words: "I may have the body of a woman, but I have the heart of a king."

After the defeat of the Armada in 1588, English traders and explorers were able to travel all over the world. England became increasingly prosperous, and the first plans were made to found colonies overseas.

2 *William Shakespeare* (1564—1616) The reign of Elizabeth I has also been called the Golden Age of English literature. The dominant figure of this time was William Shakespeare, the greatest dramatist and poet of the English language.

As a young man Shakespeare left his birthplace, Stratford-upon-Avon, and went to London, where he became an actor and theatre manager. The plays he wrote are still as popular today as they were in Elizabethan London. As a friend of his said, Shakespeare was 'not for an age, but for all time'.

Some of Shakespeare's most famous plays are Hamlet, Macbeth, Julius Caesar, As You Like it, A Midsummer Night's Dream, Romeo and Juliet and The Merchant of Venice.

3 *Oliver Cromwell* (1599—1658) The 17th century was a time of great conflict between King and Parliament. James I and Charles I wished to rule without parliament, and at the same time the Puritans, a religious sect, were persecuted for their belief. Under Oliver Cromwell, a devout Puritan, the supporters of Parliament revolted against the king, and the Civil War followed (1642—49). King Charles I was defeated and executed, and Britain became a republic with Oliver Cromwell as its head.

4

5

6

His rule lasted from 1649—1658. As a strict Puritan, Cromwell tried to make people virtuous by force. He banned the theatre and forbade music, dancing and sports on Sundays. But he also succeeded in making his country more powerful and more respected abroad than it had ever been before.

4 *Queen Victoria* (1819—1901) The long reign of Queen Victoria was a time of almost uninterrupted peace and great material progress. The rapid growth of industry made Britain the world's leading industrial nation—'the workshop of the world', as she was called—and the British Empire reached the height of its power when Queen Victoria was proclaimed Empress of India in 1876. During her long life the Queen herself became a symbol of Britain's greatness.

In 1840 Victoria married Prince Albert of Saxe-Coburg-Gotha and lived happily with him until he died in 1861. After his death she led a lonely life, withdrew from public affairs, and could only rarely be persuaded to visit London. When Victoria died in 1901 after a reign of 63 years, the world stood on the threshold of the 20th century, and many English people felt that a great age had passed for ever.

5 *Charles Dickens* (1812—1870) The Victorian Age was a time of great prosperity in England. Yet under the surface of wealth and power there was also great poverty. There was a world of difference between the mansions of the new industrialists and the slums of the factory workers.

Many voices were raised against these social inequalities, but there was one man who did more than any other to make his fellow-countrymen aware of the need for reform. He was the novelist Charles Dickens.

Dickens was born into a poor family. When his father was imprisoned for debt, the boy had to go to work in a factory. He never forgot the bitter experiences of his childhood, which were later reflected in the great novels

which brought him world fame. In 'Oliver Twist' and in 'David Copperfield' Dickens gave unforgettable pictures of the lives of the poor. Yet his anger against injustice was always warmed by humour and a deep humanity. These qualities appear clearly in 'The Pickwick Papers' and in the best-known Christmas story in the English language, 'A Christmas Carol'.

6 *Sir Winston Churchill* (1874—1965) To Britain, as to many other countries, the 20th century brought far-reaching changes, which were hastened by two world wars. Out of this time one great figure emerges—Sir Winston Churchill.

After an adventurous youth in the army and as a war correspondent in South Africa, Churchill was elected to Parliament in 1900. Between 1906 and 1929 he held many Government posts, but in the 1930s he was out of favour. Again and again he warned the country of the danger of war and the need to be prepared, but few listened to him. Only when war had broken out was he called to power.

Churchill proved a brilliant war leader. "I have nothing to offer but blood, toil, tears and sweat," he said when he became Prime Minister. His determination, sincerity and inspiring leadership contributed greatly towards the Allied victory in 1945.

Important Dates

1066	William the Conqueror invades England
1215	King John signs Magna Carta, the corner-stone of English liberty
1275	First Parliament
1533/1603	Queen Elizabeth I
1588	Defeat of the Armada—England now a great sea power
1564/1616	William Shakespeare, England's greatest poet
1603	Union of England and Scotland
1607	First British colony founded on the American mainland
1642/1649	Civil War between King and Parliament
1649/1658	England a republic under Cromwell and the Puritans
1660	England again a monarchy under Charles II
1775/1781	American War of Independence
1803/1815	Napoleonic War
1819/1901	Queen Victoria—Britain becomes a great industrial power
1914/1918	World War I
1939/1945	World War II
1953	Coronation of Queen Elizabeth II
1874/1965	Winston Churchill
1973	Britain joins the Common Market

A Warning to Beginners

In England everything is the other way round.

On Sundays on the Continent even the poorest person puts on his best suit, tries to look respectable, and at the same time the life of the country becomes gay and cheerful; in England even the richest peer dresses in some peculiar rags, does not shave, and the country becomes dull and dreary.

On the Continent there is one topic which should be avoided—the weather; in England, if you do not repeat the phrase "Lovely day, isn't it?" at least two hundred times a day, you are considered a bit dull.

On the Continent people use a fork like a shovel; in England they turn it upside down and push everything—including peas—on top of it.

On the Continent people have good food; in England people have good table manners.

On the Continent almost every nation, whether little or great, has openly declared at one time or another that it is superior to all other nations; the English fight heroic wars to combat these dangerous ideas without ever mentioning which is really the most superior race in the world.

Continental people are sensitive and touchy; the English take everything with an exquisite sense of humour—they are only offended if you tell them that they have no sense of humour.

People on the Continent either tell you the truth or lies; in England they hardly ever lie, but they would not dream of telling you the truth.

Many Continentals think life is a game; the English think cricket is a game.

George Mikes, How to be an Alien

The British Character

Importance of tea.

Love of keeping calm.

II. The United States

5 A. The Watchword is 'Attack'

An Episode from the War of Independence

1. It was a dull December morning in 1776. A dense fog lay over the wide Delaware River and the small town of Trenton, where the English troops were lying in winter quarters. On the opposite side of the half-frozen river was the small American army under the command of General George Washington. As the English had advanced inland, he had been forced to retreat across the Delaware. His little army—only some 3,000 men—in rags, hungry and running short of ammunition, was exhausted and demoralized. Only their leader still believed in a final victory.

The English had forbidden anyone to row or sail on the Delaware in order to prevent the people of Trenton from coming into contact with the rebels.

2. That December morning fifteen-year-old Kenneth Strawn stood in the dark shed where he kept his boat on the river bank. The day before, Kenneth had met a man who had asked him to help him find a boat. The stranger was an American patriot in Washington's army and Kenneth had promised to help him. Suddenly a faint tap was heard on the window pane. Kenneth immediately opened the door, let the man in and locked it behind him.

"I hope you're alone," said the stranger in a low voice.

"Yes, I am," answered Kenneth. "Here is my boat. But before you go, there's something I'd like to ask you. Did you happen to come across Lieutenant Strawn? He's my father, you know. He joined George Washington's army in early summer. We haven't heard a word from him since."

"I'm afraid I haven't met your father," replied the man, "but don't worry, he might be with a regiment in Pennsylvania . . . ."

The stranger could not say any more, because there was a noise of someone knocking loudly at the door. "Open in the King's name!"

The King's name? It must be an enemy, a Redcoat.

The stranger, as quick as lightning, jumped into the boat where he hid under a piece of canvas.

3. Slowly Kenneth walked to the door and unlocked it; he was almost thrown over by a Redcoat carrying a gun.

"What are you doing here? Who are you?" the Redcoat asked in an unfriendly way.

Christmas night, 1776. General George Washington and his forces are crossing the Delaware to attack the English in Trenton.

"I'm Kenneth Strawn. I come here daily to look after my boat."

"Who's with you? You were talking to someone."

"I'm alone."

"Will you play fair, you little beast? You're hiding a spy. Where is he?"

"There's no spy here."

"You'll pay dear for that lie, you little devil."

The Redcoat caught the boy by the shoulder and hit him hard in the face. Kenneth staggered back and saw the soldier's gun pointing at him, when suddenly the stranger leapt out of his hiding-place, knocked the gun out of the Redcoat's hand and threw him to the ground. In a moment the Redcoat was up again. Though the stranger fought like a tiger, the Redcoat was stronger and was getting the better of him. Suddenly Kenneth saw the gun on the floor. He seized it and struck the Redcoat on the head with the butt. At once the soldier loosened his grip and fell to the ground, unconscious.

"I had to do it," said Kenneth, "though I didn't like to."

"Let's hurry," said the stranger. "He's likely to recover soon."

They hastened to get the boat out of the shed. "You'd better come with me," said the stranger. "I'm sure you'll be fairly safe on the other side."

In a few moments the boat was launched. Deep went the oars into the water as they rowed through the fast-moving ice-floes to the safety of the other bank.

4. During the night of December 25th, 1776, Kenneth's boat was among those used by General Washington to cross the Delaware. Wet, half-frozen, his little force of 3,000 men marched nine miles to Trenton where they took the English by surprise. After two hours of heavy fighting, the Americans won the battle. They took about 1,000 men prisoner with hardly any losses to themselves. Washington was deeply moved. He had defeated a force twice the size of his. "From now on," he told his officers, "the watchword is 'attack'!"

There were to be many more hard times for Washington and his men, for the following month the British captured Philadelphia. But then the tables were turned. The French helped the American colonists, and with this additional strength, Washington was able to defeat the British in the end. In 1781 England asked for peace terms, and a few years later George Washington became the first President of the United States.

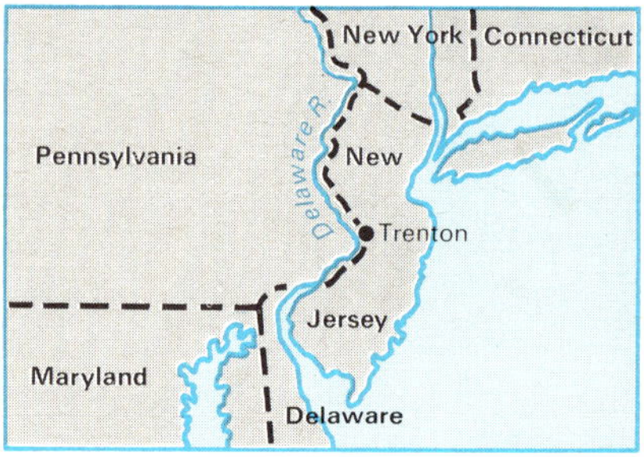

<B. The Declaration of Independence>

Once the War of Independence had begun, the colonists insisted on separation from the mother country. On July 4th, 1776, the Declaration of Independence was signed in Philadelphia unanimously by the thirteen former English colonies of America:

"We hold these truths to be self-evident,—that all men are created equal; that they are endowed by their Creator with certain inalienable rights; that among these are life, liberty and the pursuit of happiness; that to secure these rights, governments are instituted among men, deriving their just powers from the consent of the governed; that whenever any form of government becomes destructive to these ends, it is the right of the people to alter or to abolish it, and to institute new government."

Never before had a state begun its history with a proclamation of the rights of man: all men are born equal and they all have the right to govern themselves. This was an encouragement to every nation that was longing for freedom.

As the great news spread through America, from every tower in town and village bells began to ring, and soon, from one end of the country to the other, they were proclaiming that a new nation had been born. The man who had written the Declaration of Independence was Thomas Jefferson. He became the third President of the United States.

<The First Day in America>

A young Russian immigrant has just landed in New York. He has little money and no job. After an unsuccessful attempt to get a job in a restaurant, he tries to find a place to sleep in a park.

Lights began to come on in the towers around the park. It was almost dark. I found a sandy patch under a rock, rolled up my coat for a pillow, and went to sleep.

I was tired and I slept some hours. It must have been almost midnight when a light flashed in my face. I sat up. It was from the head lamp of a car on the road below me. While I watched, the engine coughed and died. A man got out. For more than an hour he knocked with tools and opened the hood and closed it again.

Then I slid down the bank. I showed him with my hands and feet and head, "Give me the tools and let me try."

He handed them over and sat on the bench.

I checked every part of the motor. In between, I cranked. I cranked until I was exhausted. Still the car wouldn't move.

I got angry. I cursed it. Then I kicked the radiator as hard as I could. The car was an old Model T, and it started with a snort.

The man came running up. He was laughing and he shook my hand and asked questions. But signs weren't enough. I showed the man my dictionary—English-Russian, Russian-English. Holding it under the headlights, he thumbed through.

"Work?" he found in English.

I looked at the Russian word beside it and shook my head.

"Home?" he turned to that.—"No," again.

I took the dictionary. "Boat. Today."

"Come home,"—he showed me the words—"with me"—he pointed to himself. "Eat. Sleep. Job." It took him quite a time between words. "Job. Tomorrow."

"Automobiles?" I said. We have the same word in Georgian.

"Automobiles!" He was pleased we found one word together.

We got in his car, and he took me through miles and miles of streets with houses on both sides of every one of them until we came to his own. We went in and we ate and we drank and ate and drank again. For that, fortunately, you need no words.

Then his wife showed me a room and I went to bed. As I fell asleep I thought to myself: Well, now, I have lived one whole day in America and—just as they say—America is a country where anything, anything at all can happen.

And in twenty years—about this—I never changed my mind.

George and Helen Papashvily

Gold-diggers at work in the Californian gold-fields. The American River can be seen in the background.

6 A. The Gold Rush

1. One November morning in 1848 Jim Roberts ran into the barber's shop of his parents in New York. He was waving a newspaper.

"Listen to this, Pa!" shouted Jim unfolding the paper.

"Gold in the American River!—This year in January, somebody building a sawmill on the American River discovered gold when deepening the river bed. That was the beginning of the biggest gold rush the world has ever seen. In San Francisco carpenters dropped their hammers, bakers their loaves, clerks their pens to rush to the American River. And now the gold fever has reached New York and other towns in the East. Shops are being abandoned and families are being deserted, while the men are hurrying westward. Anybody who can afford it will sail round South America to San Francisco. Most, however, are going overland. The Gold Rush is on!"

Mr. Roberts had stopped shaving his customer. "While fortunes are being made in California," he said, "I'm shaving people at two cents a beard in New York. If I were twenty years younger, I know what I'd do."

"And that is exactly what I'm going to do," said Jim. "I'm leaving New York next week."

"What will Sally say to that?" asked Mrs. Roberts, who was standing behind the counter. "You were going to be married next Christmas."

"She'll marry a millionaire a few months later," replied Jim with a smile.

2. Jim left St. Joseph on the Missouri early in March, 1849. He joined one of the first waggon trains leaving for the West that spring. In the prairie there was plenty of grass for the horses, and the buffalo provided sufficient meat. Those were the easy days. After a few weeks the weather changed. It rained cats and dogs for days. Drenched to the skin, people had to sleep in wet blankets. With the rain came disease. Cholera became a fellow-traveller, sweeping through waggon after waggon until more than half of the men were ill. The ones who died were buried along the route, and their graves were landmarks for those who were following. After the rain a new danger came in the shape of Red Indians. For a few days Jim and his party had been watching their smoke signals on the hills. One could well imagine what these signals meant. The train was being followed by an unseen enemy. One night by full moon the Indians attacked, but a few well aimed shots chased them away.

Jim's train crossed the Rocky Mountains, then they had to sweat in the heat of the Great Salt Lake Desert, the trap in which so many pioneers were caught. But they struggled on in the terrible sand-storms, their waggon wheels sinking deep in the dust.

It was snowing when they crossed the Sierra Mountains. A third of the waggons broke down. On leaving St. Joseph there had been 300 men in Jim's train, 120 reached California two months later after 2,000 miles of terrible hardship.

3.

San Francisco, Sept. 1849

Dear Sally,

I seem to be born lucky and have some wonderful news for you. I had been digging for several days when I suddenly struck a gold-field. Though my claim was only a hundred feet long, it brought me $ 17,000 in one week. Now I want to settle here as a farmer. The land is ideal for cattle, for fruit growing and for corn.

However, people lead a wild life here in the Golden West. The hills of California are filled with adventurers digging for gold, men who don't shrink from murder. I must tell you this, because I'm going to ask you something else. Do you still want to marry me, Sally? I've thought of you day and night since I left home. You'll be coming as soon as possible, won't you? I'll be sending you the money straight away so that you can take the boat to San Francisco round Cape Horn.

Your loving
Jim

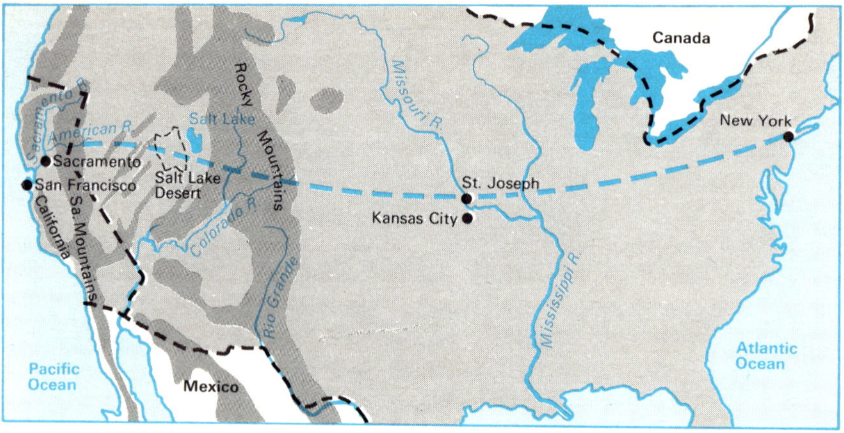

Three months later Jim and Sally were married in San Francisco. Jim left the gold-fields, bought a piece of land, and together he and Sally started to build up a new life on the rich farmland of California.

<B. The Great Migration>

Many nations, besides the British, took part in the early colonization of the USA. By the end of the eighteenth century, the population included Germans, Dutch, French and Scandinavians.

The greatest migration from Europe to the United States took place in the nineteenth century. Immigrants arrived in three waves. The first, lasting from 1815 to 1860, reached its peak in 1854, when more than 400,000 people arrived in the States. The second started in the late 1860's, and continued until the end of the century. The peak year was 1882, with 800,000 arrivals. The third great wave, 1900—1914, reached its peak in 1910, with more than a million arrivals. Since that time immigration into the USA has dwindled considerably and in 1971 there were only 370,000 newcomers.

Between 1820 and 1971, Europeans went to America in these numbers:

Germans	6,900,000
Italians	5,200,000
English, Scots, Welsh	4,800,000
Irish	4,700,000
Scandinavians and Finns	2,500,000
French	730,000
other Europeans and Russians	10,700,000

Wendy Hall

<A Fight with a Bear>

The whole camp was bedded down, and most of them were asleep, before Cleve returned to the waggon. Lying awake, staring up at the waggon cover which was faintly lit from the dying flames, Lilith heard him unroll his bed and pull off his boots. At last he stretched out with a sigh, and after a minute she could hear his regular breathing.

Sleep would not come. Several times she turned over, seeking a more comfortable position, and then suddenly, she heard another sound. Something was moving around outside the waggon. She heard a snort from Cleve's horse and she reached for her rifle, then she drew her hand back quickly.

The sounds continued, and then she could hear Cleve's horse struggling at his picket pin. "Cleve!" she whispered. "Cleve!"

"I hear it," he said aloud, calmly.

He lay perfectly still, listening. For an instant there was absolute stillness, then the sounds began again, and a bucket rattled as something turned it over.

Suddenly the horse started to rear and plunge, fighting the picket rope. Grabbing his pistol, Cleve rolled out from under the waggon and stood up and at the same moment a huge bear reared up, almost beside him. Cleve shot once ... twice ... a third time. He fired as rapidly as he could.

Blinded by the flash of the gun, the bear lunged at him. Its paw missed a blow that would have torn his head off, but it knocked him down with the lunge of his body. Cleve rolled over, but managed to cling to his pistol, and the bear crashed against the side of the waggon. He fired the pistol upward into its belly, then he scrambled to his feet and jumped back as the bear tried to rear up again. Bringing the pistol level, he squeezed the trigger again and the gun clicked, missing fire.

Cleve had no extra cartridges with him. They were all in the pockets of his coat or in the saddle pockets. Carefully, he backed away another step, straining his eyes toward the spot near the front wheel where the bear had been.

Several armed men came running. "What's happened? What was it?" they called. Cleve threw wood on the fire and some of the evergreen branches blazed up. The bear lay where it had fallen against the front wheel of the waggon, and the men approached it cautiously, their weapons ready. Three bullets had hit the bear's chest, slightly left of centre, and the three holes could have been covered by a man's hand.

It was the fourth and last shot that had saved Cleve's life, for it had gone into the bear's stomach and had broken its spine. Despite the killing shots in the chest, the bear might finally have killed him had it not been for that. He had been lucky ... very lucky indeed. *Louis L'Amour*

The moment before the assassination of Abraham Lincoln in Ford's Theatre, Washington, on April 14th, 1865. The President is sitting in a rocking-chair with Mrs. Lincoln at his side.

7 A. Death of a President

1. On November 10th, 1860, the news reached the States of the South that Abraham Lincoln had been elected President of the United States. For the first time in the history of the United States an anti-slavery president was to enter the White House in Washington.

For a long time the quarrel between the North and the South about the holding of slaves had been going on. The Northern States were against slavery, the ones of the South wanted to preserve it. After the election of Lincoln, who had always been strongly against slavery, the South acted quickly. Eleven Southern States proclaimed their secession from the Union and formed the Confederate States. Richmond in Virginia became their capital.

Abraham Lincoln's chief aim was to hold the United States together. He would even have been prepared to renounce the abolition of slavery in the South if the Union could have been preserved. However, the South wanted to separate from the North, and the Civil War began.

At first the Confederate armies were successful and they reached a point only 30 miles from the capital, Washington. The turning point of the war

came with the battle of Gettysburg in July 1863, when the Southern armies suffered heavy losses.

In January of the same year, Lincoln had proclaimed the freedom of all the slaves in the South, thus abolishing slavery in the whole of the United States. But still the war went on.

2. Washington City awakened one April morning in 1865 to the noise of cannon-fire. Lee, the commander of the Southern armies, had surrendered to Grant, the general of the North. The Civil War, which had been going on for four years, was practically at an end. Richmond had fallen into the hands of the Union troops.

The people of Washington rushed to the White House, where President Lincoln spoke to the cheering crowd.

"I have been waiting for this moment since the beginning of the war," he said. "For a long time I've had two aims—to preserve the Union and to abolish slavery. Both aims have now been achieved." He spoke of reunification, of helping to put the South on her feet again. He also said that the negroes should be given the right of voting.

In the crowd, John Wilkes Booth, an actor, had been listening to the President's speech. As the President stopped speaking, Booth said to his friend, Lewis Paine, "That's the last speech he has made." Booth was a fanatical supporter of the South. He believed that the negro was born to be the white man's slave. For months he had been carrying a plan in his mind to murder the President.

3. A few days later, on the morning of Friday, April 14th, 1865, Booth went to Ford's Theatre to fetch his mail. The owner of the theatre told Booth of a message he had just received: the President and his wife would attend the evening performance of the play 'Our American Cousin'. Now the chance Booth had been waiting for had come.

At 10 o'clock in the evening Booth arrived at the theatre and went up the stairs to the State Box. He could hear the actors on the stage. He turned the door knob. The door opened. Lincoln, facing the stage, was sitting in a rocking chair next to his wife. Booth moved along the wall, the pistol in his hand. Two other persons were sitting in the box, the President's bodyguard, Major Rathbone, and his fiancée. All were listening to the jokes on the stage. The pistol was behind the President's head. Booth pulled the trigger. There was a sound as if someone had blown up and broken a paper bag. It came in the midst of loud laughter, so that some heard it, and some did not. The President's head dropped towards his chest and he had stopped rocking. A small cloud of blue smoke hung in the air. Major Rathbone jumped up and tried

Aktivieren Sie Ihren fremdsprachlichen Wortschatz!

Grund- und Aufbauwortschatz

Ein einzigartiges Hilfsmittel zur Wiederholung und Erweiterung Ihrer Vokabelkenntnisse

Englisch
Französisch
Italienisch
Spanisch
Portugiesisch
Russisch

5 P 25-1

Klett

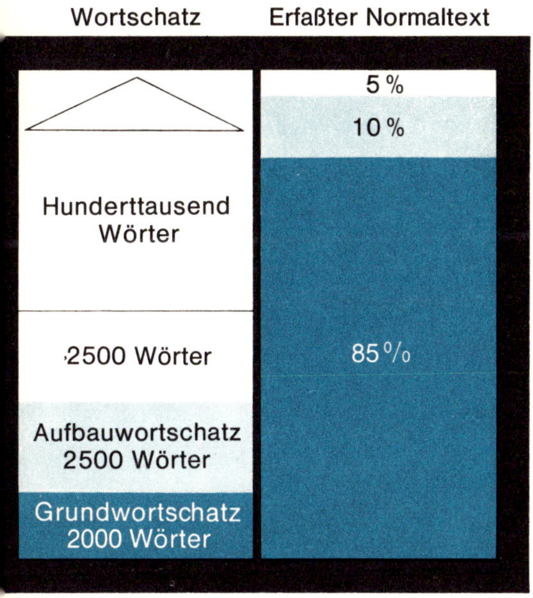

Mit dem Grundwortschatz (2000 Wörter) erfaßt man 85 % eines Normaltextes, mit dem Aufbauwortschatz (plus 2500 Wörter) weitere 10 %, zusammen also 95 % eines Normaltextes.

Was wird geboten?

4500 Wörter – ausgewählt auf Grund der internationalen Forschungen auf dem Gebiet der Worthäufigkeit und aufgeteilt in

2000 Wörter Grundwortschatz
(in alphabetischer Ordnung)

2500 Wörter Aufbauwortschatz
(nach Sachgruppen geordnet).

Sätze und idiomatische Redewendungen, die – nach ihrem Häufigkeitswert zusammengestellt – die Ausdrucksfähigkeit wesentlich steigern.
Methodische und didaktische Ratschläge für die Benutzung dieser Bücher.

Was wird erreicht?

Befestigung Ihres Wortschatzes durch systematisch angelegte Wiederholungen ■ planmäßige Erweiterung und ständige Überprüfung des Wortschatzes ■ selbständige Aneignung neuen Wortguts unter den Gesichtspunkten der Häufigkeit, Verwendbarkeit, Zugehörigkeit zu bestimmten Stoffkreisen usw. ■ rationelle Gedächtnisarbeit durch Assoziationen.

Grund- und Aufbauwortschatz

je etwa 200 Seiten, Plastic-Einband

Englisch
Bearbeitet von Prof. Dr. Erich Weis
Klettbuch 5195

Französisch
Bearbeitet von Dr. Günter Nickolaus
Klettbuch 5235

Italienisch
Bearbeitet von Prof. Dr. Paolo Giovanelli
Klettbuch 5236

Spanisch
Bearbeitet von Prof. Carl Heupel
Klettbuch 5237

Portugiesisch
Bearbeitet von Maria Luisa Amorim-Braun
Klettbuch 51959

Russisch
Bearbeitet von Dr. Helger Oleg Vogt
Klettbuch 5198

Bestellkarte

Hiermit bestelle ich zur Lieferung
über die Buchhandlung

____

in ____________________

____

Grund- und Aufbauwortschatz

- ☐ Ex. Englisch
  Klettbuch 5195, 8,40 DM
- ☐ Ex. Französisch
  Klettbuch 5235, 8,20 DM
- ☐ Ex. Italienisch
  Klettbuch 5236, 8,20 DM
- ☐ Ex. Spanisch
  Klettbuch 5237, 8,20 DM
- ☐ Ex. Portugiesisch
  Klettbuch 51959, 12,80 DM
- ☐ Ex. Russisch
  Klettbuch 5198, 12,80 DM

Grundwortschatz

- ☐ Ex. Deutsch-Englisch-Französisch
  Klettbuch 5196, 10,60 DM
- ☐ Ex. Deutsch-Französisch-Italienisch
  Klettbuch 51966, 10,20 DM
- ☐ Ex. Deutsch-Englisch-Spanisch
  Klettbuch 51967, 10,20 DM
- ☐ Ex. Deutsch-Englisch-Arabisch
  Klettbuch 51968, 14,80 DM
- ☐ Ex. Deutsch-Französisch-Italienisch-Spanisch-Englisch-Russisch
  Klettbuch 51965, 24,– DM

Preise freibleibend. Stand vom 1. 1. 1973.

____
Ort, Datum

____
Unterschrift

Postrichtige Anschrift:

____

____
Postleitzahl

____

Grundwortschatz Deutsch-Essential German-Allemand fondamental
Klettbuch 5196, 240 Seiten, 10,60 DM

Grundwortschatz Deutsch - Allemand fondamental - Vocabolario base tedesco
Klettbuch 51966, 236 Seiten, 10,20 DM

Grundwortschatz Deutsch - Essential German - Alemán fundamental
Klettbuch 51967, 235 Seiten, 10,20 DM

Grundwortschatz Deutsch - Englisch - Arabisch
Klettbuch 51968, 282 Seiten, 14,80 DM

Grundwortschatz Deutsch in sechs Sprachen (Deutsch-Französisch-Italienisch-Spanisch-Englisch-Russisch)
Klettbuch 51965, 440 Seiten, 24,– DM

Diese Bände bringen die 2000 Wörter des deutschen Grundwortschatzes mit ihren Entsprechungen in zwei bzw. fünf Fremdsprachen, und zwar nebeneinander in Kolumnen bei genauer lexikologischer Zuordnung. Der Grundwortschatz wird von etwa 3 000 idiomatischen Redewendungen ergänzt.
Dem Grundwortschatz folgt je ein Register der fremdsprachigen Grundwörter mit ihrer deutschen Entsprechung. So können von jedem Grundwort aus die Grundwörter und dazugehörigen Wendungen der anderen Sprachen gefunden werden.

Preise freibleibend. Stand vom 1. 1. 1973.

Postkarte

Bitte als Postkarte freimachen

Ernst Klett Verlag Stuttgart
Abteilung
Information und Beratung

7054 Korb
Postfach 1170

to grapple with Booth, who dropped his pistol, drew a knife, and hit the major in the arm, shouting "Revenge for the South!"

Booth jumped over the edge of the box on to the stage. He ran across the stage into the wings. Somebody tried to stop him, but in the general confusion he succeeded in escaping.

A piercing scream came from Mrs. Lincoln in the State Box. Someone shouted, "The President has been shot!"

The lights went on and showed hundreds of faces filled with fright and anger. A young doctor, who was in the theatre, examined the President. "His wound is mortal," he said. "It is impossible for him to recover."

Lincoln died the next day. Thus one of the greatest Presidents the United States has ever seen met his death. His murderer was cornered a few weeks later in a Virginian barn and shot.

Lincoln's work, however, was carried on in spite of resistance in the South. The negroes not only remained free but were also given the right of voting. As they belonged to the lowest class of the population, poor and uneducated, their struggle to gain full rights as American citizens has been long and difficult, and it still continues today.

<B. What is New York?>

One of the oldest cities in the States. In 1614, the Dutch founded a trading post on the Island of Manhattan (an Indian word meaning 'Celestial Burial Ground') and called it New Amsterdam. Later in the seventeenth century it was taken over by the English, who renamed it New York.

The second largest city in the world, with a population of over eight million; the most important city in the United States, ten times as big as the Federal Capital, Washington.

A cosmopolitan city, whose population includes more than 50 different nationalities. Among the most numerous are Italians, Germans, Irish, Russians and Poles. Here you can eat the food of almost every country in the world, and read daily newspapers published in fifteen languages.

A powerful financial centre. Wall Street, where the New York Stock Exchange and many great banking houses are situated, dominates the money markets of the world.

The Home of the United Nations, whose permanent headquarters, designed by Le Corbusier, stand on eighteen acres of international territory overlooking the East River.

Wendy Hall

<**Night movement—New York**>

In the night, when the sea-winds take the city in their arms,
And cool the loud streets that kept their dust noon and afternoon;
In the night, when the sea-birds call to the lights of the city,
The lights that cut on the skyline their name of a city;
In the night, when the trains and waggons start from a long way off
For the city where the people ask bread and want letters;
In the night the city lives too—the day is not all.
In the night there are dancers dancing and singers singing.
In the night the sea-winds take the city in their arms.

Carl Sandburg

<**My First Payday**>

Carl Sandburg, the celebrated American poet, was born in Illinois in 1878. The son of a poor Swedish immigrant, he had to leave school at the age of eleven and go to work.

I was eleven when I got my first regular job. Before that there had been only little jobs here and there, after school hours or on Saturdays. But now I was wearing long pants and every Friday was payday.

I worked for Callender & Rodine on the second floor of a building on Main Street. They sold land and houses. The office was large, and I would guess it was twenty feet from one wall to the other. Mr. Callender was a heavy man with a large yellow moustache. His head was wide between the ears, and he had a big, round stomach, a 'bay window'. Mr. Rodine was thin and had a rosy face.

I unlocked the office door about a quarter to eight each morning, Monday through Friday. I cleaned the office, digging in for the dust in the corners and between the floor boards. Then I swept the dust out into the hall, and swept the hall along the six or eight feet to the top of the wide steps leading down to the street. Then I swept the steps. Reaching the bottom, I swept all the dirt on to the sidewalk of Main Street and across the sidewalk. With two or three last great efforts I swept a basketful of dust and paper out on the street to join other sweepings and layers of dirt. If a strong east wind was blowing, my sweepings would soon be all over Main Street.

This morning service of mine for Callender & Rodine took less than half an hour. I was pleased and thankful when on Friday morning Mr. Callender would bring his right hand out of a pocket and, with a look on his face as though he had almost forgotten it, hand me a piece of money with "Here you are." I would take the money, say "Thanks," run down the steps, and on the sidewalk open my hand to look at what it held. There it was, twenty-five cents, a silver quarter of a dollar.

Carl Sandburg

May 26th, 1927. Edsel Ford drives the fifteen millionth Model T car from the assembly line. At his side sits his father, Henry Ford.

8 A. The Man who put America on Wheels

1. The news came as a complete surprise to the USA that winter morning in 1914. It was in the newspapers that the Ford Motor Company had announced a minimum wage of five dollars a day for all its workers. At the same time the day's work was shortened from nine to eight hours. Until that time the Ford Motor Company had been paying the usual wages, which were just over two dollars a day.

American industrialists were alarmed. Such high wages would ruin America's industry. No employer would be able to keep his workers at the present rate.

Meanwhile, thousands of workers were queueing at the Ford factory in Detroit. From all over the country they came, filling the empty freight trains, even clinging to the buffers, in the hope of a five-dollar job. More than ten thousand disappointed men stood at the gates, which had been closed, for there were no more vacancies. The police were called, and instead of the job they had hoped for, the waiting crowds received streams of water from the fire hose.

Henry Ford, however, had set the ball rolling. His idea was that high wages and low selling prices would increase the buying power of the masses. He believed that the prosperity of the USA depended on such principles.

2. Henry Ford was a car builder. He was not the first that had come on the idea of the horseless coach. The Germans, Daimler and Benz, were its inventors, but Ford was the first to realize what so many people had been dreaming of: he made it possible for anybody with an average income, including every Ford worker, to buy an automobile.

One day Ford announced that he was going to make only one car—and it would be Model T.

"I will build a car for the masses," he said. "And what is more, it will be a good car."

How could Ford fulfil his promise? He could, because he was the first to use the assembly line for mass production.

Nowadays everybody knows what an assembly line is like. Nobody can imagine a big motor car factory without it: an endless belt which moves slowly on while the different parts of a machine are assembled on it and put together by workers. Each man does one kind of job at a fixed time. Sometimes all a man has to do is to turn a screw. As the machine moves on, more and more parts are added until the complete product leaves the belt. The assembly line cut the time required for the construction of Model T from 14 hours to 1 hour and 33 minutes. And the price fell from $ 1,200 to $ 295.

3. In nineteen years Ford produced fifteen million Model T cars—the car that became affectionately known as 'Tin Lizzy'. 'Lizzy' was a machine of a kind that never existed before and never will be seen again. Nothing that followed could compare with her. She changed the life of a nation. 'Lizzy's' wheels were turning day and night all over the States, in rain and sunshine, in the plains and on the hills.

'Lizzy' was black. "People may choose any colour they like," said Henry Ford, "provided they choose black."

'Lizzy' was ugly. She had no speedometer. To see if she had petrol you had to lift the seat cushion, unscrew the cap and poke a stick into the tank. The one thing, however, she could never be accused of was failure. Model T became a people's car.

At the age of nineteen Model T died. The jokes against it had begun to hurt: "A Ford is like a bathtub. It's useful, but you don't want to be seen in it." Other motor-car makers, above all the mighty General Motors, following Ford's example, were able to reduce the costs of much more attractive cars. Fewer and fewer wanted Model T's.

4. For a long time 'Old Henry' refused to admit that Model T was outmoded, but the falling sales spoke a language of their own. At last Ford decided to make a new car. That was the beginning of Model A. In a plant that made 1,800,000 cars a year everything stopped. Every machine in it had to be re-made, hundreds of new machines had to be invented. The birth of Model A took nine months. It was still the cheapest car on the market, but it had four-wheel brakes, a windscreen wiper, and the buyer could choose among several different colours.

The Ford Motor Company produced 6,000 cars a day for five years, at the end of which Model A died, too. For a second time Ford had to close his plant. New Models followed, and the Ford Empire grew and grew.

When in 1947 Henry Ford closed his eyes for ever at the age of 83, the Ford Motor Company had produced well over 30 million cars. His work and his ideas are marching on. The Ford moving assembly line system has generally been adopted for car production in the whole world.

B. Conversation: On a Motor Trip

Can you give me a lift?
Where shall I drop you? Drop me at the next corner, will you?
I'll pick you up on the way back.
Drive carefully.—I'll ride in the back.
What make is that car? It's a Ford.
I bought it second-hand.
What's the top speed? How fast does it (she) go?
At a speed of 80 miles per hour.
He changes gear, he puts on the brakes.
The car has a breakdown.
We have a puncture—a flat tyre.
We are out of petrol. The tank is empty.
Where is the nearest filling-station?
Fill it up, please!
How much, sir? Three gallons, please.
Check the engine oil, please.—The oil in the engine is low.
Put in two pints of fresh oil.
Will you check the pressure of the air in the tyres?
We had an accident the other day.
The car had a smash. We bumped into another car.
They overtook on a bend.
I was fined for speeding.

<American and British English>

1. Differences in pronunciation

a) Words ending in *-ary* and *-ory* have a stress on the next to last syllable in American:
secretary *Br* [ˈsekrətri] *Am* [ˈsekrəˈtɛri];
laboratory *Br* [ləˈbɔrətri] *Am* [ˈlæbərəˈtɔri].

b) Americans often pronounce *r* in positions where it is not pronounced in British English:
bar *Br* [bɑː] *Am* [bɑr];
fear *Br* [fiə] *Am* [fiər].

c) ɑ, ɔ, juː in British English become æ, ɑ, uː in American:
bath *Br* [bɑːθ] *Am* [bæθ]; hot *Br* [hɔt] *Am* [hɑt];
news *Br* [njuːz] *Am* [nuːz];
New York *Br* [ˈnjuː ˈjɔːk] *Am* [ˈnuː ˈjɔrk].

d) Other words which are pronounced differently:
tomato *Br* [təˈmɑːtəu] *Am* [təˈmeitəu]; clerk *Br* [klɑːk] *Am* [klərk];
address *Br* [əˈdres] *Am* [ˈædres]; lieutenant *Br* [lefˈtenənt] *Am* [luːˈtenənt].

2. Differences in spelling

a) Words ending in *-or: Br* colour, neighbour; *Am* color, neighbor
b) Words ending in *-ter: Br* centre, theatre; *Am* center, theater
c) Words ending in *-ize: Br* civilize(-ise), organize(-ise); *Am* civilize, organize
d) Words in which *l* is doubled in British English: *Br* traveller; *Am* traveler
e) Simplified spellings in American: *Br* though, although, through; *Am* tho, altho, thru

3. Differences in vocabulary

Americans and English people often use different words to mean the same thing. Here are some common examples:

Br	*Am*	*Br*	*Am*	*Br*	*Am*
luggage	baggage	autumn	fall	(bank-)note	bill
lorry	truck	tram	streetcar	bill	check
pavement	sidewalk	fellow	guy	sweets	candies
petrol	gas	porter	doorman	lift	elevator
biscuit	cookie	flat	apartment	cupboard	closet
holiday	vacation	chemist's	drug store	postman	mailman

<America and the Americans>

The Many Faces of America

America is the general name given to the two huge continents of North America and South America, joined together by the smaller states of Central America. North America consists of Canada, the USA and Mexico. Yet today, when we speak of America and the Americans, we usually mean the United States and its citizens.

The USA is a country of great contrasts. In climate it ranges from the arctic cold of Alaska to the tropical heat of Florida; in landscape from the endless plains of the Middle West to the snowy peaks of the Rocky Mountains. It is as large as the whole of Europe, and the 3,000-mile journey from east to west by the fastest train takes at least two days and three nights.

The USA is a land of abundance. It produces 13% of the world's wheat, 20% of its cotton, 25% of its milk, 30% of its butter, and 75% of its oil. At the same time the USA is the most highly-industrialized country in the world. One city alone—Detroit, the centre of the car industry—produces more cars in a year than the car industries of Britain and France together.

Automation, or production of goods by entirely automatic machines, instead of by human labour, is more advanced and more general than in Europe. The push-button factory has come into being. At one of the Ford plants in Michigan, 4,800 engines are produced each day, entirely by machine. No single process is done by humans. A radio factory which formerly employed 200 workers now needs only two to supervise machinery by remote control. On the other hand, far more people are now needed to maintain the machinery which does the work.

The people of the USA are a mixture of many different races, and the majority of them are of European origin. During the two main immigration waves in the 19th century more than 35 million people left Europe to make a new home in America. The total population of America in 1972 was 208 million, and it is still growing fast.

There is still another face of America—a face with a dark skin. There are over 20 million negroes in the USA, the descendants of the former slaves. It is more than 100 years since the slaves were freed, but the negroes' struggle for equal rights still goes on.

The USA has been called the melting pot of nations. Out of the settlers, pioneers, slaves and immigrants of the past have grown the Americans of today, citizens of the world's richest country.

1 Maine
2 New Hampshire
3 Vermont
4 Massachusetts
5 Rhode Island
6 Connecticut
7 New Jersey
8 Delaware
9 Maryland
10 Pennsylvania
11 West Virginia
12 Indiana
13 Alabama
14 Mississippi
15 Louisiana

The Americans

The Melting Pot. Although the first colony in North America was British, other countries also sent settlers across the Atlantic. In 1614 the Dutch established a trading post on Manhattan Island, which later became New Amsterdam and then New York. Swedish colonists settled in Delaware, French Huguenots in South Carolina, Germans in Pennsylvania. The British, however, remained in the majority, and in 1790 they still made up 92% of the population.

The great immigration waves of the 19th century brought a continuous stream of European settlers to America—Germans, Italians, English, Scots, Welsh, Irish, Russians, Scandinavians and Finns. Very many of these were fugitives from religious or political oppression in their own countries and, in spite of the difference in language and customs, they had a common aim—to live their own lives in freedom.

The love of freedom was not the only thing these people had in common. Wherever the immigrants settled they had to overcome the same difficulties, to solve the same problems of government, to defend themselves against common enemies. All these factors helped to fuse the many different races into one people. At first the immigrants still thought of themselves as English, German, Dutch or Italian. Later they began to call themselves New Englanders or Virginians, after the region in which they had settled. Then, after the Civil War, as the United States rapidly developed into a rich and powerful country, strong national feelings grew among the people, who saw themselves more and more as members of a great and united nation—the Americans.

The Indians and the Negroes. There are still two racial minorities which have not yet become fully integrated into the American nation. They are the Indians and the negroes. By 1900 the Indian population had shrunk to 300,000 after nearly three centuries of desperate resistance against the white man and his way of life. Today they are increasing again, but they still prefer to keep to themselves. A few work in the white man's towns, but the majority still live in the reservations provided by the American government.

In the 100 years since the end of slavery and the Civil War the negro population of America has risen from 4 million to over 20 million. In the North negroes attend the same schools as whites. They have the right to vote, and two negroes have represented Northern States in Congress. In the former slave-holding States of the South, however, their progress towards equality has been slower.

Still today, talented negroes do not always find it easy to get the jobs they deserve, and many negro families have to put up with poor housing accommodation, even in the North. The Federal Government, however, has shown itself

to be firmly on the side of the negroes in their struggle for equal rights, and much is being done, though slowly, to prevent racial discrimination all over the United States.

Politics and the State

The President and the Government. The President is the head of state and at the same time the leader of the Government and commander-in-chief of the armed forces. His powers are considerable. He appoints the Cabinet, negotiates treaties with foreign governments, and can recommend laws to the Government. He can also veto any bill which has been passed by the Government. The President is elected for a period of four years. The candidates for the presidency are chosen by the two great parties, the Republicans and the Democrats, and for months before the election all eyes are on the two candidates as they travel about the country from meeting to meeting. The political differences are often very slight, and the presidential election campaign sometimes appears to be more a battle of personalities than of policies.

Congress, the Parliament of the United States, consists of two Houses—the Senate (Upper House) and the House of Representatives (Lower House). The Senate is made up of 100 Senators, two from each State, elected for a period of 6 years. The House of Representatives has 435 members (Congressmen), elected for 2 years. Both Houses can introduce new laws, and the Senate must also approve or reject all appointments or treaties suggested by the President. All taxation laws must originate in the House of Representatives.

Each of the 50 States has its own government under a Governor, whose position is similar to that of the President in the Federal Government. The States are bound to observe the Federal Laws, but they have considerable freedom to manage their own affairs in such matters as education, public health, and the punishment of criminals.

Power and Responsibility. In little more than 300 years the USA has grown from a small colony into the most powerful country in the world.

After the War of Independence the Americans' first task was to protect their huge country against interference from other nations. 'America for the Americans' was their slogan, and for many years they followed the so-called policy of 'isolationism'. Although they welcomed immigrants from all over the world, they believed that America should avoid foreign alliances.

During this long period of isolationism the Americans took a number of measures to protect their own continent and their interests in the Pacific. In 1867 they bought Alaska from Russia; in 1898 they bought the Philippines from Spain and occupied the Hawaiian Islands. In 1904 they gained control of

the Panama Canal. All these measures, together with America's growing power, brought the USA more and more in contact with other nations, and the first decisive step away from isolationism was taken in 1917, when the USA entered World War I.

Between the two World Wars the USA withdrew again from international politics; but, when World War II broke out in 1939, it soon became clear that America could no longer isolate herself from world events. All over the world, in Asia as well as Europe, American soldiers fought and died for the American concept of democracy and freedom. When the war ended in 1945, a great part of Europe lay in ruins, and the leadership of the Western World passed to America.

Great power brings great responsibility. The Americans realized that they could never again turn their backs on the rest of the world. Characteristically they adapted themselves quickly to their new role. One of their first international measures after the war was the Marshall Aid Plan which helped to rebuild the shattered economy of Europe. But America's burden of responsibility was not confined to material help alone. As the work of post-war reconstruction went on, the nations of the world grouped themselves into two great rival power blocks—the Communist countries of the East, led by the Soviet Union, and the nations of the West, under the leadership of the USA.

Important Dates

1492	Columbus discovers the New World
1607	First English colony at Jamestown
1620	Pilgrim Fathers land at Plymouth
1664	New Amsterdam taken from the Dutch — becomes New York
1773	Boston Tea Party
1776	Declaration of Independence
1775—81	War of Independence
1789—97	George Washington, first American President
1840—70	Drive to the West
1860	Abraham Lincoln becomes President
1861—65	American Civil War
1903	The Wright brothers make the first successful flight
1917	USA enters World War I
1929	World Economic Depression
1941	USA enters World War II
1945	First atom bomb dropped on Hiroshima (Japan)
1961—63	John F. Kennedy President
1969	First American moon landing

1

2

Important People

1 *George Washington* (1732—1799) was born in Virginia, the son of a rich tobacco planter whose grandfather had emigrated to America from England. Washington was brought up like an English gentleman and, as a young man, served in the British army. When war broke out between the American colonies and England, Washington became commander-in-chief of the colonists' army. Under his strong leadership, and with French help, the colonists defeated the British, and in 1789 Washington became the first President of the USA.

It was no easy task to govern a new country, but Washington's wisdom and strong character won him great respect. The new capital of the USA was named Washington D.C. in honour of the man who was 'first in war, first in peace, and first in the hearts of his countrymen'.

2 *Abraham Lincoln* (1809—1865) was born of very poor parents in a small log cabin in Kentucky. He had to work as soon as he was old enough, and he grew up tall and strong, but with little education. Later he studied law in his spare time and became a lawyer. He was elected to Congress in 1846.

At this time, work on the southern cotton plantations was done by negro slaves. Lincoln was an opponent of slavery, and, when he became President in 1860, the Southern States rebelled and tried to break away from the USA.

The Civil War followed, in which 600,000 Americans died. In 1865 the Southern States were defeated. America was re-united and 4 million slaves were set free. A few days after the end of the war Lincoln was shot in the theatre by an actor and died the next day.

3 *Walt Whitman* (1819—1892). Until the middle of the 19th century American literature did not develop a character or style of its own, but remained strongly influenced by English writers. Then, as the United States rapidly grew in

power and importance, new writers arose who drew their inspiration more and more from America and the American people. The most important of these was the poet Walt Whitman. He saw the Americans as a young race of pioneers. Again and again in his poems he celebrated the United States as the land of liberty and democracy. His works reflect the restless energy of a growing nation and his vision of its great future.

'We the youthful sinewy races, all the rest on us depend,
Pioneers! O Pioneers!'

4 *Thomas A. Edison* (1847—1931). Edison, one of the world's most famous inventors, began work at the age of 12 as a newspaper boy on long-distance trains. Later he became a telegraph operator and finally set up his own factory for making electrical apparatus. Then began the long series of inventions that made him famous. Edison took out more than 1000 patents for his different inventions, many of which still play an important part in our daily lives. Among the best-known were the electric light bulb and the gramophone.

5 *John D. Rockefeller* (1839—1937). Rockefeller began his professional life as an assistant book-keeper with a small salary. He ended it 50 years later as a multi-millionaire and the richest man in the world.

Rockefeller made his money in the oil industry. In 1867 he put all his savings into an oil company, and thirteen years later, by ruthless business methods and hard competition, his Standard Oil Company had gained control of 90% of all American oil refineries. In 1882 he formed his company into a 'trust'—a huge association of big firms, with which no small firm could compete. In 1911 the National Oil Trust was dissolved by the state, and Rockefeller retired. He had not only made a vast fortune out of oil. He also owned ore-fields, coal-fields, and large shares in the railways and the banks.

His business methods had made Rockefeller into one of the most hated men in the United States. Later, however, he won popularity by his great gifts to science, education and medical research. In 1913 he established the Rockefeller Foundation with a capital of $150,000,000 to work for 'the benefit of mankind' and to fight such plagues as malaria and yellow fever.

6 *John F. Kennedy* (1917—1963). During World War II John F. Kennedy served as an officer in the American navy. In 1946 he entered Congress and in 1953 became a senator. The young senator's ability and ambition quickly brought him to the front of the political stage and in 1960 the Democratic Party chose him their presidential candidate. He won the election by a narrow majority and, at the age of 43, became the youngest president in the history of the United States.

Kennedy's youth and energy were an inspiration not only to his own people but to many nations of the West. He proposed new laws to secure civil rights for the negroes of America, and his efforts to ban the use of nuclear weapons raised hopes of better relations between the West and Russia. But Kennedy did not live to realize any of his plans. After less than three years in office, in November 1963, he was shot and killed by an assassin in the streets of Dallas, Texas.

Anecdotes

1. He didn't think so. One day an American school was visited by a lady who talked to the children about Christopher Columbus. She told them what a good thing it was that he had discovered America, so that they all could go to such a fine school. Did not everybody think so?

"Oh, yes!" shouted all the children. Only a little boy in a corner looked most unhappy and said nothing.

The lady turned to him asking kindly, "Don't you think so, too?"

"No, I don't," he answered, "for I am a Red Indian."

2. Poor Boy. A European woman, newly-arrived in America, was asked how her daughter liked the United States.

"Wonderful!" said the woman. "She has married an American, and he helps her in the house, washes the dishes, looks after the baby—in fact, he does everything for her."

"And how is your son getting on?"

"Oh, the poor boy!" said the woman. "He doesn't like it at all. He married an American girl and has to help her in the house, wash the dishes, look after the baby—in fact, he has to do everything for her."

III. The Commonwealth

9 A. From Prison Camp to Sovereign State

1. From earliest times travellers had spoken of a 'Great South Land' somewhere in the Southern Seas. But no eye had seen that legendary country, no ship had touched that unknown shore—not until the 17th century, when Dutch seamen discovered the huge island we now call Australia.

They found it an empty wilderness, populated only by a few black-skinned aborigines, one of the most primitive peoples in the world. The Dutch saw little to interest them and made no attempt to found colonies. Many years later Captain Cook explored the east coast, which he claimed for Britain. Then, in 1787, eleven ships set sail from England with 700 men and women and 300 soldiers on board, bound for 'The Southern Unknown Land', as many people still called it. The 700 'passengers' on this 12,000-mile voyage were neither colonists nor adventurers; they were convicts from the prisons of England, criminals who had been sentenced to transportation for life. In those days the English penal laws were the harshest in Europe. The prisons were overcrowded, and transportation was a common punishment for even such small crimes as the theft of five shillings.

2. Captain Phillip, the commander of the expedition, had no illusions about the difficulties that lay ahead. Yet he was determined to carry out his instructions to found and maintain a colony on the east coast of Australia.

After a voyage of 8 months Captain Phillip and his 'settlers' landed, and a terrible struggle for existence began. Among the convicts and their soldier-guards there was not a single experienced farmer. The few animals they had brought with them died or were lost in the bush. Water was scarce. Important crops like wheat were unknown in Australia. The cow, the sheep, and other animals from which we get our food did not exist there. Instead of these the settlers found new and strange plants and curious animals like the kangaroo.

For the first few years Captain Phillip's colony was nothing more than a prison camp, in which the guards and the governor were hardly better off than the prisoners themselves. They had a two years' supply of food, but three years passed before the next ship came from England, just in time to save the little colony from starvation.

3. Gradually conditions improved. Free settlers began to arrive from England. Convicts who had finished their prison sentences were given their freedom and

The founding of a colony. Captain Phillip and his officers drink to the health of King George III and the future of their first settlement in Australia.

a piece of land. New colonies were founded along the coast, and villages and small towns began to grow up. Explorers crossed the Blue Mountains and discovered the endless sun-baked deserts of Central Australia.

Between 1820 and 1830 settlements were established along the west coast of Australia and in 1840 the transportation of convicts from England was stopped.

Then suddenly something happened which changed Australian history. The eyes of the world turned to Australia at the sound of one word. Gold! The great Californian gold rush was still in full swing; and now from Australia came fantastic stories of men who had found nuggets worth thousands of pounds. Fortunes were waiting for men to come and take them out of the earth. And the men came—hundreds of thousands of them from all over the world. Just as in California seamen left their ships, farmers their fields; men of all kinds, good and bad, rushed to the goldfields. In the 10 years between 1851 and 1861 more than £120,000,000 worth of gold was taken from the earth, and the population of Australia jumped from 500,000 to over a million.

4. The story of modern Australia begins from that time. Railways and the telegraph brought the widely-separated coastal colonies closer together, and among the people there was a growing desire for unity and independence. They wanted to put the 'convict past' behind them and make a new start in freedom. The former gold-diggers took to farming. The first sheep farms were established which were to make Australia one of the biggest wool producing countries of the world.

At last, in 1900, the different colonies united under one government, and later Australia took her place with Canada, New Zealand and South Africa as a self-governing member of the Commonwealth.

B. Conversation: Paying a Visit

Is Mr. Gordon at home?—May I see Mrs. Gordon?
My name is Gundermann. Petra Gundermann. My sister Doris asked me to call on my way through London.
Oh, yes, come in, will you?
I hope I'm not intruding.
Not at all. We are very pleased to see you.
May I introduce my brother, Dick?
This is Petra Gundermann. Petra, this is my sister, Joan.
How do you do?—How do you do?
How are you?—We're glad to see you.
Do sit down. Will you have a cigarette?
No, thank you. I don't smoke.
Tea is just ready. Would you like some?
Yes, please.
How do you like London?
I love it. It's most fascinating.
Oh, I'm glad to hear that. Is this your first visit to England?
Yes, it is, but I hope it won't be my last.
I hope so, too. Would you care to see the garden?
I'd love to. May I just wash my hands, please?
Yes, the first door at the top of the stairs.
I'm afraid I must go now.
Come again whenever you like. Do come and see us again before you return to Germany.
Good-bye and thank you.
Remember us to Doris when you write home.
Yes, I will. Good-bye.

<A Ship Sails up to Bideford>

A ship sails up to Bideford;
Upon a western breeze,
Mast by mast, sail over sail,
She rises from the seas,
And sights the hills of Devon
And the misty English trees.

She comes from Eastern islands;
The sun is on her hold;
She bears the fruit of Jaffa,
Dates, oranges, and gold.

She brings the silk of China,
And bales of Persian dyes,
And birds with sparkling feathers,
And snakes with diamond eyes.

She's gliding in the starlight
As white as any gull:
The East is gliding with her
In the shadows of her hull.

A ship sails up to Bideford;
Upon a western breeze,
With fruits of Eastern summers
She rises from the seas,
And sights the hills of Devon
And the misty English trees.

Herbert Asquith

<The Lights on the Islands>

One night we passed two islands, steeply humped against faint reflected moonlight; and on each of them, high up, shone a steady yellow gleam.

"Not lighthouses," I said to Laura. "Villages."

We gazed as the ship slid by and the humps receded into the darkness and even the lights were obscured by the shoulder of a hill, never to be seen by us again. So peaceful and secret; so self-contained.

One of the ship's officers joined us, off duty.

"Yes," he said, following our gaze. "One of them is a leper colony and the other a penal settlement."

God, is there no escape from suffering and sin?

V. Sackville-West, No Signposts in the Sea

Every year thousands of Commonwealth students come to Britain to study. The majority return later to their own countries.

10 A. Journey's End

1. The total population of the Commonwealth today is about 750 million. Eighty seven per cent of these are coloured people. Some are the original inhabitants of their countries, like the peoples of India or the negroes of Nigeria, others are the descendants of former slaves, like the negroes of the West Indies.

The first African slaves were brought to the West Indies about 400 years ago to work on the sugar plantations. Jamaica, the chief island, was at that time a Spanish colony and remained so until it was captured by the English in 1655. The slave trade continued until 1807, and later, in 1833, Britain abolished slavery and ordered her colonies to set their slaves free.

Nowadays all citizens of the Commonwealth enjoy equal rights, no matter what colour their skins may be. The standard of living among the coloured peoples, however, is still fairly low compared with that of the British, and this caused tens of thousands of West Indian negroes to immigrate into Britain during the 1950's and 1960's in the hope of better jobs and living conditions.

2. Among these immigrants was John Baker, the great-grandson of a former negro slave. He had heard people say that there were good jobs to be had in England. He had done well at the grammar school in Kingston, Jamaica, and his aim was to study physics at London University, then to take a post as a physicist in industry.

In order to pay for his studies John Baker worked in the evenings as a lift-boy in a West End hotel. In London he saw plenty of negroes who were earning good wages as bus conductors, lorry drivers, porters, waiters, waitresses and nurses. It seemed to him that as a qualified physicist he would have the chance of an excellent job. There was only one thing he did not realize. Negroes in England are still rarely to be found in the higher professions.

3. When John Baker had finished his studies, he began to look for a position as a physicist. He applied first for a post in the research department of a firm of plastic manufacturers, and a week later he had to appear for an interview.

In the firm's waiting room five other applicants were sitting—all young English graduates. John Baker was the only negro present. He noticed one or two of the other applicants look at him rather curiously, but he did not worry. He was sure that his qualifications were as good as theirs.

At last it was his turn. The staff manager was polite but rather vague. He scarcely glanced at John Baker's papers. "Thank you, Mr. Baker," he said at the end. "We shall let you know our decision."

John Baker went home and waited impatiently for news. A week later he received a letter, which began as follows:

Dear Mr. Baker,

We regret to inform you that the post for which you applied has now been filled. . . .

No reason was given. John Baker was puzzled and disappointed, but he did not give up hope. During the next few months he applied for dozens of posts with private firms, but in every case the answer was the same: "We're sorry, but the vacancy has been filled." Everybody was very polite. Nobody told him the real reason for his lack of success. But gradually John Baker understood: a barrier stood between him and his career. It was his colour.

In despair John Baker wrote to a government department and asked them to give him a job. This time he was successful. The British Government offered him a post as welfare officer. In this position he would be expected to look after the welfare of poor negro families in London. It was a job, but it was not the work for which he had been trained. This made him hesitate.

4. Then he saw an advertisement in the newspaper. The Government of Nigeria offered positions as instructors to science graduates. All his friends advised him to apply for the job. Nigeria, like Jamaica, was a member of the Commonwealth. The passport with which he had come to England would also allow him to enter Nigeria, and there was no language difficulty, for English is used in all Commonwealth countries.

John Baker applied for the post, and a fortnight later he was asked to appear for an interview. This time there was no polite refusal. Nigeria had just gained her independence and urgently needed qualified instructors of all kinds, especially scientists, so as to train her young workers for new industrial projects. John Baker was just the kind of man they were looking for.

When he landed in Africa, John Baker, a free and educated man, ended the journey which his ancestor had started as a slave four centuries before.

<B. Choosing a Career>

The number of jobs open to young people is greater than ever. What career should the boys and girls who are leaving school each summer choose? When they have passed their school leaving examinations and have received their General Certificate of Education at Ordinary Level (GCE 'O' Level) they have a big choice. Every school has a career teacher who will advise them. So will the officers of the 'Youth Employment Service'. The newspapers are full of offers.

Do you want a career that

1. offers you special training?
2. means work among interesting people?
3. means meeting people and helping them?

THE WESTMINSTER BANK
WILL TRAIN YOU TO BECOME
A FIRST CLASS BANK CLERK

If you are such a person and you can answer YES to all these questions then write to the Staff Manager, Westminster Bank Ltd, London.

We shall train you to become a perfect bookkeeper. Apply in own handwriting.

THE FROSTED FOODS Co., Ltd,
High Wycombe.

Are you interested in becoming a saleswoman in London's finest store? Write to Staff Manager, **HARRODS.**

Why not join Britain's Biggest Exporters?
If you want to know more write to
Ford Motor Company, Ltd, Dagenham.
We shall train you to become fully qualified secretaries, shorthand typists, mechanics, engineers.

Young men leaving school this summer, make your career with **BATA,** Britain's most modern shoe manufacturers. All training and residential expenses paid. Additional allowance from £117 to £220 a year. Fares paid home three times a year.
BATA require young men to train for management posts. We produce 14 million pairs of shoes a year and export 35% of the total shoe exports of the United Kingdom.

Do you want to become a fully qualified nurse? Apply to the **WELSH HOSPITAL, Cardiff.**

<Queen Elizabeth's First Christmas TV Talk>

Twenty-five years ago my grandfather broadcast the first of these Christmas messages. Today is another landmark because television has made it possible for many of you to see me in your homes on Christmas Day. My own family often gather round to watch television, as they are at this moment, and that is how I imagine you now.

I very much hope that this new medium will make my Christmas message more personal and direct.

It is inevitable that I should seem a rather remote figure to many of you—a successor to the Kings and Queens of history: someone whose face may be familiar, but who never really touches your personal lives. But now, at least for a few minutes, I welcome you to the peace of my own home.

That it is possible for some of you to see me today is just another example of the speed at which things are changing all around us. Because of these changes I am not surprised that many people feel lost and unable to decide what to hold on to and what to discard, how to take advantage of the new life without losing the best of the old.

But it is not the new inventions which are the difficulty. The trouble is caused by unthinking people who carelessly throw away ageless ideals as if they were old and outworn machinery.

They would have religion thrown aside, morality in personal and public life made meaningless, honesty counted as foolishness, and self-interest set up in place of self-restraint.

At this critical moment in our history we will certainly lose the respect of the world if we abandon those fundamental principles which guided the men and women who built the greatness of this country and Commonwealth.

Today we need a special kind of courage, not the kind needed in battle, but a kind which makes us stand up for everything that we know is right, everything that is true and honest. We need the kind of courage that can withstand the subtle corruption of the cynics so that we can show the world that we are not afraid of the future.

It has always been easy to hate and destroy. To build and to cherish is much more difficult. That is why we can take a pride in the New Commonwealth we are building.

I believe in our qualities and in our strength. I believe that together we can set an example which will encourage upright people everywhere.

I hope that 1958 may bring you God's blessing and all the things you long for. And so I wish you all, young and old, wherever you may be, all the fun and enjoyment and the peace of a very happy Christmas.

11 A. The Suez Canal—Waterway of the World

1. One evening in 1875 Lionel Rothschild, the London banker, while entertaining some friends at his home, heard that a Government messenger wished to speak to him about an urgent business matter.

Rothschild found the messenger waiting in his study.

"Please excuse me, sir, for disturbing you at this late hour," said the messenger. "But the Prime Minister has asked me to enquire about the possibility of an immediate loan."

"For what amount?" asked Rothschild.

"Four million pounds," said the messenger.

"And what is your security?"

"The British Government."

A few days later it was announced that Mr. Disraeli, the British Prime Minister, had used this enormous sum to buy nearly 180,000 Suez Canal company shares from the bankrupt ruler of Egypt, thus giving Britain a large share in the new canal.

2. Though registered under an Egyptian name, the Suez Canal was, strictly speaking, a French project, built by a Frenchman, Ferdinand de Lesseps, with French money. It was 103 miles long and connected the Mediterranean with the Red Sea.

The British Prime Minister's action, taken without the consent of Parliament, meant that Britain and France together now completely controlled the Canal, but in England Disraeli had to face a storm of criticism. Why, asked MPs, had the Prime Minister spent such an enormous amount on a 'ditch dug in the sand'?

But Disraeli was a clever statesman, who well knew what he was doing. At that time Britain still ruled over the greatest Empire the world had ever seen. The Canal was of vital importance to her sea-routes. To reach her rich territories in India and the Far East, British ships now no longer had to make the long and dangerous voyage round the Cape of Good Hope, the Suez Canal having shortened the distance by 4,000 miles.

From that time onwards British influence in Egypt grew ever stronger. In 1888 an international treaty was signed which allowed ships of all nations, whether armed or not, to use the Canal in peace or war. But during the first ten years of the 20th century international rivalry began to grow, and, as war-clouds gathered over Europe, Britain proclaimed Egypt a British protectorate and took over the defence of the Suez Canal.

During the First World War the Turks, once rulers of Egypt, now allies of Germany, advanced through Palestine and managed to reach the Canal, but were

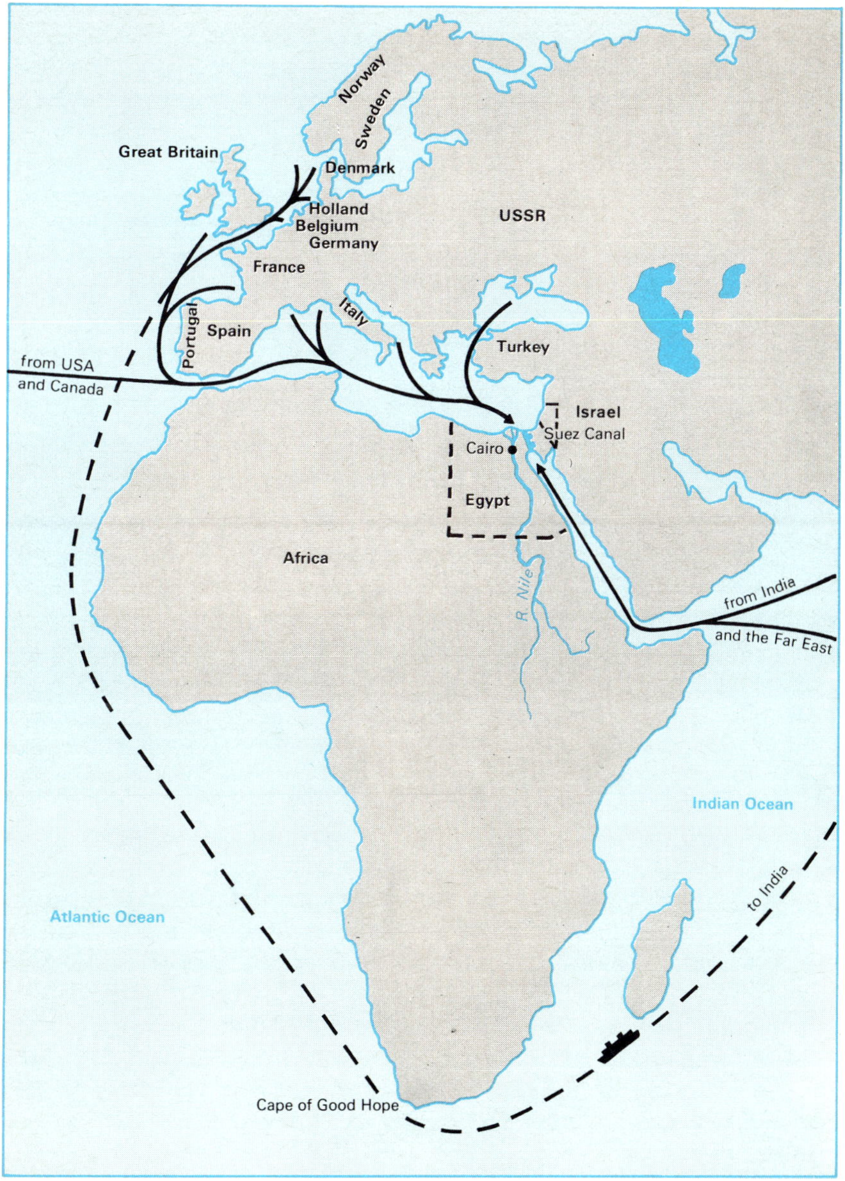

The Suez Canal
artery of world trade

— — — —	Cape route to India 10,700 miles
———	Suez route to India 6,200 miles

driven back after a fierce battle. For the rest of the war the Canal was defended by troops from different parts of the Empire.

3. During the years between the two world wars the old concept of Empire began to change. Among colonial peoples all over the world, and especially in India, resistance to British rule was growing fast. The Egyptians, too, demanded their freedom, and in 1936 Britain gave up the protectorate, though still retaining the right to keep her troops along the Suez Canal.

In 1939 the Second World War began, the Suez Canal again becoming an important military objective. First the Italians, then the Germans under their brilliant leader, Field Marshal Rommel, advanced eastwards across North Africa towards Egypt and the Canal.

In August 1942, English newspapers appeared with the headline: 'Rommel at the Gates of Alexandria'. Only 50 miles lay between the Germans and the Canal. Then came the successful British attack, and Rommel began his long retreat, which ended a year later with the surrender of the German and Italian forces. The War in Africa was over and the Suez Canal still remained in the hands of the British.

4. After the end of the war a great part of Europe lay in ruins. Power had shifted to America in the west and the Soviet Union in the east. The old British Empire had become a thing of the past. In its place arose the new concept of the Commonwealth—a family of free and independent states, with Britain as an equal partner.

The demands for independence could no longer be ignored. In 1947 the British left India, and that country celebrated its first Independence Day. This was followed, as the years passed, by further Independence Days all over the world as colony after colony was given its freedom. The last British troops left Egypt. But the Canal Company still controlled the waterway, Britain and France being the main share-holders.

Then, in 1956, Egypt again appeared in the headlines of the British newspapers: 'Nasser nationalizes the Suez Canal'. Thus, just as Disraeli, with one stroke, had shut Egypt out of the Suez Canal Company, so now the Egyptian president turned the tables and claimed the Canal for Egypt.

Britain and France made a last attempt to regain control. In the autumn of 1956 Israeli, British and French forces invaded Egypt. But world opinion, including America and the Soviet Union, was against them, and the United Nations condemned their action, thus forcing them to withdraw.

Since the 1967 war between Israel and the United Arab Republic, the Suez Canal has been closed, and once more ships have to travel around the Cape of Good Hope to and from Europe.

<B. Conversation: Passengers on an Ocean Liner>

Mr. A: Hallo! Nice to see you again. Aren't we cabin neighbours?

Mr. B: I believe we are.

Mr. A: Where have you been since the voyage began? I didn't see you in the dining-saloon at all.

Mr. B: No, I couldn't touch a thing. I stayed below deck—spent three days lying flat in my berth.

Mr. A: There was a lot of rolling and pitching after we left the port of New York.

Mr. B: Oh, don't talk about it! I'm a very bad sailor. Haven't you ever been seasick?

Mr. A: No, I don't know the meaning of the word. I always take pills against seasickness. They always do the trick.

Mr. B: I get seasick even if the passage is not rough but smooth.

Mr. A: I'm sorry to hear that. We have had excellent meals these days.

Mr. B: I'll have to eat double portions for the rest of the voyage to get my money's worth of food.

Mr. A: I'm glad to see you've got back the old fighting spirit. Will you join me for a drink at the bar below the bridge?

Mr. B: With pleasure. But first I'm going to walk a few rounds from bow to stern for my health.

Mr. A: Right you are. See you later.

<Anecdote: Gunboat Diplomacy>

Towards the end of the 19th century the British government decided to send a gunboat to Zanzibar, where there was unrest among the natives. The captain of the gunboat received the following instruction from the Prime Minister:

"You will turn your guns on the royal palace, land and present our demands to the Sultan."

"And what if the Sultan refuses our demands?" asked the captain.

"That's quite unthinkable," said the Prime Minister. "But if he does—then return to your ship and sail away."

The demands were hard. The Sultan considered them carefully, then sent his Grand Vizier on board the gunboat. During the negotiations the Vizier asked:

"And what do you intend to do, if my master refuses your demands?"

The captain glanced towards the cannons of his ship and said solemnly:

"Then I fear I shall have no choice but to carry out the second part of my instructions."

Within half an hour the Sultan had accepted the British demands.

Mahatma Gandhi

12 A. Mahatma Gandhi

1. In 1877 all India was firmly under British rule. During the past 200 years, from a few small trading stations on the coast, the British had gradually gained control of the whole country. They had defeated their main trading rivals, the French, and by treaty and conquest they had brought the many independent states under British domination. A serious rebellion among Indian troops had been crushed, and in London Queen Victoria had just been proclaimed Empress of India. The British Empire was at the height of its power. Outwardly all was peaceful; but under the surface, especially among educated Indians, unrest and the desire for freedom were steadily growing.

At that time a young Indian boy of 9 was living with his parents in the little town of Porbandar on the west coast. He was a shy boy, small for his age, and not very strong. His name was Mohandas Gandhi.

Gandhi was highly intelligent and, on reaching the age of 20, he travelled to London to study law. After qualifying, he returned to India and two years later went to South Africa to work as a lawyer among the Indian immigrants there. He often took up their cause in the courts. During the Boer War he

organized a team of Indian stretcher-bearers and won praise from the Boers and the British. Later he gave up his profession to lead the coloured people in their struggle for better living conditions. He began to publish a newspaper and organized strikes to protest against racial discrimination in South Africa. This led to his being arrested and imprisoned.

2. In 1914 Gandhi returned to India to continue the struggle in his own land. The independence movement was rapidly gaining strength, but it was still limited to politicians and educated people.

Gandhi realized that the success of the movement depended on his winning the support of the masses. Although he came from a wealthy family and could have enjoyed a comfortable life, he decided to devote himself to the independence movement among the people.

He went among them barefoot and in simple clothing, speaking to them in words that they could understand. He was a deeply religious man, who hated any kind of violence, and he showed his people how to fight for their freedom by peaceful means—by strikes and by refusing to pay taxes.

Gandhi's influence spread rapidly among the people, who trusted him as one of themselves and followed him without question. In 1930, when the British introduced new taxes, he called the people to protest against the tax on salt, the production of which was a British monopoly. Even the poorest Indian peasant understood the importance of salt, and thousands of them followed him on his famous march to the coast, where he publicly made salt from sea water.

3. To the British Gandhi represented an insoluble problem. It would have been easier to crush an armed rebellion than to deal with Gandhi's peaceful methods. Again and again he was put in prison for breaking the tax laws, but this only strengthened his power over the people, many of whom regarded him as a saint and a martyr. They called him 'Mahatma', which means 'great soul'.

During the Second World War Britain appealed to India to support the struggle against Japan, but Gandhi continued to demand freedom for his people. "Leave India now" was his answer, and he used all his influence to oppose the war effort.

When the war ended, it was clear that independence could no longer be delayed. Step by step the transfer of power from London to Delhi was prepared, the last British troops were withdrawn in 1947, and India became free.

Gandhi's aim had been achieved, but there was still one great problem which even he had not been able to solve. The population of India was divided into two great religious groups, the Hindus, who were in the majority, and the Moslems. Gandhi himself was a Hindu, and he had always hoped that it would be possible for the Hindus and the Moslems to live in peace under one govern-

ment. The Moslems, however, feared that such a government would be under the control of the Hindus, and they insisted on having their own state. Thus the great country was divided into two independent nations—India, the home of the Hindus, and Pakistan, the land of the Moslems.

4. In the first months after independence there was a great danger of riots breaking out between the Hindus and the Moslems in Calcutta. Gandhi prevented a massacre by going fearlessly among the people, appealing to them to avoid violence.

His message of brotherhood, however, made him many enemies among the extremists on both sides. Threatening letters were sent to him, and a bomb exploded in the garden of the house where he was staying in Delhi. His followers warned him against showing himself in public, but Gandhi would not listen to them.

Then, on January 30th, 1948, Gandhi attended a prayer meeting in Delhi. As he entered, a young Hindu fanatic stepped forward out of the crowd and fired three shots. Gandhi spoke the name of God and fell. In a few minutes he was dead.

Gandhi died with many tasks unfinished. The conflict between the Hindus and the Moslems remained unsolved. But his great work for India was carried on by his successor, Nehru, who, in 1949, proclaimed India a free republic within the Commonwealth.

<B. Perfect Control>

The country is India. A British officer and his wife are giving a large dinner party. They are sitting with their guests—among them an American naturalist— in their large dining-room which has a marble floor and wide glass doors opening on to a veranda. A lively discussion starts between a young girl, who insists that women have outgrown the jumping-on-a-chair-at-the-sight-of-a-mouse era, and a colonel, who says that they haven't. The American does not take part in the discussion but watches the other guests. As he looks, he sees a strange expression come over the face of the hostess. She is staring straight ahead. With a slight gesture she summons the native boy standing behind her chair and whispers to him. The boy's eyes widen: he quickly leaves the room. Of the guests, none except the American notices this or sees the boy put a bowl of milk on the veranda just outside the open doors. In India, milk in a bowl means only one thing—bait for a snake.

The American realizes there must be a cobra in the room. His first impulse is to jump back and warn the others, but he knows the tumult would frighten the cobra into striking. So he speaks quickly: "I want to know just what control everyone at this table has. I will count slowly up to three hundred—that's five

minutes—and not one of you is to move. Those who move will have to pay five pounds. Ready!"

The 20 people sit like stone images while he counts. He is saying "... two hundred and eighty ..." when, out of the corner of his eye, he sees the cobra come out from under the table and move towards the bowl of milk. Screams ring out as he jumps to slam the veranda doors.

"You were right, Colonel," the host exclaims. "A man has just shown us an example of perfect control." "Just a minute," the American says, turning to his hostess. "Mrs. Wynnes, how did you know that a cobra was in the room?" A faint smile lights up the woman's face as she replies: "Because it was crawling across my foot."

<The Blind Men and the Elephant>

It was six men of Hindostan
To learning much inclined,
Who went to see the Elephant,
(Though all of them were blind):
That each by observation
Might satisfy his mind.

The first approached the Elephant,
And happening to fall
Against his broad and sturdy side,
At once began to bawl:
"Bless me, it seems the Elephant
Is very like a wall."

The second, feeling of his tusk,
Cried, "Ho! what have we here
So very round and smooth and sharp?
To me 'tis mighty clear
This wonder of an Elephant
Is very like a spear."

The third approached the animal,
And happening to take
The squirming trunk within his hands,
Then boldly up and spake:
"I see," quoth he, "the Elephant
Is very like a snake."

The fourth stretched out his eager hand
And felt about the knee,
"What most this mighty beast is like
Is mighty plain," quoth he;
"Tis clear enough the Elephant
Is very like a tree."

The fifth who chanced to touch the ear
Said, "Even the blindest man
Can tell what this resembles most;
Deny the fact who can,
This marvel of an Elephant
Is very like a fan."

The sixth no sooner had begun
About the beast to grope,
Than, seizing on the swinging tail
That fell within his scope,
"I see," cried he, "the Elephant
Is very like a rope."

And so these men of Hindostan
Disputed loud and long,
Each in his own opinion
Exceeding stiff and strong,
Though each was partly in the right
And all were in the wrong.

John Godfrey Saxe

<The Commonwealth and its Peoples>

What is the Commonwealth?

The Commonwealth is an association of over 30 independent countries and the 26 smaller countries, or dependencies, which they administer. It occupies nearly a quarter of the world's surface and has a total population of over 913 million.

The Queen and the Commonwealth

All the countries of the Commonwealth were formerly colonies of the British Empire and were governed from London. Gradually, as the colonies became stronger and better able to govern themselves, they demanded and were given their freedom. Thus the Empire slowly developed into the Commonwealth, with Britain no longer its ruler but an equal partner of the other free countries. Today more than 90% of all Commonwealth peoples belong to free and independent states. Some of these, like Australia and Canada, are monarchies, with Queen Elizabeth II as their head of state. Others, like India and Ghana, are republics under their own presidents. All of them, however, acknowledge the Queen as the Head of the Commonwealth.

A Multi-racial Association

Until 1947, the independent Commonwealth countries contained about 70 million people, the great majority of whom were white. Then India and Pakistan, with their huge coloured populations of nearly 500 million, gained their freedom. Now more than 87% of the free peoples of the Commonwealth are coloured. When the Commonwealth Prime Ministers meet in London, less than half of them are white. The multi-racial character of the Commonwealth today is based on the principle of equal rights for all races. Predominantly negro states, for example, have negro majority governments. This led in 1961 to a quarrel between South Africa, which is ruled by a white minority government, and the other Commonwealth states. The result was that South Africa left the Commonwealth.

Since 1945 only four other countries have left the Commonwealth—Burma, Eire (Southern Ireland), Southern Yemen and Pakistan (1972). All the others, in spite of great differences of race, religion and politics, chose to remain in the Commonwealth on gaining their independence.

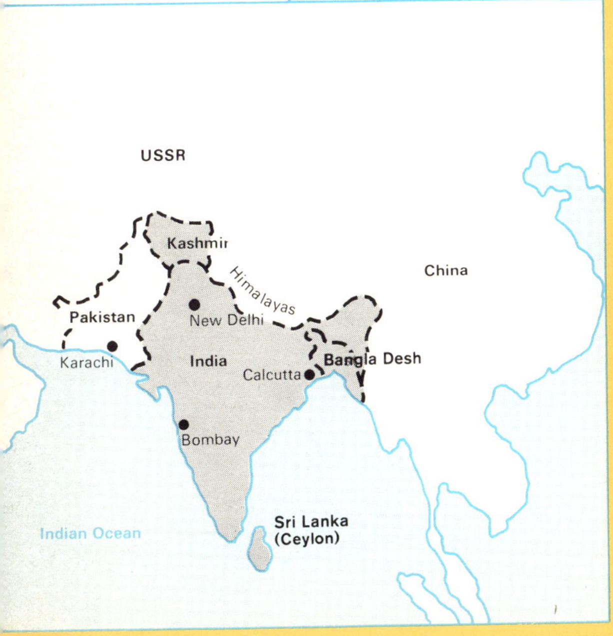

Some Commonwealth Countries

Canada

Area: 3,900,000 sq.miles
Population:
21,000,000
Languages:
English, French
Religion:
Christian
Head of State:
Queen Elizabeth II

Republic of India

Area: 1,200,000 sq.miles
Population:
520,000,000
Languages:
Hindi, English and 13 other officially recognized languages
Religions:
Hindu (78%), Moslem (10%), Christian (2·5%) and many others
Head of State:
President of India

Sri Lanka (Ceylon)

Area: 25,332 sq.miles
Population:
12,000,000
Languages:
Sinhalese, Tamil, English
Religions:
Buddhist (70%), Hindu (25%), Christian (1%), Moslem (0·5%)
Head of State:
President of Sri Lanka

Ghana

Area: 92,000 sq.miles
Population:
8,545,000
Languages:
English and more than 50
Negro languages and dialects
Religions:
traditional native beliefs,
Moslem, Christian
Head of State:
President of Ghana

Australia

Area: 3,000,000 sq.miles
Population:
12,200,000
Language:
English
Religion:
Christian
Head of State:
Queen Elizabeth II

New Zealand

Area: 104,000 sq.miles
Population:
2,800,000
Languages:
English, Maori
Religion:
Christian
Head of State:
Queen Elizabeth II

Common Ties

What holds the Commonwealth together? Apart from the symbol of the Crown there is a common tradition of law and of parliamentary government. English is also an official language in all Commonwealth countries. Of even greater importance are the economic ties. The Commonwealth controls nearly a quarter of world trade, and a good deal of this is 'within the family'. There is also a world-wide programme of economic aid, by which the richer countries give help to the poorer. Britain alone, for example, spent more than £ 175,000,000 in 1970 on economic aid for the Commonwealth, especially for India, Pakistan and the new African states.

Important People

Discoverers, adventurers, seamen, soldiers, business men and politicians—such were the men who built the British Empire and held it together for more than three hundred years.

Gradually Britain had to realize that her colonies could not remain for ever under British rule. One by one, as they grew stronger and more able to govern themselves, they began to demand their freedom. Mahatma Gandhi of India and Jomo Kenyatta of Kenya—men of all races and colours arose to lead their peoples on the difficult road to independence. Thus the Empire of yesterday was slowly transformed into the Commonwealth of today—a multi-racial association of free and independent nations.

1 *Sir Walter Raleigh* (1552—1618). One of the most brilliant figures at the court of Queen Elizabeth I was Sir Walter Raleigh. As a young man he fought in the Netherlands and Ireland. Then, with the approval of the Queen, he planned to establish the first English colonies in North America. His expedition failed, but Raleigh never lost interest in the idea and formed a company to found colonies in the New World. His efforts prepared the way for future colonists.

Later Raleigh explored South America in a vain hope of finding the legendary 'City of Gold', El Dorado, and in 1596—97 he led two successful attacks against the Spaniards, Britain's great rivals for sea power.

The death of Elizabeth meant Raleigh's downfall, for King James I, who succeeded her, distrusted the bold adventurer and, after an unfair trial, Raleigh was sentenced to death for treason.

For more than 12 years Raleigh lived as a prisoner in the Tower of London, studying science and writing his History of the World. But all his efforts to gain the King's favour failed and he was executed on Tower Hill in 1618.

2 *Captain Cook* (1728—79). James Cook, the son of a Yorkshire farm worker, was apprenticed to a shopkeeper, but soon left this work to go to sea. He was a good seaman and an excellent navigator and quickly rose to the rank of captain.

Cook made many scientific expeditions to the Pacific. On one of these he became the first white man to land on New Zealand. He also explored the east coast of Australia, named it New South Wales, and took possession of it in the name of his king. Today Australia and New Zealand are both important members of the Commonwealth.

On all his expeditions Cook showed a kindly interest in the natives, and his kindness usually won their confidence. Yet it was at their hands that he finally met his death. In 1779 he made his last expedition to the Pacific, where he discovered the Hawaii Islands. One day a small boat was stolen from his ship, and Cook landed and demanded that the boat should be given back. The natives suddenly attacked him, and, before he could return to his ship, he was struck down and killed.

3 *Robert Clive* (1725—74). 'An ill-mannered good-for-nothing.' That was what people called young Robert Clive. He had to be removed from four different schools because of his bad behaviour, and at last his father decided to send the boy overseas to earn his living. So, at the age of 18, Robert Clive sailed to India as a clerk in the East India Company.

Thus began the career of the man who laid the foundation of the British Empire in India. At that time India was divided into a number of small states, and the French and British East India Companies were fighting for power. Clive, who was fearless, daring and a born soldier, joined the army and soon became a captain. After a series of brilliant victories against the French, Clive succeeded in overthrowing the powerful and cruel Nawab of Bengal. By treaties of friendship with other Indian rulers he gradually built up British power in other parts

4

5

6

of India, and in 1765 the East India Company officially took over the government of Bengal, with Clive as its Governor.

Clive was hungry for power. He also made a huge fortune, and his enemies accused him of dishonesty in his dealings with the Indian rulers. His last years were spent in disgrace, but no one could deny that he had been a just administrator, a great ruler, and a brilliant soldier.

4 *Cecil Rhodes* (1853—1902). Because of bad health Cecil Rhodes was sent to South Africa at the age of 16. Within two years he had made a fortune in the South African diamond rush; within five he was in control of big gold-mining interests. In 1881 he entered politics, and nine years later he was Prime Minister of the Cape and the richest and most powerful man in South Africa.

At that time the struggle for colonies in Africa was in full swing. Rhodes believed passionately that British rule was the best for the people of Africa and he used great power to gain large territories for Britain including Bechuanaland and Rhodesia, which was named after him.

Rhodes' efforts to extend British rule led to war with the Dutch colonists in South Africa. Out of this war a new state arose—the Union of South Africa. But Rhodes did not live to see it. He died in 1902 and was buried in the Matoppo Hills of Rhodesia. His last words were, "So much to do, so little done."

Rhodes left his huge fortune to found the Rhodes Scholarships at Oxford for students from the Commonwealth, the USA and Germany.

5 *Rudyard Kipling* (1865—1936). The last quarter of the 19th century was the golden age of the British Empire. Queen Victoria had been proclaimed Empress of India, the world was at peace and Britain was its leading power, immensely rich and immensely strong.

During this time a young, unknown journalist, the son of an English official in India, began to publish stories and poems about life in the frontier posts

and among the regiments of the Indian Army. He was Rudyard Kipling, and he quickly became famous as a new voice in literature—the voice of imperialism.

'Take up the White Man's Burden' was Kipling's message. Like Cecil Rhodes he saw the White Man as a heroic figure, whose duty was to bring order, justice and culture to other races in the world.

Today Kipling's imperialistic ideals are out of date, but a number of his stories and military ballads have become recognized as literary classics and his animal stories are still read by children all over the world.

6 *Jan Smuts* (1870—1950). Born in South Africa of Dutch descent, Jan Smuts went to Cambridge in 1891 to study law. In 1895 he returned to South Africa, where he became a strong opponent of British colonial policy. During the Boer War (1899—1902) he fought against the British. Later, as a minister of the new South African government, he worked tirelessly for better understanding between the Boers and the British.

During the First World War Smuts gave his full support to Britain, and in 1919 he became Prime Minister of South Africa. In 1924 he was defeated by the Nationalist Party, which was strongly anti-British. On the outbreak of the Second World War he was returned to power and brought his country into the war on the side of Britain. He became the first Commonwealth officer to hold the rank of Field Marshal.

In 1945 Smuts helped to draw up the charter of the United Nations and a year later led his country's delegation to the UN. In 1948 he was once again defeated by the nationalists. Smuts spent the last two years of his life as the leader of the opposition, protesting strongly against the government's policy of racial segregation. All his efforts, however, were in vain. Eleven years after his death South Africa left the Commonwealth because of her racial policy, and declared herself a republic.

Important Dates

1583	Newfoundland becomes the first English colony
1588	Defeat of the Spanish Armada
1607	First colony on the American mainland founded at Jamestown, Virginia
1620	Pilgrim Fathers sail to America
1756—63	Seven Years' War against France—British rule established in Canada and India
1769—71	Captain Cook's voyages of exploration to New Zealand and Australia
1776	American colonies proclaim their independence as the United States

1814—78	The naval bases of Malta, Cyprus, Aden, Hong Kong and Singapore pass into the British Empire
1877	Queen Victoria proclaimed Empress of India
1867—1907	Canada, Australia, New Zealand become self-governing
1899—1902	Boer War
1909	Union of South Africa founded and granted self-government
1914—18	World War I
1926	Imperial Conference—the expression 'British Commonwealth' adopted to include all self-governing states in the Empire
1931	Statute of Westminster—Recognition of full independence of Canada, Australia, New Zealand and the Union of South Africa
1939—45	World War II
1947	India and Pakistan become independent
1948—72	The Republic of Ireland (Eire), Burma, the Union of South Africa, Southern Yemen and Pakistan leave the Commonwealth. Twenty-five former colonies (including twelve African states) become independent and join the Commonwealth.

Opinions about the Commonwealth

1. *Field-Marshal Smuts:* 'I think the expression "Empire" is misleading. We are not one State or nation or empire, but a community of States, which I prefer to call "the British Commonwealth of Nations".' (1917)

2. *Sir Robert Menzies, Prime Minister of Australia:* 'It is an error to suppose that when the first republic entered the Commonwealth door the old sentiment flew out of the window. We still have an attachment to each other which none of us would deny. That is why we see in our newly independent nations such eagerness to remain in the Commonwealth. That is why I can sit in a Prime Ministers' Conference and feel immediately as much at home as if I were sitting in my own Cabinet.' (1960)

3. *Mr. Duncan Sandys, Secretary of State for Commonwealth Relations:* 'Britain has no desire to hold on to her remaining Colonies a day longer than is necessary. Politically, they involve us in much unwelcome controversy with the outside world; and economically they bring us no profit. We could, of course, give all our Colonies their independence overnight, as some members of the United Nations are pressing us to do. But we think we have a responsibility to the inhabitants, which we must fully discharge. We have a duty, not only to lead them to independence, but also to prepare them for the responsibilities which this involves.' (1962)

IV. The USA and the World

13 A. Lindbergh's Flight

1. The prize the twenty-five-year-old American, Charles Lindbergh, was competing for in May 1927 had been offered by a New York hotel owner as early as 1919—25,000 dollars for the first New York-Paris flight.

The Atlantic Ocean had already been crossed by plane from Newfoundland to Ireland by two Englishmen in 1919; the English had sent an airship to America and back; the Germans had flown their airship, the ZR 3, from Friedrichshafen to New York; but the prize for the flight New York—Paris was still to be won. Shortly before Lindbergh's attempt to fly to Paris, two Frenchmen had started from Paris to New York. Their plane had been lost sight of over the Atlantic, and they had never been heard of again.

Lindbergh was already an expert pilot before he started on his flight to Paris. He had been a lieutenant in the American Air Force and later had flown the mail between Chicago and St. Louis. For his flight across the Atlantic Ocean he chose a small single-engined plane, 'The Spirit of St. Louis'.

2. The night before the flight he slept badly. There were so many things to think about. Early in the morning of May 20th Lindbergh drove to the airfield where the last preparations were being made to his plane. Would the weather allow him to start? He hoped so. There were a few clouds in the sky, but they were harmless. At 7.30 a.m. he was ready. Every detail had been thought of. He fastened his safety-belt, pulled his goggles down over his eyes and took off, accompanied by the good wishes of millions of Americans. Before the beginning of a big boxing-match in New York, forty thousand spectators were told to rise from their seats and pray for Lindbergh.

At 9.30 a.m. Lindbergh left behind him the coast of the United States. Although he had only been flying for some hours he began to feel tired. His legs were stiff and cramped. He did not dare to eat. An empty stomach was better for keeping awake. Then he saw the coast of Nova Scotia, the Canadian province north-east of the United States. Forests and lakes passed underneath him. Twelve hours after the take-off, about 1,100 miles from New York, 'The Spirit of St. Louis' was caught sight of near St. John's, the capital of Newfoundland. Then Lindbergh left the American continent for the weary flight of 2,000 miles to the Irish coast. Below, he could see white icebergs on the grey Atlantic. Over the Atlantic he was met by huge clouds and strong winds. It became bitterly cold. 'The Spirit of St. Louis' was tossed about like a leaf in the wind.

Charles Lindbergh, the first man to fly alone across the Atlantic, landed in Paris on May 21st, 1927. A huge crowd had gathered to welcome him.

With his flashlight Lindbergh inspected the wings of the plane. Ice was forming on them. His plane was in danger. After two hours of flying through the darkness, the moon appeared, lighting up the clouds. Lindbergh became tired, and soon he was being tricked by visions. The clouds changed into dragons and monsters ready to swallow up 'The Spirit of St. Louis', but the little plane continued its way eastwards towards Europe. Lindbergh wanted to sleep. His eyelids were heavy, his back ached, his arms were stiff, but to fall asleep would be certain death. He used every trick he knew to keep awake. He sang, pinched his arms and checked the controls of his plane again and again. He was glad that 'The Spirit of St. Louis' was not able to fly without his help.

After 24 hours of flying he was again troubled by visions. He saw islands with beaches, hills and woods. So he thought, but in reality there was nothing but the seemingly endless ocean. Then after 27 hours he sighted several small fishing boats. The coast of Europe could not be far. Suddenly there were hills ahead of him. Were they the hills of Ireland, Spain or France that were to be seen in the distance? It was the coast of Ireland. With his heart full of joy he looked down on the Irish landscape, on small farms, on cattle grazing in the fields. It was wonderful to see people on the roads looking up at him. But he had to fly on. Paris was still 600 miles away. Two hours later England appeared. His course took him over Devon and Cornwall, then over the Channel until he reached the French coast.

3. At 10.p.m. on May 21st, $33\frac{1}{2}$ hours after he had left New York, he saw the lights of Paris. He was given an overwhelming reception by the French. As soon as 'The Spirit of St. Louis' stopped on the runway thousands of Frenchmen ran across the field to greet the great aviator. He had hardly left the plane when he was seized and carried away by the wildly cheering crowd. For the next half hour his feet did not touch the ground.

His reception in Europe was nothing compared with the one that lay in store for him in the United States. There he received the greatest welcome ever given to an American. Lindbergh had become a national hero.

<B. Machines in Daily Life>

The Americans were the first to introduce machines into daily life, but their use soon spread to other countries. Let us see what part machines play in the life of modern London.

1. Praed Street, Paddington, London. It is eleven o'clock on a Sunday night. All the shops are closed with the exception of one: The Coin Laundry. It is brightly lit, but there is nobody in it. Neither attendant, nor customer. Suddenly a young man with a basket full of dirty linen opens the door. Two coins in a machine, and a packet of soap powder is in his hand. Then he opens one of the 24 washing-machines, throws in the linen and soap powder and goes away after having put one 10p piece in the slot. Half an hour later he comes back again, takes his washing, now clean, and disappears.

2. Park Lane Underground Garage, under Hyde Park, has parking space for 1,100 cars. The garage is open day and night. You drive your car down a tunnel and stop in front of a barrier. A machine at your window holds out a ticket. As soon as you have taken the ticket, the barrier rises automatically and closes behind you. Don't look for an attendant, for there is none. Just choose your bay and walk out of the garage by the pedestrian exit.

Your first sight of a garage employee will be when you drive out of the garage. At the car-exit barrier a man checks the time and day of your having entered the garage on the ticket. You pay for the time your car was parked.

3. On June 10th, 1965 a British jet carrying 80 people from Paris to London became the first passenger-carrying plane in the world to use an automatic landing system. All the pilot had to do was to apply the brakes after landing. The automatic control assures safe landing in any weather.

Man's work replaced by machines. Automation is the word. Planes fly automatically controlled, and the pilot is only there in case of emergency.

A new world, an automated world is developing.

<The Young Dead Soldiers>

The young dead soldiers do not speak.
Nevertheless they are heard in the still houses.
(Who has not heard them?)

They have a silence that speaks for them at night
And when the clock counts.

They say,
We were young. We have died. Remember us.

They say,
We have done what we could
But until it is finished it is not done.

They say,
We have given our lives
But until it is finished no one can know
what our lives gave.

They say,
Our deaths are not ours,
They are yours,
They will mean what you make them.

They say,
Whether our lives and our deaths were for peace and a new hope
Or for nothing
We cannot say.
It is you who must say this.

They say,
We leave you our deaths,
Give them their meaning.
Give them an end to the war and a true peace,

Give them a victory that ends the war and
a peace afterwards,
Give them their meaning.

We were young, they say.
We have died.
Remember us.

Archibald Macleish

In August, 1963, a huge crowd of 200,000 people, white and coloured, marched through Washington to demand civil rights for negroes.

14 A. We, too, are America

1. "We coloured people are nothing but a bundle of resentments and sufferings which are going to explode somewhere," said a Mississippi woman one day as she stood in front of a St. Louis restaurant. She was looking at a notice 'For Whites only'.

The explosion—and no one would have then taken it for that—came in December, 1955, the day Mrs. Rosa Parks boarded a bus in Montgomery, Alabama.

Mrs. Rosa Parks was a coloured woman, in her early fifties. When the bus arrived, Mrs. Parks boarded it as she had done many times before. Once on the bus, she obeyed a familiar practice. A part of the bus—from the front to the middle—was reserved for white people, the part from that point to the rear was reserved for negroes. Mrs. Parks sat in the first seat behind the white part—that is to say, the first negro seat.

It was the rush hour in Montgomery, and the bus was being rapidly filled. Several negroes and whites had to stand. Shortly after Mrs. Parks had sat down, the white bus driver ordered her and three other negroes to stand up and let whites have their seats. This meant that Mrs. Parks would have to stand while a white man sat in her seat. The other three negroes moved when told to do so. Rosa Parks refused, "I'm not going to move," she said. Mrs. Parks was arrested. There was no disturbance on the bus when she was being led away by the police. Some white people were heard to murmur about "damn niggers" and a few negroes giggled. The entire incident was over in five minutes. But from this small episode the negro revolt began.

2. Twenty-four hours after Mrs. Parks' arrest a large gathering of local negro leaders was being held to discuss a plan of action. It was decided to call a bus boycott for the following Monday. This meant that seventeen thousand negroes —75 per cent of the bus-riding population—would have to walk to work on Monday morning.

A young negro Baptist minister, Dr. Martin Luther King, accepted the task of distributing pamphlets to spread the news among Montgomery's fifty thousand negro citizens.

The following Sunday, the day before the boycott, the Baptist church in Montgomery was packed. Three thousand people were standing outside waiting for the call of action, the call that Martin Luther King and other negro leaders would be giving. After other speakers had finished, Martin Luther King walked to the rostrum.

"We are here today to say to those who have mistreated us for so long that we are tired of being segregated and humiliated. We are tired of being kicked about by the brutal feet of oppression. Now we have no alternative but to protest. For many years we have shown patience. We have sometimes given our white brothers the feeling that we liked the way we are being treated. But we have come here tonight to be saved from the patience that makes us patient with anything less than freedom and justice."

By then, the angry negroes were ready to walk, march, and if necessary fight. Only the non-violent preaching of Martin Luther King kept them from starting a riot.

3. As the buses drove on Monday morning through the part of the town where the negroes lived, they were empty. The white reaction was bitter. Martin Luther King and other negro leaders were jailed. Despite these acts the protest continued for a whole year. The case was taken to the United States Supreme Court which ruled against segregated seating on municipal buses, and bus segregation came to an end in Montgomery.

The Montgomery story had its effect upon other Southern cities. King formed the Southern Christian Leadership Conference whose first aim was to attack segregation on buses. The struggle against school segregation followed. Martin Luther King became the driving force of the negro revolt. As a disciple of non-violence he was able to involve thousands of American white people in the negro's struggle. "The non-violent man not only refuses to shoot his opponent but he also refuses to hate him," he said in a speech in Chicago. He believed that the man who turns the other cheek is going to win the battle.

In 1964 Dr. Martin Luther King, the preacher of non-violence and the champion of negro civil rights, was awarded the Nobel prize for Peace. In 1968 he was shot and killed in Memphis, Tennessee, but his work still goes on.

B. Conversation: At the Doctor's

Doctor: Next, please.

Patient: Good afternoon, doctor.

Doctor: Good afternoon. You are not a patient of mine, are you?

Patient: No, I'm in England on an exchange visit. I'm German and I come from Berlin.

Doctor: I'll have to have some particulars. What's your name, age and present address?

(Patient gives particulars)

Now, what's the trouble, young lady?

Patient: I've got a bad cold and a sore throat.

Doctor: Have you taken your temperature?

Patient: Yes, it was normal this morning, but yesterday evening it was 100 and I had a bad headache.

Doctor: Let me feel your pulse. Well, that's quite normal, too. I want to look at your throat. Open your mouth, please. Now say 'Ah'! Yes, your throat is a little inflamed. You must gargle three times a day and take a tablet every two hours. I'll write you a prescription. Take it to the chemist's. He will give you some throat tablets and a bottle of gargle.

Patient: What do I owe you, doctor?

Doctor: Nothing, my dear. The National Health Service will pay the fee for your visit and your medicine.

Patient: But I'm a foreigner. I'm only here for a short stay.

Doctor: That doesn't make any difference. You're entitled to free treatment. Come to my surgery again at the end of the week.

Patient: Thank you very much, doctor. Good-bye.

<Boyhood on a Missouri Farm>

In my schoolboy days I had no aversion to slavery. I was not aware that there was anything wrong about it. No one arraigned it in my hearing; the local papers said nothing against it; the local pulpit taught us that God approved it, that it was a holy thing, and that the doubter need only look in the Bible if he wished to settle his mind—and then the texts were read aloud to us to make the matter sure; if the slaves themselves had an aversion to slavery, they were wise and said nothing. In Hannibal we seldom saw a slave misused; on the farm, never.

There was, however, one small incident of my boyhood days which touched this matter, and it must have meant a good deal to me or it would not have stayed in my memory, clear and sharp, vivid and shadowless, all these slow-drifting years. We had a little slave boy whom we had hired from someone, there in Hannibal. He was from the eastern shore of Maryland, and had been brought away from his family and his friends, halfway across the American continent, and sold. He was a cheery spirit, innocent and gentle, and the noisiest creature that ever was, perhaps. All day long he was singing, whistling, yelling, whooping, laughing—it was maddening, devastating, unendurable. At last, one day, I lost all my temper, and went raging to my mother and said Sandy had been singing for an hour without a single break, and I couldn't stand it, and wouldn't she please shut him up. The tears came into her eyes and her lip trembled, and she said something like this:

"Poor thing, when he sings it shows that he is not remembering, and that comforts me; but when he is still I am afraid he is thinking, and I cannot bear it. He will never see his mother again; if he can sing, I must not hinder it, but be thankful for it. If you were older, you would understand me; then that friendless child's noise would make you glad."

Mark Twain

I, too, am America

I, too, sing America.

I am the darker brother.
They send me to eat in the kitchen
when company comes
but I laugh,
and eat well,
and grow strong.

Tomorrow
I'll sit at the table
when company comes.
Nobody'll dare
say to me,
"Eat in the kitchen"
then.

Besides, they'll see how beautiful I am
and be ashamed,—

I, too, am America.

Langston Hughes

In 1965 Edward White became the first American to leave a spacecraft in orbit. For 21 minutes he floated in space.

15 A. The Space Race

1. On October 4th, 1957, the USA was in a fever of excitement about the baseball match that was to take place the following day between the Milwaukee Braves and the New York Yankees. It was the topic from Boston to Los Angeles—in homes, schools, offices, subways. It was even talked about that evening in the Russian Embassy in Washington, D.C., during a reception given for a group of American scientists. All conversation, however, stopped when a high Russian official held up his hand for silence. He had a most important announcement to make: The USSR had sent up a satellite into outer space. At that moment the first man-made satellite was circling round the earth. Sputnik I was its name. It weighed 184 pounds and was 23 inches in diameter, the size of a medicine-ball. Never before had man succeeded in doing this. The space age was born.

The Milwaukee Braves won the match the next day, but they had to share the front page of the newspapers with Sputnik I. The news about Sputnik I came as a shock to the USA—to the American people and above all to the American scientists who had believed they were leading in space science.

2. However, if Sputnik I was a shock, it was also a challenge. America took up the challenge. At Cape Canaveral, now Cape Kennedy, scientists like Wernher von Braun worked day and night, and a few months later, on January 31st, 1958, the first American satellite was sent into space. The space race was on.

Again it was the Russians who were ahead when on September 12th, 1959, Lunik II was landed on the moon. The following month, the first pictures of the moon's far side were taken from Lunik III. On August 20th, a capsule containing two dogs was successfully recovered from Sputnik V. It was the largest satellite launched up to that time.

3. Scarcely has an exploration in history been as carefully planned as man's trips into space. When Columbus sailed west from the shores of Portugal, he knew far less what he had to expect than did the first space men. Nothing was left to chance. During their ground-training the space men have to experience as many of the conditions of space flight as possible. They are trained to withstand the sudden acceleration necessary for launching the rockets into space, because the pressure on the body during the launching is enormous. They get used to being tossed about, to reading the instruments, to receiving the orders from the ground-control centre. They also experience the feeling of weightlessness. When travelling in space, the gravity of the earth has no hold upon them. In a weightless space ship, there is no up and down, no floor or ceiling in the usual meaning of the word. Walking is impossible. This difficulty can be overcome by wearing magnetic shoes, or by pulling oneself along on objects in the cabin or special guide-ropes. Weightless eating is also a problem. Liquids cannot be poured into cups, cooking in the ordinary way is also impossible, as the food would rise out of the pot while being cooked. The soup, the steaks, the pudding would float in the air. Nor would it be suitable to use an ordinary spoon as the food would not stay on it. Spoons must have a lid, liquids must be squeezed from plastic bottles into the mouth.

To overcome all these difficulties 5,500 firms with several million workers are occupied in the space flight industry in the USA. It is already larger than the automobile industry. The space age has just begun, and already there is a shortage of trained men and women in the many fields of space exploration. Thousands of highly trained young people will have to fill new jobs. Over a hundred American colleges and universities are now offering courses in space science.

4. On April 12th, 1961, the Russian Yuri Gagarin became the first man to fly into space. He successfully circled round the earth in 108 minutes and reached an altitude of 188 miles. Seldom did Moscow witness such scenes of rejoicing. No sooner had the news of Gagarin's space flight disappeared from the

world's newspapers than three weeks later the astronaut Alan B. Shepard became the first American in space with a fifteen-minute flight in a Mercury capsule, reaching an altitude of 115 miles and landing in the Atlantic 302 miles from Cape Canaveral.

More Russian and American astronauts flew into space, one of them a Russian woman, who did 49 orbits in three days. Both Soviet and American astronauts left their capsules and floated around their space ships in suits made of special materials. Then, in August 1965, it was the American astronauts Conrad and Cooper who broke the world record by staying 190 hours and 56 minutes in space and circling 120 times round the earth. It was the distance and time needed to reach the moon and come back. Thus they prepared the way for astronauts to land on the moon itself.

It was an Apollo Mother Ship which, in July 1969, took the first three American astronauts to the moon, 240,000 miles away. On nearing it, the Apollo went into orbit. A smaller spacecraft detached itself from the main capsule and landed two of the spacemen on the moon. Finally the two astronauts rejoined the mother ship for the return to earth.

Meanwhile the space race between the USA and the USSR goes on.

<B. Walk in Space—A Dialogue>

It was the third orbit of Gemini 4 with Astronauts McDivitt and White on board, and into space stepped Edward White. From the moment he began his 17,500 m.p.h. walk, White saw the planet Earth 120 miles away. White kept in communication with McDivitt and Gemini Control:

White: I'm looking right down and it looks like we're coming on the coast of California. I'm going in slow rotation to the right. I'm getting to work on getting some pictures, Jim.

McDivitt: O.K. Get out in front where I can see you again ... Where are you?

White: Right out in front now ... There's no difficulty at all in recontacting the spacecraft. I'm very thankful in having the experience to be first.

McDivitt: Ed, will you please roll around? Right now we're pointing just about straight down to the ground ...

White: O.K. ... The sun in space is not blinding but it's quite nice ... I can sit out here and see the whole California coast.

McDivitt: They want you to get back in now.

White: *(laughing)* I'm not coming in ... This is fun.

McDivitt: Come on.
White: Hate to come back to you but I'm coming.
McDivitt: O.K., come in then.
Control: You've got about four minutes to Bermuda.
White: All right. I'll open the door and come through there ... Aren't you going to hold my hand?
McDivitt: No, come on. Let's get in here before it gets dark.
White: It's the saddest moment of my life.
McDivitt: Well, you're going to find it sadder when we have to come down.
Control: Gemini 4. You getting him back in?
McDivitt: He's standing in the seat now.
Control: O.K. You're going to have Bermuda in about 20 seconds.

<A Fight with a Shark>

Santiago, an old fisherman, has caught a giant fish after a terrific struggle. Exhausted, the old man ties the fish to the side of his boat and turns towards the land. But he soon has worse enemies to fight—sharks.

When the old man saw him coming he knew that this was a shark that had no fear at all and would do exactly what he wished. He prepared the harpoon and made the rope fast while he watched the shark come on.

The shark closed fast astern and when he hit the fish the old man saw his mouth open and his strange eyes as he drove forward in the meat just above the tail. The shark's head was out of water and the old man hit it with his blood-mushed hands driving a good harpoon with all his strength. He hit it without hope but with resolution and complete malignancy.

The shark swung over and the old man saw his eye was not alive and then he swung over once again, wrapping himself in two loops of the rope. Three-quarters of his body was clear above the water when the rope came taut, shivered and then snapped. The shark lay quietly for a little while on the surface and the old man watched him. Then he went down very slowly.

"He took about forty pounds," the old man said aloud. He took my harpoon too and all the rope, he thought, and now my fish bleeds again and there will be others.

"But man is not made for defeat," he said. "A man can be destroyed but not defeated." I am sorry that I killed the fish though, he thought. Now the bad time is coming and I do not even have the harpoon. The shark is cruel and able and strong and intelligent. But I was more intelligent than he was. Perhaps not, he thought. Perhaps I was only better armed.

Ernest Hemingway, The Old Man and the Sea (abridged)

A member of UNICEF in Thailand taking children to be medically examined.

16 A. UNO Fights Sickness and Starvation

1. The slow destructive illness we know as tuberculosis is called the 'quiet death' in India where it kills 500,000 people a year.

Hundreds of miles outside the capital, New Delhi, there lies Sachakhera. It is a tiny village, far from the nearest town. Nevertheless UNO has entered the house of a poor Indian family. In the kitchen the young mother listens attentively to a blue-turbaned man. This man explains to her how the United Nations and the Indian Government are working together to stop the spread of TB. Would she bring her children to the shaded side of the street, where a table is standing, and have them inoculated?

The Indian woman knows little of medicine and she glances at the village leader, who is standing at the door. He nods his head, and a few minutes later she takes her children across the street to be inoculated.

That same year in which the youngsters of Sachakhera lined up for the doctor's needle, 45 million people were tested for TB and 14 million inoculated in Asia alone.

2. Every year about 300 million people in the world caught malaria and three million of them died. Rich soil was completely worthless, because the farmers had been struck down by this terrible disease. The malaria-carrying mosquito was the absolute master of millions of acres of good land in Asia, Africa, and Latin America. It was a challenge to UNO.

A dull November fog was enveloping the UNO Headquarters in New York as representatives of some 80 countries assembled to discuss the situation. That year, 1951, the mosquito's deadly sting had been felt worse than ever. In some places 80 out of 100 people were laid low with malaria. UNO decided to strike back and to strike hard. That day in November it declared war on the death-carrying insect. The answer to the problem of how to wipe out the mosquito was DDT. 'Operation Malaria' had top priority. DDT factories were set up in all the malaria affected areas of the world.

One of the most striking examples of how malaria can be beaten with modern means comes from India—a country which needs more productive land to feed its 500 million people. In 1950, at the foot of the Himalayas, half a million acres of fertile land were a jungle swamp because of malaria. About 77 out of 100 children were victims of the disease.

Then came UNO's attack by planes and helicopters. Tens of thousands of tons of DDT were thrown over the area. As a result, the mosquito has almost been wiped out in that region. The production of food rose 30%. But the best news is that only 3 out of 100 children have malaria.

All this has been achieved by the United Nations Children's Fund—UNICEF—one of the UN organizations in which the United States and the Soviet Union work side by side with other countries, including the Federal Republic of Germany. UNICEF is at work to improve the health and welfare of children in underdeveloped regions. Already, with UNICEF supplies, millions of children have been protected against disease or saved from hunger.

UNICEF was awarded the Nobel Prize in 1965.

3. This age may be that of the washing machine, the family car and the bathroom, but only in highly industrialized countries. For the great mass of the world's population it is still the age in which man tills the soil behind the primitive wooden plough as his ancestors did 2,000 years ago. He is underfed and badly clothed. In underdeveloped regions he lives only 40 years on an average, in some countries only 27. In countries with a normal living standard, life expectation is 63.

Though sending food and medical supplies to the underdeveloped regions of Africa, Asia and Latin America is necessary, it does not solve the problem in the long run. People must be helped to help themselves. This is where UNESCO (United Nations Educational, Scientific and Cultural Organization) steps in.

Children at a village school in Central Africa enjoying their morning 'milk break'. The milk is provided by UNICEF.

UNESCO brings education to those regions where most people cannot read or write. No country is able to stand on its own feet in the modern world without adequate education for everybody. UNESCO helps by financing the foundation of schools and universities.

UNESCO's efforts cannot show such quick results as those achieved by UNICEF. Knowledge cannot be produced like medicine or food. The process is slow and difficult, and will take fifty years at least. Will there be enough qualified teachers? Only time will show if the battle against ignorance can be won.

<Research Unlimited>

Dr. Peter Marshall (1902—1949) was Chaplain of the United States Senate from 1947 to 1949. Here is the text of one of his sermons.

During the lifetime of most of us, science and invention have made their greatest strides. Everybody over forty can remember the mood of optimism that marked the first decade of the twentieth century. People then were living in the days of the first telephones perfected for general use, the first express trains, the first uses of electricity and the first internal combustion engine. Great things were in prospect.

Since most of us were born, the automobile has been developed, until there is now one car for about every five persons in America. Electric lighting and electricity for many home uses is commonplace.

The radio and television, which can bring music, drama, advertising and the latest news into your living-room or bedroom, are now taken for granted.

The airplane no longer amazes, but whisks us across the continent from breakfast to supper. Motion pictures have become a weekly diet. Electric eyes open doors at our approach, and radar enables us to see in the dark. Penicillin and sulfa drugs have conquered many a germ, and atomic energy has opened a vast new world. All of this since most of us were born . . .

These latest inventions and discoveries have made war more terrible, and while they have given us many conveniences and comforts, they have made life more complicated, peace more difficult and the human heart more troubled.

Spiritually, we have not kept pace with our progress in the realm of science and invention. Some people have thought that the more science we have, the more religion can be discarded. But that is not so.

All the high hopes built on scientific gifts and invention have crashed to the ground, as we have been forced to face the realistic fact that man can be so insane and so corrupt that the more power you give him, the more widely will he destroy himself.

That is why the atomic scientists, those brilliant men who delved into the secrets of nuclear energy, are so troubled and conscience-stricken.

We are now at the place where we see that progress simply must be made in the realm of morals and ethics and character, if civilisation is to be saved. The time has come when we must face the solving of the world's true problems —the human problems . . .

The problem of lying—which is called propaganda . . .,
the problem of selfishness—which is called nationalism . . .
the problem of greed—which is often called profit or good business . . .
the problem of licence disguised as liberty . . .
the challenge of materialism—the hook that is baited with security . . .

These are the problems that confront us now.

But why are there so few spiritual discoveries to match the progress made by science? The answer lies in a lack of researchers.

We have money, we are well-clothed, we are comfortably housed, we have automobiles and all the latest gadgets in our homes. But we are spiritually undernourished. We have neglected spiritual food. Without spiritual exercise, our souls are soft and flabby.

The challenge today, pointed and heated by the atomic bomb, is still what it always was: a challenge to spiritual research.

Exercises

1

1. Comprehension Test

a) On the morning of June 15th, 1215 a peasant had seen a great number of people going to Runnymede. They were accompanied by soldiers and seemed to be rather excited. In the evening the peasant asked one of the soldiers questions.
1. Who were all these people that came to Runnymede in the morning?
2. Why had King John made the barons and wealthy merchants angry?
3. And why did they come to Runnymede?
4. What was it that the King should not do in future?
5. Did the King sign the document at once?
6. Why did King John not keep his promises?

b) When the peasant returned home he told his neighbour everything he had heard from the soldier:
"The soldier told me that a great number of barons and merchants had come to Runnymede in the morning. They had been made angry by King John ..."

Go on with the peasant's report.

Let's prepare the next exercise

Shall we go to the cinema? The 'Palace' and the 'Empire' are not far away.	**Both** (the) cinemas are quite near.
But we can't go to the 'Palace' and the 'Empire' as well.	We can go to **either** of the cinemas but we can't go to both.
What's on?—'King John' is on at the 'Palace' and 'Richard III' at the 'Empire'.	
Peter doesn't like these films, nor does Tom.	Peter doesn't like these films. Tom does **not** like these films **either.** *or:* Tom **doesn't either.**
Peter says: "I want to see a western or no film at all."	*Peter says:* "I want to see **either** a western **or** no film at all."
Peter doesn't go to the cinema. Tom doesn't go to the cinema.	**Neither** Peter **nor** Tom go to the cinema.—They like **neither** of the films.

2. Preparing a Talk about King John

Change the numbered sentences using 'both', 'either', 'not either', 'either . . . or' or 'neither'.

There are two fifth forms at the secondary technical school in Wimbledon, 5A and 5B.

1. Mr. Benson teaches history to 5A and 5B.
2. 5A and 5B have had lessons about William the Conqueror and King John and want to talk to each other about these subjects.
3. They have not enough time to talk about William the Conqueror and King John.
4. They can choose one of these subjects.
5. 5A does not want to talk about William the Conqueror, 5B does not want to talk about William the Conqueror.
6. One boy in 5A does not like the first subject, and he does not like the second subject.
7. They can have their meeting on Thursday, they can also have it on Friday.
8. 5A and 5B decide on having the meeting on Friday.
9. They can meet in the room of the 5A, they can also meet in the room of the 5B.
10. 5A and 5B choose the room of 5A because it is larger.

3. From a Talk about King John

All the boys in both the classes agree that King John was England's worst king.

Ex.: (his father, his brothers—to love)

a) **Neither** his father **nor** his brothers loved him.

b) His father did not love him, his brothers did **not either.**

1. (his people, his family—to have a good word to say for him)
2. (the English, the French—to help him)
3. (the barons, the merchants—to want to give him money)
4. (the townspeople, the peasants—to want to fight for him)
5. (the lords, the bishops—to trust him)

4. Something about King John

Emphasize the words in bold type using 'all' or 'at all'.

Ex.: **The barons** hated King John.—**All the barons** hated King John.

1. **The lords** and **merchants** had to give large sums of money to King John.
2. Some peasants even had to give **their money** to King John.
3. When King John had signed the Charter he said **nothing** about his plans.
4. Soon after King John had signed the Charter he swept **over** the country with his soldiers.
5. The barons and merchants were **not sorry** when they heard of King John's death.

5. Magna Carta

Put in 'every', 'nobody', 'all' or 'no'.

From the 63 clauses of Magna Carta:
... should be put into prison without a fair trial.
... should be forced to pay taxes without the lords' and bishops' consent.
... baron should keep his lands.
... townspeople should keep their goods and other possessions.
... free man should be hindered in his business.

<6. Frank's First German Breakfast—An Interpreting Exercise>

The Wagners in Tübingen are having Frank from Birmingham as their guest for six weeks. As Frau Wagner does not know any English, Günter has to be the family's interpreter. *Fill in what Günter says:*

1. *Frau Wagner:* Guten Morgen, Frank! Hast du gut geschlafen?
   Günter: Mother wants to know whether you ...
2. *Frank:* Very well, thank you. Of course I was very tired after the long journey.
   Günter: ...
3. *Frau Wagner:* Das Frühstück ist fertig. Nehmt bitte Platz. Frank, setz dich bitte neben Günter.
   Günter: ...
4. *Frau Wagner:* Frank, willst du während deines Aufenthaltes in Deutschland etwas Deutsch lernen?
   Günter: ...
5. *Frank:* Yes, I do. I already know a very little German, and I hope my knowledge of German will improve. I can understand a little, but I'm not used to speaking German.
   Günter: ...
6. *Frau Wagner:* Wir können dir kein englisches Frühstück anbieten.
   Günter: ...
7. *Frank:* Don't worry about that. When I am in Germany I want to see how the Germans live, and what they eat.
   Günter: ...
8. *Frau Wagner:* Nun bedient euch bitte! Frank, magst du den deutschen Kaffee? Und Brot mit Butter und Marmelade?
   Günter: ...
9. *Frank:* Everything is excellent. Your coffee is very good. Did you make the jam yourself, Mrs. Wagner?
   Günter: ...
10. *Frau Wagner:* Ja. Aber du kannst auch Honig haben. Sonntags gibt es bei uns immer Eier. Vermißt du Speck und Eier nicht?
    Günter: ...
11. *Frank:* Not at all. We don't get bacon and eggs at home every day.

<7. Translate as quickly as you can — Revision of indefinite pronouns>

1. Ich habe
   ... wenig Geld und wenige Bücher.
   ... etwas Geld und einige Bücher.
   ... ein wenig Geld und einige (wenige) Bücher.
   ... kein Geld und keine Bücher.
   ... viel Geld und viele Bücher.
   ... nicht viel Geld und nicht viele Bücher.
   ... einige Münzen und einige Bücher.

2. Er versteht
   ... etwas Englisch.
   ... Englisch.
   ... kein Englisch.
   ... wenig Englisch.
   ... nicht viel Englisch.
   ... ein wenig Englisch.
   ... einige Wörter.

3. Da ist
   ... jemand an der Tür.
   ... niemand an der Tür.
   ... etwas in meinem Auge.
   ... nichts in meiner Tasche.

4. Hörst du
   ... etwas?
   ... jemanden?
   ... nichts?

Let's prepare the next exercise

Bob is **four feet** tall.—Tom is **five foot six** tall.
The blue dress costs £8 (*say:* **eight pounds**).
The yellow costume costs £11·50 (*say:* **eleven pound fifty**).

8. In a Big Shop—A Reading Exercise

Read the prices for the following articles correctly:

a very good pair of sun-glasses	from £2·10	to £2·75
a pair of swimming-trunks	from £1·60	to £2·70
a nice summer dress	from £6	to £8·75
a good white shirt	from £2·43	to £3·99
a pair of trousers	from £5·15	to £6·75
a sun hat	from £1·05	to £1·70
a pair of tennis shorts	from £2·99	to £3·15
a pair of tennis shoes	from £1·35	to £2·50
a tennis racket	from £2	to £5·53

<9. Test your pronunciation>

Pronounce the following words very carefully:

[ʃ] *or* [tʃ]: shoes — choose; sheep — cheap; shop — chop; share — chair; shows — chose; she's — cheese.
[tʃ] *or* [dʒ]: chain — Jane; choose — juice; chop — job.
[s] *or* [z]: so — zoo; sea — New Zealand; bus — busy; Lassie — lazy; price — prize; to seize, he says, size, souls, surprise, season, Susan.

<10. Translation: Wie König Johann die Normandie verlor>

1. Nachdem Johann zum König von England gekrönt worden war, wurde ihm auch noch die Lanze der Herzöge der Normandie gegeben. 2. Das bedeutete, daß er jetzt Herr beider Länder war. 3. Als Johann die Lanze [entgegen-]nahm, ließ er sie zu Boden fallen. 4. Alle Leute, die das sahen, sagten: „Dieses Zeichen wurde Johann von Gott gegeben, damit er die Normandie seinem jungen Neffen Arthur überläßt *(Infinitiv)*." 5. So beschlossen sowohl die französischen als auch die normannischen Barone, Arthur gegen Johann zu helfen. 6. Als Johann eines Tages in der Normandie war, hörte er zufällig, daß Arthur sich auf einer Burg ganz in der Nähe aufhielt. 7. Er entschloß sich, seinen Neffen gefangenzunehmen *(to take prisoner)*. 8. Am frühen Morgen erreichte er mit seinen Soldaten die Burg. 9. Da Arthur auf den Angriff seines Onkels überhaupt nicht vorbereitet war, war es nicht schwer für Johann, ihn gefangenzunehmen. 10. Sowohl französische als auch normannische Barone zogen gegen den König zu Feld, nachdem sie gehört hatten, daß Arthur gefangengenommen worden sei und Johann den Befehl gegeben habe, seinen Neffen zu töten. 11. Johann wurde besiegt, und die Normandie, die 140 Jahre lang mit England vereint gewesen war, war verloren.

2

1. Comprehension Test

1. What are the most important facts described in the Railway Story?
2. Which of the thoughts expressed in the Railway Story seem ridiculous nowadays?—Why?
3. A traveller coming from the Continent by train always arrives at Victoria Station. If he wants to go to Cambridge from there he must cross London and reach Liverpool Street Station first. What is the reason for this?
4. What are the rivals of the railway today?
5. Would you prefer travelling by train, car or plane? Give the reasons.

<2. Trains in England and America>

English:		**American:**	
1 line	3 luggage van	1 track	3 baggage car
2 engine	4 passenger coach	2 locomotive	4 passenger car

3. What people had to do during the first journey in 1830 — Revision

Passengers on one of the first trains were told by an engineer what they had to do before and during the journey.

1. Stay in your seats during the journey.
2. Keep hold of the small children.
3. Leave the dogs and cats at home.
4. Take only a light meal before the journey.
5. Take some drinking-water with you.
6. Put scarves round your heads because of the strong wind.
7. Pay for the journey in advance.

What else may the engineer have told the passengers?

a) *Now change the above sentences using 'to have to'.*
1. Passengers **had to** stay in their seats during the journey.
2. They ...

Go on.

b) Mrs. Davis, who didn't listen to the engineer, asked her husband questions, and Mr. Davis told her what passengers **'were to'** do.
1. Shall we be allowed to walk to and fro in the carriage during the journey? No, we **are to** stay in our seats ...
2. Is it necessary to ...

Go on.

4. Excited Passengers — Revision

One day in September 1830 about 200 people travelled on the train between Liverpool and Manchester. Most of the people were rather excited. This is what you could hear among them:

a) *Add the correct question tags.*
1. It is rather exciting, ...?
2. Many people will watch us, ...?
3. They won't come too near the engine, ...?
4. We shan't travel faster than 35 miles an hour, ...?
5. It's not good to eat too much during the journey, ...?
6. My son won't be sick, ...?
7. You didn't forget your money, ...?
8. You've bought the tickets for me, ...?
9. The engine driver knows everything about the engine, ...?
10. It won't be too cold during the journey, ...?

b) *Add sentences with 'so', 'nor', 'neither', 'not either'.*
1. I'm so excited. ...
2. I hope there won't be an accident. ...
3. I don't think that it is possible to drive faster than 35 miles an hour. ...

4. I can't believe that it is possible to read or write on the train. ...
5. My wife has not yet arrived. ...
6. I can't remember where I put my ticket. ...
7. My daughter has never been on a train before. ...
8. I'm afraid it will be rather cold during the journey. ...

5. 'to have' + Object

a) *Change the words in italics into expressions with 'to have'.*
It is the first day of Miss Baker's holidays which she spends in the Swiss Alps.

Ex.: When she wakes up in the morning she *looks* out of the window.
When she wakes up in the morning she **has a look** out of the window.

1. Then she gets up and goes to her nice little bathroom *to wash.*
2. Before breakfast she *walks* for a quarter of an hour.
3. After breakfast she *smokes.*
4. Then she takes her bathing-costume, goes to the swimming-pool and *swims.*
5. After that she feels tired and *rests.*
6. During lunch she *chats* with her neighbour.
7. After lunch she goes up to her room and *sleeps.*

b) *Now ask questions with 'to have' + object and answer them. You must use a form of 'to do' with your questions, because 'to have' does not mean 'to possess' here.*

Ex.: **Does** your father **have lunch** at home with you?
No, he **doesn't.** He **has lunch** at his office, because it would take him more than an hour to come home and go back to his office.

You can use the following expressions with your questions and answers:

to have breakfast, tea, supper, a cup of coffee, a glass of orange juice, a sandwich, a good time, a word with someone, a lot of work to do, a ride in the car, any letters last week, a nice holiday.

6. Preparing a Journey—Revision

a) Mr. Warner wants to go to Italy with his wife and his two daughters.
A week before the journey he sees
1. ... that his car is not quite in order. So he **has it overhauled.**
2. ... that his best suit is dirty. So ...
3. ... that his hair is too long. So ...
4. ... that his summer shoes must be repaired. So ...
5. ... that his watch is out of order. So ...

b) The day before the journey Mrs. Warner asks her husband:
1. Did you have the car overhauled?
2. Did you ...?
Go on.

Let's prepare the next exercise

Mother: Will you help me with the housework this morning, Mary?
Mary: But I want to play tennis, Mother.
Mother: Oh **do help** me. I feel so tired today. Hilf mir **doch,** bitte.
And then Mary **did** help her mother. ... hat **schließlich doch** geholfen.

7. An Anxious Wife

Mr. Harrison wants to go by plane for the first time in his life. His wife, who has never been on a plane either, is very anxious and asks him

1. ... to stay on his seat during the flight.
2. ... to follow the instructions of the stewardess.
3. ... to fasten his seat-belt when necessary.
4. ... to eat only a light meal on the plane.
5. ... to drink only fruit juice during the flight.
6. ... to take a seat near the exit.
7. ... to call the stewardess if he is sick.

a) *Now say what Mrs. Harrison told her husband.*
1. "**Do stay** on your seat during the flight."
2. "**Do** ..."

Go on.

b) Did Mr. Harrison follow his wife's instructions?—Yes, he did.
1. He **did stay** on his seat during the flight.
2. He **did** ...

Go on.

<8. Expressions and idioms with 'to do' and 'to make'>

Expressions with 'to do':

to do the housework	to do someone a favour
to do the ironing	to do one's homework
to do a room	to do right
to do the washing	to do wrong
to do the shopping	to do well in a test

Idioms with 'to do':

that will do	*that's enough, all right* That will do. You need not work any longer today.—This room will do for the girls.
to do without	*to live without* Young children cannot do without milk.
I can do with	*I don't need more than* I can do with only a sandwich for lunch.

I could do with	*I should have, should like* My coat is rather old. I could do with a new one.—I could do with a cup of tea or coffee.
to have done -ing	*to have finished* Have you done writing?

Expressions with 'to make':

to make a plan	to make a journey
to make a cake	to make the beds
to make a mistake	

Idioms with 'to make':

to make money	*to earn money* Can a person learn how to make money?
to make a good football player	*to become a good football player* You'll make a good football player, Tom.
to make fun of s.o.	*to laugh at s.o.* Although he had fallen into the water, nobody made fun of Bill.
to make haste	*to hurry* Make haste or you will be late for school.
to make for	*to go towards* Tom made for the playing-field.
to make up	*to invent (a story)* Can you make up a story about Robin Hood?
to make o.s. at home	*to feel as if at home* Make yourself at home.

a) *Fill in a form of 'to do' or 'to make'.*

1. How does this blind man ... his money?—He ... baskets.
2. My friend often ... jokes, but he never ... anything wrong.
3. Our neighbour could ... with a new hat.
4. She ... hats and ... her work well.
5. Please ... it as I do, and you won't ... any mistakes.
6. In the morning I ... the beds and ... all the housework.
7. I have to ... haste for I must still ... the shopping.
8. You always ... your homework, but in spite of that you often ... mistakes.
9. Do you like to ... the cooking?
10. Do you ... cakes yourself?—Yes, I try to ... my best.
11. Mother ... all our dresses herself.

b) *Translate the sentences under a) into German.*

c) *Can you make up a story with some of the idioms with 'to do' and 'to make'?*

<9. Translation: Die Kuh auf den Eisenbahnschienen>

1. Vor hundert Jahren waren [die] Eisenbahnen in England noch nicht so gut, wie sie jetzt sind, und [das] Reisen [war] deshalb weniger angenehm. 2. Das kleine Seebad Selsey, das heutzutage von vielen Leuten besucht wird, konnte man zu jener Zeit nur einmal am Tage mit einem langsamen Zug erreichen. 3. Dieser Zug war so langsam, daß man zwei Stunden brauchte, um die Entfernung von zehn englischen Meilen zurückzulegen *(= zu reisen)*. 4. Eines Tages fuhr Mr. Smith, der seine Ferien in Selsey verbringen wollte, in diesem Zug. 5. Nach einiger Zeit hielt der Zug plötzlich an. 6. Mr. Smith, der draußen weder Häuser noch Menschen sah, fragte den Schaffner *(guard)*, was los sei. 7. „Wir haben anhalten müssen, weil eine Kuh auf den Schienen ist", antwortete der Schaffner. „Natürlich werden wir das Tier wegtreiben müssen, bevor wir unsere Reise fortsetzen können", fügte er hinzu. 8. Schließlich gelang es dem Lokomotivführer und dem Schaffner, die Kuh wegzujagen, und eine Viertelstunde, nachdem der Zug angehalten hatte, begann er sich wieder in Bewegung zu setzen. 9. Ungefähr zehn Minuten lang konnten die Fahrgäste ihre Reise genießen, aber dann hielt der Zug plötzlich noch einmal. 10. Mr. Smith guckte aus dem Fenster, rief den Schaffner und fragte ihn mit einem Lächeln: „Ist [schon] wieder eine *(another)* Kuh auf den Schienen?" 11. „Nein, mein Herr", erwiderte der Schaffner trocken, „es ist dieselbe Kuh."

3

1. Comprehension Test

1. Describe Derek's plans for the future and his problems at school.—What are your own future plans?
2. Compare what you have read about Derek's and Kevin's school with your own school. What is the difference?
3. What kind of a family are the Robinsons? Describe their daily life and their holidays. How can they afford to pay for a TV set, a refrigerator, a washing-machine and their yearly holidays at the seaside?
4. What does social security for a family mean? How can the State afford to grant it?

2. From a report on child-workers (1830)—'must'

1. Tens of thousands of children work in the new factories and coal mines.
2. As men often cannot find work, women and children earn the necessary money for the family.
3. It is no exception that children of seven or eight years spend up to sixteen hours a day in factories or coal mines.
4. Sometimes even younger children help to support their families: one case is known where a child of three works in a coal mine.

5. In the coal mines these children push or draw carriages with coal along passages which often are not more than eighteen inches high.
6. Here they crawl along on all fours never seeing the sun or having time to play.
7. Other children work at the pumps standing knee deep in water all day long.
8. These poor children live in dirty houses and sleep in shifts because there are no beds for all of them.
9. They work more or less continuously until they die or become ill.
10. Children also work on Saturdays and clean the machines on Sundays.

a) *Put this text into the past tense and change the sentences using 'to have to', 'to be obliged to' or 'to be forced to'.*
Begin like this: In the first half of the nineteenth century tens of thousands of children **were forced to** work in the new factories and coal mines.

b) Does Derek have to work like children in the nineteenth century?—
No. As long as he is a child he **need not** work in factories and coal mines.
He **need not** earn ...

Go on saying what Derek need not do and use the suitable sentences.

c) *What is Derek's and Kevin's life like?*

3. What young boys and girls must not do

a) *Change the sentences using 'must not' instead of 'not to be allowed to'.*

Ex.: Boys and girls under 16 years are not allowed to stay in restaurants after they have finished their meal if they are not accompanied by a grown-up person.
Boys and girls under 16 years **must not** ...

1. Boys and girls under 17 years are not allowed to drink spirits in a restaurant.
2. The restaurant owner is not allowed to sell spirits to boys and girls under 17 years, not even if they want to buy the spirits for somebody else.
3. Boys and girls under 16 years are not allowed to take part in a public dance.
4. Boys and girls between 16 and 18 years are not allowed to stay at a public dance longer than 10 p.m. if they are not accompanied by a grown-up.
5. Boys and girls between 16 and 18 years are not allowed to stay at a public dance longer than 12 p.m., even if they are accompanied by a grown-up.
6. Boys and girls under 16 are not allowed to smoke in public.

b) Robert, a boy of 17 years and Tom, his 15-year-old brother, want to go and see their relations in Blackpool next week.
What will Robert be allowed to do and what not? And Tom?
Use the sentences under a) and the expressions 'to be allowed to' and 'must not'.

Let's prepare the next exercise: 'may'—'might'

Mr. Roberts: I can't find the car key. Where is it?
Mrs. Roberts: It **may** be in your pocket.
Mr. Roberts: But it isn't. I **might** have lost it.
Mrs. Roberts: You **might.** But look, what is that in your left hand?
Mr. Roberts: Oh, the car key!

'May' and 'might' are used in the sense of 'perhaps'. They express a possibility.

4. Kevin Goes to the Beach

a) Kevin is preparing to go to the beach one afternoon.
Kevin: "Mother, I can't find my swimming-trunks."
Mrs. Robinson: "They **may** be on the chair beside your bed."
Kevin: "No, they aren't. Can I have Derek's swimming-trunks?"

Here are other things the boy can't find:
sun-glasses, comb, purse, tennis-racket, coloured shirt, towel, beach shoes.

Make up similar conversations.

b) Before Kevin leaves, his mother says: "Take some sandwiches with you. You **might** get hungry after swimming."

Then she gives some more advice:
to take some extra money—to want to buy something to drink; to take an umbrella—to rain; to take a book—to want to read; to take a pullover—to feel cold after swimming; not to swim out too far—to get tired.

5. The Robinsons in Blackpool

The Robinsons and their two sons Derek and Kevin are enjoying Blackpool's sandy beach for a fortnight. The two boys always want to do something that their parents cannot allow them to do.

Ex.: Kevin: **May** I eat ice-cream instead of lunch today?
Mrs. Robinson: No, you **may not.** You **might** be sick afterwards.

Then Kevin wants
... to swim very far out although it is a stormy day.
... to spend all his pocket-money on the slot-machines.
... to take their black cat into the water.
... to stay at another seaside resort for a few days.

Derek wants
... to give up school after the holidays.
... to become an ice-cream man in Blackpool.
... to drink some alcohol, because he has a sore throat.
... to sleep on the beach in the night.

<6. Life in the Welfare State>

Fill in 'might' or the substitute verbs of 'can' and 'must' and connect them with the verbs that follow.

Ex.: English families ... (to save) money?
Are English families **obliged** to save money?

1. No Englishman ... (to save) money, if he does not want to.
2. But he ... (to get) ill. What will happen to him then?
3. Thanks to the National Health Service he ... (not to pay) a penny in such a case.
4. But he ... (to be) without work one day. And he ... (not to earn) money when he is over 65.
5. He need not worry. The State ... (to pay) him a pension.
6. Therefore he ... (to pay) National Insurance to the State as long as he works.
7. ... the Robinsons (to buy) new furniture for their living-room last year?
8. No, they could not afford it, because they ... (to pay) for their new car, their TV set, their refrigerator and their washing-machine.
9. Could the Robinsons' parents afford to live that way? No, they couldn't. They ... (to save) money for illness, unemployment and old age and they ... (not to buy) so many things for their household. ...

Let's prepare the next exercise: 'will'—'would'

a) Many German girls go to England every year. Some of them **will work** in households, and others **will take** jobs in hospitals or training colleges.

'Will' expresses that something happens again and again.

b) When Bettina stayed in England her friends **would tell** her when her English was not correct. They **used to take** her for week-end trips when they went for one themselves.

'Would' or 'used to' express that something happened again and again in the past.

7. Talking about Sons and Daughters

The Robinsons meet the Jacksons on Blackpool's beach. The Jacksons have two daughters, Susan, aged fifteen, and her seventeen-year-old sister Betty. Both families talk about their sons and daughters.

Mrs. Robinson: "Kevin is a difficult boy. Every morning when the alarm-clock has rung he stays in bed. He does not get up until I go to his room and switch the light on. He is always tired in the morning, because he stays up too long in the evening watching TV. Then he reads his favourite books in bed. Mostly he forgets to clean his shoes and to pack his school things in the evening.

He does that in the morning and has no time for a proper breakfast. He only drinks a cup of milk in the kitchen. Then he rushes to the bus stop to get his school bus. Sometimes he even forgets to comb his hair."

a) *Say what Mrs. Robinson tells Mrs. Jackson in the following way:*
"Every morning when the alarm-clock has rung, Kevin **will stay** in bed. He **won't get up** until I go to his room ..." *Go on.*

b) Having heard about Kevin Mrs. Jackson says: "When Betty was younger, it was the same with her. Every morning after the alarm-clock had rung, she **would stay** in bed. She **would not get up** until ..." *Go on.*

c) *Do exercise b) again but use 'used to' instead of 'would'.*

d) Mrs. Robinson: "Derek is quite the opposite of Kevin. Every morning when the alarm-clock has rung he **does not stay** in bed any longer. He **gets up** before I go to his room and ..." *Go on. Change what Mrs. Robinson said about Kevin so that it will be suitable for Derek.*

<8. New Year's Eve at the Bakers'—A Story in Pictures>

New Year's Eve = the night before the 1st of January

He is putting the clock on.

He is putting the clock back.

<9. Translation: Ein Inselabenteuer>

1. Letztes Jahr wollten Robinsons ihre Ferien nicht in Blackpool verbringen, sondern gingen statt dessen in ein schottisches Seebad, und manchmal machten sie Ausflüge mit dem Boot. 2. Es gab eine Menge felsiger Inseln in der Nähe der Küste, die Derek und Kevin besuchen wollten. 3. Eines Tages gingen ihre Eltern für den Nachmittag weg und sagten zu ihren Söhnen: „Ihr dürft nicht mit einem Boot wegfahren. Das könnte gefährlich sein." 4. Aber die Abwesenheit ihrer Eltern gab Derek und Kevin die Gelegenheit, mit dem Boot eines Fischers zu einer der Inseln zu fahren. 5. Als sie die Insel einige Stunden lang ‚erforscht' hatten, wollten sie zurückfahren. 6. Aber das Boot war verschwunden! 7. Sie hatten das Boot nicht hoch genug aus dem Wasser gezogen, und die Wellen *(waves)* hatten es weggetragen. 8. Was würde jetzt geschehen? Was sollten sie tun? 9. Würden sie zum Strand zurückschwimmen können? 10. Falls nicht, würden sie hier bleiben müssen, bis jemand sie fände. 11. Wie lange würden sie ohne zu essen leben können? 12. Wenn nur der Fischer ihnen nicht erlaubt hätte, sein Boot zu nehmen! 13. Nach ungefähr 3 Stunden sahen sie ein Boot kommen. 14. Sie winkten und riefen, bis sie gesehen und nach Hause gebracht wurden. 15. Sie fürchteten, ihre Eltern würden sie bestrafen, aber Herr und Frau Robinson waren so froh, sie wiederzuhaben, daß sie vergaßen, sie zu bestrafen.

4

1. Comprehension Test

a) 1. What advantages would there be if a tunnel were built between Folkestone and Calais?
2. Would there be any disadvantages? If so, what?
3. Why would it not be practical, if a motorway were built instead of a railway?
4. What might happen in case of a war?
5. What might happen in case of an earthquake?

b) *Make up a list of points for and against the tunnel project. Now talk about the advantages and disadvantages using your list.*

Let's prepare the next exercise:

Present Tense after 'when', 'before', 'as soon as', 'until'

We'll visit you **when we come** to London.
I'll leave here **as soon as** I have the necessary money.

You have learned that in English a future action is expressed by the future tense. But: the present tense must be used in adverbial clauses of time beginning with 'when', 'before', 'as soon as' and 'until'.

2. A Visit is Announced

One day Mr. and Mrs. Winter in London get a letter from their German friends, Mr. and Mrs. Thiele, in which they announce their visit.
Change the infinitives into the right tense and fill in suitable conjunctions.

Ex.: We'll send you a telegram ... we (to know) the exact date.
We'll send you a telegram **as soon as we know** the exact date.

1. Wait ... you (to get) our telegram ... you (to book) rooms at a hotel.
2. We'll ring you up ... we (to arrive) in London.
3. We'll leave here ... grandmother (to be) back from hospital.
4. ... she (to be) back she'll look after the children.
5. Now wait ... we (to write) again ... you (to do) anything to prepare our visit.

<3. Train your fantasy>

The German 'erst' = not ... until
not ... before

Ex.: You can't visit us until ...
You can't visit us **until you have done** your homework.

1. I shall not go away from here until ...
2. We shall not find our seats in the theatre until ...
3. I can't finish my work before ...
4. Mr. Barton can't pay for his house until ...
5. You shan't have any sweets until ...
6. She'll not be able to read an English newspaper before ...
7. You can't buy a new car until ...
8. The boys will not return from their holiday until ...

4. An Anxious Wife

Mr. Winter wants to go to Victoria Station to wait for his German friends, the Thieles.

a) Before he leaves Mrs. Winter says:
Do put your coat on. **If** you **don't, you'll catch** a cold.
Do take a bus. If you ..., (to be late).
Do take some money. ... (not to be able to buy a ticket).
Do look at the time-table. ... (not to find the right platform).
Do take your glasses. ... (not to read the time-table).

b) Mr. Winter does what his wife says.
He puts his coat on. If he didn't he would perhaps catch a cold.
He takes a bus. If ...

Go on.

c) When Mr. Winter has left the house he thinks:
What should I do if the Thieles did not arrive?
What should I do if . . . (the bus—to be late); . . . (I—to lose my purse); . . . (I—not to recognize the Thieles); . . . (the Thieles—to forget their money); . . . (they—not to find a porter for the luggage).

d) *Can you find out what Mr. Winter would do if all the things under c) happened?*

5. 'Should' in If-clauses

On the boat train an Englishman has given a guide-book about London to Mr. Thiele. There he reads:

Even if **you should arrive** (selbst wenn Sie . . . sollten) in London in the middle of the night, **you would find** a room.

If you should . . .
(to lose your money—the police—to tell you what to do); (to lose your way in the city—every Englishman—to help you); (to arrive with only foreign money—every bank—to change it); (to want to see the famous sights of London—a tourist office—to give advice); (to look for an address—to get help at a police station); (to rain—the museums—to shelter you from it).

6. Test: If-clauses

Change the infinitives in brackets into the right tenses.

1. If there had not been so many difficulties, the Channel tunnel (to be built) years ago.
2. If a tunnel is built, travellers (to be able) to go the whole way from London to Paris without getting out of their cars.
3. If a terrible storm (to rage) on the sea, travellers will not take any notice of it.
4. If a tunnel were built, people (to be taken) from England to France in 30 minutes.
5. Would it not be more practical if a motorway (to be built) instead of a railway?
6. If a motorway were built, the exhaust fumes of the cars (to make) a much more expensive ventilation system necessary.
7. If goods can be transported by railway, freight costs (to be) 50 per cent less than they are today.
8. If the tunnel (to begin) at Folkestone, this city would become the gateway to the Continent.
9. The tunnel would probably have been destroyed if it (to be built) before the Second World War.
10. The First World War (to be) two years shorter if supplies could have been sent through a tunnel.

<7. Word-formation>

Form opposites of adjectives by putting the prefix in- or im- in front of them and give their German meaning.

Prefix in-: *Ex.:* correct — incorrect (unrichtig, fehlerhaft)
(complete, expensive, definite, dependent, direct, exact)

Prefix im-: *Ex.:* possible — impossible (unmöglich)
(proper, perfect, personal, polite)

<8. 'happy' — 'lucky'>

happy, happiness:	Mrs. Robinson is **happy** because her husband need not stay in hospital any longer. In her **happiness** she has invited some friends to welcome him.
lucky, luck:	Kevin is **lucky:** he won a radio at the fair. That was **good luck!** Derek spent a lot of money, but didn't win anything. That was **bad luck. Better luck** next time!
Phrases:	lucky day; lucky fellow; lucky penny

Put in 'happy' or 'lucky'.

1. You were ... that you have won such a lot of money. 2. But money alone does not make you .... 3. In our holidays we were not ... with the weather. It rained all the time. 4. But Colin was quite ... in spite of the weather, because he made a lot of friends. 5. When the holidays begin, everybody is ... and looking forward to travelling. 6. There was a bicycle race in Blackpool for boys and girls between 15 and 18. Kevin was ... and won the prize.

<9. How to use your dictionary (I)>

a) *Here are two lists of words. Most of the English words are unknown to you. Look up in your dictionary which of the words of list 2 suit to those of list 1. Write down the correct order of words in list 2.*

List 1

Glühbirne — prüfen — auswechseln
Kette — rostig — ölen
Schlauch — flicken — Flicken
Schutzblech — abschrauben — Schraubenzieher
Felge — lackieren — Pinsel
Klingel — zerlegen — ausprobieren
Sattel — anschrauben — Schraubenschlüssel

List 2

bell — bulb — chain — to check — to mend — mudguard — to oil — paint-brush — patch — to replace — rim — rusty — saddle — screwdriver — to screw on — spanner — to take apart — to test — inner tube — to unscrew — to varnish

b) *Look up the English pronunciation of the unknown words in a dictionary.*

c) *Look for other English nouns and verbs that have something to do with your bike. Think of:* Rahmen, Lenker, Handgriff, Rücktritt, Pedale, polieren, spannen...

d) *Form sentences with the word groups.*

e) *Now you will be able to do one of the following compositions:*
1. What my bicycle looks like (Description)
2. What I ought to do every fortnight to keep my bike in order

<10. Translation: Im Hyde Park>

1. Sollten Sie jemals nach London kommen, vergessen Sie nicht, die berühmte Rednerecke *(Speakers' Corner)* im Hyde Park zu besuchen. 2. Hier kann jeder frei über alles sprechen. 3. „Wenn ich Sie wäre", hörte ich einen Sprecher sagen, „würde ich kein Fleisch mehr essen, sondern nur Obst und Gemüse. 4. Wenn Sie das tun, werden Sie länger leben. 5. Selbst wenn Sie schwer arbeiten sollten, werden Sie sich niemals müde fühlen. 6. Wenn Sie krank werden sollten, werden Sie sich schnell erholen. 7. Bald werden Sie sich fühlen, als ob Sie zehn Jahre jünger wären. 8. Aber falls Sie nicht aufhören, Fleisch zu essen, werden Sie sich öfter müde fühlen, öfter krank werden und wahrscheinlich eher *(sooner)* sterben. 9. Es ist schade, daß so viele Leute die falschen Lebensmittel essen. 10. Wenn ich früher gewußt hätte, wie gut Obst und Gemüse für meine Gesundheit sind, würde ich niemals Fleisch gegessen haben. 11. Sie werden nicht wissen, wie schlecht Fleisch für Sie ist, bis Sie aufhören, es zu essen." 12. Wie gefiel Ihnen der Sprecher? 13. Er hätte besser sein können, nicht wahr?

5

1. Comprehension Test

1. Who were the first English settlers in America? When did they leave England?
2. In what way were the 'United Colonies' independent of England? What did they have to do?
3. What was the reason for the American War of Independence? When did it start?
4. Describe the situation of the American army before it crossed the Delaware under General Washington.
5. Why was French help so important for the American army at the end of the War of Independence?
6. What is the meaning of the stars and stripes in the American flag?
7. Why do Americans celebrate the 4th of July? How do they celebrate it?

<8.> Do you remember Paul Revere? Tell the story of his ride.

2. The Position of Adverbs of Indefinite Time — Revision

Put the adverbs in suitable places.

George Washington was born on February 22nd, 1732, and spent his boyhood near Fredericksburg.
1. (often): His favourite friend was Richard Henry Lee, with whom he played.
2. (sometimes): Did the boys write letters to each other?
3. (seldom): The boys wrote letters to each other.
4. (already): Did they write about matters of war and state at that time?
5. (often): No, they did not. They read books together about foreign countries.
6. (always): They had been good friends.

Let's prepare the next exercise: The Position of Adverbs

1. George **always** wanted to find a friend.
2. Did he **ever** find one?
3. When he had **finally** found one, he was very glad.
4. **At once** the two friends began spending their free time together.
5. They went **regularly** to visit each other.
6. It was **certainly** a good friendship.

The adverb can be put:
1. *before the verb, if there is no auxiliary,*
2. *in questions, after the first auxiliary and the subject,*
3. *after the first auxiliary in the compound forms of the verb,*
4. *at the beginning or at the end of the sentence,*
5. *after the verb, if there is no direct object,*
6. *after the simple forms of 'to be'.*

3. Young Washington and the Wild Horse

Choose adverbs from the following list and put them in suitable places.
You can sometimes use the same adverb twice.

(extremely, certainly, often, always, already, ever, unfortunately, normally, early, soon, at once, anxiously, finally, usually, still, suddenly, firmly, rather, immediately, again, sadly, at first)

1. Young George Washington galloped over the fields near his parents' farm when he was learning to ride. 2. He was a good rider at the age of nine. 3. When George was eleven years old there was one horse on the farm which was strong and wild. 4. Nobody had succeeded in riding this horse. 5. It was a man's job to train a wild horse, but George wanted to do that himself. 6. One morning he went to the fields with some boys and tried to catch the horse. 7. The boys thought that they would never manage to catch it. 8. But they got the horse and George sprang upon its back. 9. The boys watched the horse and its brave rider. 10. Up to now this horse had thrown off every rider. 11. But George stayed on it. 12. After the first rounds the horse seemed to be resolved

to throw off its rider. 13. It sprang into the air with an enormous leap. 14. But that was its last leap, because it fell and broke its neck. 15. George went home to his mother. 16. She asked him: "Have you been in the fields? How is the wild horse?" 17. "It's dead, Mother," George answered. "I killed it." And he told her what had happened. 18. First his mother was upset, but then she said: "I'm proud of my son, who speaks the truth."

Let's prepare the next exercise

A man **quickly** entered a travel agency and asked for the cheapest route to New Orleans. The travel agent answered his questions **in a friendly way.**

Adverbs usually have the ending -ly. If the adjective already ends with -ly it can be used adverbially with the phrase 'in a ... way' or 'in a ... manner'.

But there are a lot of adjectives which can be used as adverbs without being changed. These are

1. *the adverbs of time: daily, weekly, monthly, yearly, early*
2. *adverbs in the following expressions: to walk fast; to run fast; to answer right; to answer wrong; to speak loud; to speak low; to buy cheap; to buy dear; to sell cheap; to sell dear; to play fair; to work hard; to stand firm; to sit still; to look s.o. full in the face.*

4. Crossing the Delaware

Put in the right form of the adverbs.

1. On the 25th December, 1776, when the English Redcoats were (happy) celebrating Christmas at the small town of Trenton, Washington's men were in camp on the opposite bank of the Delaware. 2. They had worked (hard), did not have enough to eat and were (poor) dressed. 3. The soldiers did not know (exact) what they were going to do that day, but their leader, Washington, had spoken to them (friendly) and asked them to stand (firm). 4. Colonel Knox (sad) thought back to the time when he had been a bookseller and had (secret) dreamed of being a publisher one day. 5. Now that dream was far away and he was an officer in Washington's army. 6. Suddenly General Greene walked (fast) towards him, looked him (full) in the face and said: "It will soon be dark and we can start the crossing." 7. "But there's ice in the river," Knox replied. "The crossing will be difficult." 8. They spoke (low) because they did not want to worry the soldiers. 9. When it was almost dark, Washington galloped along the lines of soldiers calling (loud) for General Greene, asking him to start the crossing. 10. When the soldiers moved to the river, their hearts were heavy. 11. Many of them now believed that they were going to die. 12. It was hard work to row through the icy water. 13. The ice-floes made it impossible to land (direct) in Trenton, but they got across, (quick) marched through the snow towards the city, captured it and won one of the most famous victories in American history.

5. On a Ship to New York

I was sitting on the deck of my ship to America in the hot afternoon sun. People around me were drinking Coca Cola and chatting to each other. This is what I heard them say:

Ex.: "When I went to the travel agency to buy my ticket, I met an old friend." *(zufällig)*
"When I went to the travel agency to buy my ticket, **I happened to meet** an old friend."

1. "When my husband discovered that he had forgotten his wallet in the main dining-saloon, he went back to fetch it." *(eilig)*
2. "If you ring me up in my hotel before 10 o'clock tomorrow morning, you will reach me." *(bestimmt)*
3. "New York is rather a busy city, but my hotel is in a quiet street." *(hoffentlich)*
4. "Look at those clouds in the sky. It will rain soon." *(wahrscheinlich)*
5. "I could take you to Washington in my car after our arrival in New York."— "I promised some friends to stay in New York for a fortnight." *(leider)*
6. "Oh, I must try to find cheap hotels. I haven't much money." *(nämlich)*
7. "When I came from the tea-room an hour ago, I met Mr. Clark." *(zufällig)* "He enjoys the voyage very much and is sorry that it will be finished by tomorrow." *(anscheinend)*
8. "All of us will have a nice time in America." *(hoffentlich)*

Let's prepare the next exercise

Was machst du **denn** da?	What are you doing there?
Das ist **eigentlich** gar nicht so schlecht.	That's not so bad.
Das wird **wohl** das Richtige sein.	This will be the right thing.
Wie hat er es **nur** fertiggebracht, diese Stellung zu bekommen?	How did he manage to get that job?
Du wirst **doch** kommen?	You will come, won't you?
Wer kommt sonst **noch?**	Who else is coming?
Da bist du **ja** endlich!	There you are at last!

There are some small German words which are often not translated into English. Sometimes quite different expressions are used for them in the English sentences.

6. A Translating Exercise

Try to understand the following English sentences and translate them into good German using the small words of the left column.

denn: Where is the car key?
Where was your fountain pen?
Is he really so poor?
Are you leaving the party? But why so early?

eigentlich: Where exactly did it happen?
What do you want anyhow?
That's not a bad idea.
She is quite a nice girl after all.

wohl: I think we must go now. That is indeed possible.
He knows that all right. Now you see that I was right.
That may well be. He might come yet.
That's hardly the right thing to do.
There is little chance that it will stop raining today.
I can read English all right, but I can hardly speak it.
I told you that a hundred times at least.
I wonder if Mr. Smith will come today.

nur: How on earth did he find out my address?
All were there except Miss Miller.
You know that well enough.
Why did he take up that profession, if he doesn't like it?

doch: Do sit down.
He did come after all.
You don't really mean that, do you?
If only the doctor would come soon.
Don't!
Surely you know that Miss Miller is leaving the firm.
That's really too bad.

noch: Say that once more. What more do you want?
Anything else? He has only $10 left.
He is twice as old as she is.
That makes the story even more interesting.

ja: He is an old man, after all.
It really is not so bad.
Can you speak French? If so, please help me translate this letter.
Will she come?—I think so.
You know that my pension is very small.
I told you so, didn't I?

<7. Two difficult pairs of words>

to sit, sat, sat **to lie, lay, lain**
to set, set, set **to lay, laid, laid**

Fill in the right verb.

1. I'm so glad you've come to see our new house. But I'm afraid we can't s... in the s...ing-room, as I haven't l... the carpet there yet.
2. Please s... down while I am l... the table. But you can't s... in this arm-chair, because Peter has l... his dirty shoes on it.

3. You can have an egg for tea if you like. Our hens are l... very well at the moment.
4. Well, now I have l... the table, let's have some tea. It's a pity it's too cold to s... in the garden.
5. I hear that you are going to Canada in a few days. When do you s... off?
6. Didn't you say your ship is s... sail tomorrow and is l... ready in the harbour? I wish I could make such a long voyage.

<8. How to use your dictionary (II)>

You want to say in English, "Steck den Brief in einen Umschlag," and you don't know the word for 'Umschlag'. You can look it up in your dictionary. Here is what you would find there:

Umschlag *m (Brief)* envelope; *(Buch)* wrapper, cover, jacket; *(Kragen)* collar; *(Einfassung)* hem; *(Ärmel)* cuff; *(Hose)* turn-up; *(Wetter)* change; *(Veränderung)* alteration, turn; *med* compress, poultice; *com* turnover; *(Umladung)* transfer (*od* reshipment) of load

Which is the word you need?

Here are more examples from your dictionary which show you the difficulty of translating:

verschreiben *irr tr* to use in writing; *(Arznei)* to prescribe; *(vermachen)* to make over (to); *(falsch schreiben)* to write incorrectly; *r* to make a slip (in writing *od* of the pen); *fig* to sell o.s. to; to set o's heart upon, to devote o.s. to

ruhig *a (Seele, See, Wetter)* calm; *(geräuschlos)* silent; *(bewegungslos)* still; *(innerlich ~)* tranquil; *(heiter)* serene; *(gefaßt)* composed; *(friedlich)* peaceful; *(kaltblütig)* cool; *(Farbe)* sober; *~ adv* safely

a) *There are a lot of abbreviations in the sections of your dictionary printed above. On one of the first pages of your dictionary you will find a list of abbreviations. Find out what the following abbreviations mean:*

m, med, com, od, irr, tr, r, fig, a, adv

b) *Now translate the following sentences with the help of your dictionary:*

1. Als Catherine krank war, verschrieb ihr der Arzt eine gute Medizin.
2. Alan verschreibt sich oft in seinem Diktat.
3. Sir Francis Drake verschrieb sich seiner Königin mit ganzem Herzen.
4. Mutter macht Catherine dreimal am Tag einen warmen Umschlag.
5. Vergiß nicht, eine Briefmarke auf den Briefumschlag zu kleben!
6. Dein Buch braucht einen neuen Umschlag.
7. Moderne Hosen haben keinen Umschlag.
8. Glücklicherweise war die See ruhig, und niemand wurde seekrank.
9. Als der Lehrer die Klasse betrat, waren die Jungen ziemlich ruhig.
10. Der Jäger und der Schimpanse standen völlig ruhig, nachdem sie den Löwen gesehen hatten.

<9. Translation: Ein teurer Name>

Use English verbs for the German adverbs in italics.

1. Niemand würde sich heute an Button Gwinnett erinnern, wenn er nicht zufällig unter jenen fünfundfünfzig Männern gewesen wäre, die 1776 die Unabhängigkeitserklärung unterzeichnet haben. 2. Er war ein einfacher und nicht sehr bekannter Ladeninhaber in Savannah, Georgia, und der unbedeutendste unter den Männern, deren Unterschriften man auf jenem berühmten Dokument findet. 3. Dies war *anscheinend* der Höhepunkt seiner Karriere; ein Jahr später starb er. 4. Aber seine wirkliche Karriere hatte zu dieser Zeit kaum begonnen. 5. Das glauben Sie *wahrscheinlich* nicht, nicht wahr? 6. Dann hören Sie zu: 7. Später, als die Unabhängigkeitserklärung Geschichte geworden war, sammelten die Leute *gern* Unterschriften auf Briefen und Rechnungen von jenen Männern, die sie die Väter der Vereinigten Staaten nannten. 8. Die Unterschriften von vierundfünfzig dieser Männer konnte man leicht finden, aber die Unterschrift des fünfundfünfzigsten, die von Button Gwinnett, war viel schwerer zu finden. 9. Da er ein unbedeutender Mann gewesen war, hatte er nicht viele Dokumente unterschrieben. 10. So mußten die Leute, die einen vollständigen ‚Satz *(set)* der Väter' haben wollten, teuer für eine Unterschrift von Button Gwinnett bezahlen, nach einiger Zeit sogar mehr als £10.000. 11. Eines Tages sah ein Mann in Wolverhampton, England, alte Akten *(files)* durch und entdeckte *zufällig* drei Unterschriften von Button Gwinnett. 12. Sie können sich vorstellen, daß er sie *schleunigst* verkaufte.

6

1. Comprehension Test

1. What started the Californian Gold Rush in 1848?
2. Look at the map and describe Jim Roberts's journey to California. Why was the second part of the journey more difficult than the first? What were his adventures during this journey?
3. What kind of people went to California at the time of the gold rush?
4. You have heard in our text that people left their homes because they wanted to become rich in the Californian gold fields.—There are other reasons for leaving one's home. What are they? Think of the first English colonists in America or the negroes in the Southern States of America before 1863.

2. On the Way to California (this — that; these — those)

Tommy:	**This** is my tent. I want to sleep in it in California. **These** are my boots. I need them when I am standing in the American River looking for gold.
Andy:	Look at **that** big gun over there. Is it yours?
Jack:	Yes, it's mine. They say you may need a gun in California.
Andy:	Look at **those** boxes in our waggon. What do they contain?

Jack: Matches. They say you can't buy any matches on the way to California.
First gold-digger: Have you found any gold **this** week?
Second gold-digger: No, I haven't. **These** last two weeks have been rather bad. But I remember **those** days just after my arrival. I found a lot of gold then. **That** was a good time for me.

Put in 'this', 'that', 'these' or 'those'.

Jim and his companions are having a day's rest after six days of moving on. Jim thinks back to ... times in New York. What a rush during ... last week before his departure! All ... things that had to be bought! ... week has been quieter. Nothing but moving on and on. The weather was wonderful at first, but ... last two days it has not stopped raining. He had to change his shirts several times, and now he is wearing the nice shirt made of wool Sally gave him on ... last day they had together. When he puts his hand in one of its pockets he suddenly finds a letter from Sally in it. ... really is a surprise! Jim hopes to find plenty of gold in ... famous areas of California. And Sally will marry him as a millionaire. Isn't ... a nice thought? While Jim is thinking Andy has taken his guitar and is singing the song which all gold-diggers sing on their way to California. It is the tune of 'Oh, Susanna', but with a new text:

I soon shall be in Frisco,
And then I'll look around;
And when I see the gold-lumps there,
I'll pick them off the ground.

Oh, California,
That's the land for me;
I'm bound for California
With my washbowl on my knee.

<3. In a Big Shop>

Mr. Robertson and his wife go shopping for their summer holiday. They want to buy sun-hats, light shoes, a bathing-costume, swimming-trunks, a blanket for the beach, shorts, a light blouse, ...
What else could they need for a summer holiday?
The shop assistant shows Mrs. Robertson two sun-hats, a white one and a yellow one.

Shop assistant: Which hat do you like, **this one** or **that one?**
Mrs. Robertson: I think I'll take the white one.

Go on with this conversation.

4. All Kinds of Gold-diggers

Form relative sentences with determinative pronouns.

Ex.: Some gold-diggers have a lot of money. They can afford everything.
Those who have a lot of money can afford everything.

1. Some men had no money. They tried to earn some during their journey. 2. Many gold-diggers did not have enough food. They bought some in St. Joseph. 3. Some men were not honest. They stole food and money from their fellow-travellers. 4. Some men did not have the right clothes. They bought what they needed in

St. Joseph. 5. Many gold-diggers did not have a waggon of their own. They joined groups with waggons and oxen. 6. Most of the gold-diggers travelled in groups. They chose a leader. 7. Several of the gold-diggers were bearded. They were imitated by the others. 8. Some men had a breakdown with their waggons. They were helped by their companions. 9. Some gold-diggers had not bought enough meat. They tried to kill buffaloes or wild birds.

Let's prepare the next exercise

People who wanted to become rich, went to California in 1849.
Anybody who could afford it went by ship round South America.
The ones who found gold, often lost it again.

The German 'wer' (= alle diejenigen, die) *is expressed in English with 'people who'; 'anybody (anyone) who'; 'a person who'; 'the ones who'; 'those who'.*

5. Going to California

For every group of gold-diggers it was necessary to choose a leader, because the waggons were for most of their journey far away from sheriffs and judges. The leader had to keep order among his men.

Make up relative clauses using 'people who', 'anybody (anyone) who', 'a person who', 'the ones who' or 'those who'.

Ex.: Some people stole. They were punished.
People who stole were punished. **A person who** stole was punished.

1. Some people wanted to take another route. They had to leave the group. 2. Some persons became ill. They were looked after. 3. Some gold-diggers stole food or money. They were often driven away from their group. 4. Some destroyed waggons or hurt animals of their fellow-travellers. They were severely punished. 5. Some people did not want to make Sunday a day of rest. They were allowed to leave their group and move on by themselves.

6. A Cycling Tour — Relative Clauses with and without Relative Pronouns

Form relative clauses with determinative adjectives and leave out the relative pronoun where possible.

Ex.: A lot of boys took part in the cycling tour. They had bicycles.
Who (which boys) took part in the cycling tour?
Those who (that) had bicycles.
Some boys were chosen as leaders for the different groups of boys. They had a lot of responsibility.
Who (which boys) had a lot of responsibility?
Those chosen as leaders for the different groups of boys.

1. Some boys did not take enough food with them. They were often hungry. Who ...? 2. Some bicycles had not been overhauled before the tour. They broke

down. Which ...? 3. Some boys had no raincoats with them. They often got wet through. 4. A few boys did not have their hair cut during the cycling tour. They had rather long hair afterwards. 5. Some bicycles were painted by the boys. They were the most beautiful.

<7. In Father's Car through the Black Forest—An Interpreting Exercise>

One Sunday the Wagners want to drive to the Black Forest with their English guest Frank. Günter is again the family's interpreter.

Fill in what he says:

1. *Herr Wagner:* Wo würdest du gern sitzen, Frank?
   Günter: Father wants to know where you ...
2. *Frank:* May I sit in the front of the car beside you, Mr. Wagner?
   Günter: ...
3. *Herr Wagner:* Wollen wir zuerst die Autobahn *(motorway)* benutzen oder den nächsten Weg nehmen?
   Günter: ...
4. *Frank:* I should prefer to see your famous 'Autobahn'.
   Günter: ...
5. *Herr Wagner:* Wie gefällt dir unsere Fahrt?
   Günter: ...
6. *Frank:* Very much, Mr. Wagner. Your 'Volkswagen' runs very well. Is it better than a Ford?
   Günter: ...
7. *Herr Wagner:* Für mich ist der Volkswagen gerade richtig. Er ist billiger als ein Ford und braucht weniger Benzin.
   Günter: ...
8. *Frank:* How fast can you go and how fast are you allowed to go on the 'Autobahn'?
   Günter: ...
9. *Herr Wagner:* Ich kann nicht schneller als 120 km in der Stunde fahren. Für die Autobahn gibt es keine Geschwindigkeitsbegrenzung. Dort kann jeder so schnell fahren, wie er will.
   Günter: ...
10. *Herr Wagner:* Kannst du fahren, Frank?
    Günter: ...
11. *Frank:* No, I can't. I'm not allowed to yet. I have to wait until I am 18.
    Günter: ...
12. *Herr Wagner:* Wenn du mit einem Wagen nach Deutschland kommst, wird es etwas schwierig für dich sein, weil hier alle Autos auf der rechten Seite fahren.
    Günter: ...
13. *Frank:* I think I can get used to that.
    Günter: ...

<8. A Short Story in Pictures>

<9. Translation: Eine andere Art Goldgräber>

1. Ein Engländer mit Namen Tomkins war Soldat im zweiten Weltkrieg. 2. Er war unter denen, die vom Anfang des Krieges an in der Armee gewesen waren, und sehnte sich danach, zu seiner Familie zurückzukehren. 3. Er hoffte, nach Hause geschickt zu werden, und erzählte dem Arzt des Regiments, daß er plötzlich taub *(deaf)* geworden sei. 4. Der Arzt jedoch glaubte ihm nicht und dachte sich einen Plan aus, um die Wahrheit über Tomkins herauszufinden. 5. Zwei andere Soldaten versprachen, dem Arzt zu helfen. 6. Als sie allein mit Tomkins waren, begannen sie sich gegenseitig [etwas] von einer Kiste Gold zuzuflüstern, die unter jenem großen Birnbaum in der Nähe der Kirche vergraben worden war. 7. Sie wollten früh am nächsten Morgen dorthin gehen, um das Gold auszugraben. 8. Tomkins hatte natürlich alles gehört, ging sofort zu dem Birnbaum und begann zu graben. 9. Er hatte Glück: Nach einer Viertelstunde entdeckte er die Kiste. 10. Schnell brach er sie auf, aber sie enthielt nur einen schweren Stein und ein Stück Papier mit den folgenden Worten darauf: „Wenn du so taub bist, wie du sagst, wie konntest du [dann] hören, was wir über die versteckte Kiste gesagt haben?“ 11. Ist Tomkins danach nach Hause geschickt worden? Was denkst du?

7

1. Comprehension Test

1. What was the situation in the Northern and Southern States of America when Abraham Lincoln was elected President?
2. How did the Southern States act after Lincoln's election?
3. What were Lincoln's aims during the Civil War? Did he reach them?
4. Tell the story of Lincoln's death.

<5.> What was the situation of the slaves in the Southern States of America before slavery was abolished? Think of the story 'Follow the North Star'.

2. Past and Past Perfect — Revision

Dates from Lincoln's life:

1. *1809:* born in a log cabin in Kentucky. Lincoln's parents came from Virginia to Kentucky. His grandfather was killed by Indians.
2. *1816:* Lincoln's father Thomas goes to Indiana and builds a simple log cabin. The family spent one whole year in a hut which had walls only on three sides.
3. *1818:* Lincoln's mother Nancy dies. Lincoln's mother sent young Abe to school for a few days every year to give him some education.
4. *1819:* Lincoln's father marries again: Sarah Bush Johnston. Sarah Bush Johnston's husband died a few years before Lincoln's mother.
5. *until 1828:* Lincoln works in the woods, cutting down trees. Lincoln's father was a farmer and carpenter.
6. *between 1828 and 1831:* He works on a boat that carries food and other goods to and from New Orleans. Sarah Bush Johnston always thought that Abe should learn more than to cut trees.
7. *1831:* He leaves his parents' home and starts working as a clerk in New Salem. Lincoln read all the history and law books he could get.
8. *after 1831:* For 20 years he pays back money he owes to someone. Lincoln opened a shop of his own. But this was not a success.

Now use the past tense and the past perfect and say the sentences like this:

Ex.: Lincoln **was born** in 1809 in a log cabin in Kentucky. What had happened before? His parents **had come** from Virginia to Kentucky. His grandfather **had been killed** by Indians.

3. Past Simple or Past Continuous? — Revision

Put in the right forms of the past tense.

Abe Lincoln's adventure on a Mississippi boat.

1. One evening at about 8 o'clock the men (to stop) the boat. 2. Allen Gentry (to fasten) the boat to a tree and Abe Lincoln (to count) the money which they had earned that day, when they suddenly (to hear) somebody whistling. 3. As they (not to see) anybody they (to go on) with their work. 4. While Allen (to cook) their supper on a small fire Abe (to write) some notes in their log-book. 5. Suddenly seven negroes (to rush) towards them from behind the bushes. 6. They (to shout) and (to throw) stones at them. 7. While two negroes (to bind) Allen, three others (to jump) into the boat; the remaining two watched the path leading to the scene. 8. While Allen (to lie) on the ground Abe (to fight) with the negroes in the boat. 9. While Abe (to defend) himself against the negroes, Allen (to manage) to free himself. 10. When the negroes (to see) Allen coming to the boat they (to flee). 11. While Abe (to look for) the oars Allen (to cut) the anchor rope. 12. Half an hour later the boat (to move) quietly on the stream. The men (to look for) a safer place for the night.

Let's prepare the next exercise

a) A policeman to another policeman at 11 o'clock in the morning: "**This morning has been** very difficult for me. I **have received** the news that a dangerous burglar **has been seen** in our street."	a) *The present perfect is used for actions within a period of time that is not yet finished. Think of expressions like 'this morning', 'this week', 'today', etc.*
b) In the evening the policeman and his wife have guests. During the evening he tells them: "**This morning was** very difficult for me. I **received** the news that a dangerous burglar **had been seen** in our street."	b) *The past tense can also be used with these expressions, for example when you describe at 8 o'clock in the evening what happened in the morning.*

4. Miss Foster's Busy Day

Miss Foster is a secretary in a big New York firm. One Friday morning she has a lot of work to do:

1. She has to type an urgent letter to Mr. Brown.
2. She has to type a report about the last business conference.
3. She has to write letters of invitation for the next business conference.
4. She has to ring up Mr. Walker's wife to tell her that Mr. Walker cannot come home for lunch.
5. She has to ring up a telephone firm to tell them that the telephone in the room next to hers is not in order.
6. She has to book hotel rooms for Mr. Walker's next business trip.
7. She has to interview a young girl who has applied for a post in the firm.
8. She has to fetch traveller's cheques for Mr. Walker from the bank.
9. She has to order books for Mr. Walker.
10. She has to show a new secretary where to put the copies of the letters.

a) At 11 o'clock Miss Foster has done half the work Mr. Walker has given her. He comes into her room and asks her:
"**Have you typed** the letter to Mr. Brown yet?"—"Yes, **I have just typed** it."
"**Have you . . .?**"—"No, **I haven't . . . yet.**"
"**Have you . . .?**"

Go on.

b) In the evening Miss Foster is invited to a party. During the evening she tells her friends what a busy morning she has had in the office:
"**This morning I typed** an urgent letter to Mr. Brown. **I typed** . . ."

Go on.

5. 'ever' and 'never' + Present Perfect—Revision

a) *A newspaper reporter asks a businessman questions:*

Reporter:	*Businessman:*
"**Have** you **ever been** to England?"	"Yes, I **have been** to England several times."
"**Have** you **ever spent** Christmas in England?"	"No, I **have never** had a chance to do that."
"**Have** you **ever been** to London?"	"Yes, of course, I **have been** there three times."
"Have you ever . . .?"	

Go on with this interview.
(to go to Stratford-on-Avon; to see a Shakespeare performance; to live with an English family; to taste a plum-pudding; to spend Guy Fawkes' Day in England; to prepare an open fire; to go to the British Museum; to see Queen Elizabeth; to see an English film)

Can you think of more questions and answers?

b) *Now ask the boys and girls questions with 'ever'.*

Ex.: **Have** you **ever had** a chance to fly?
No, **I have never had** a chance to fly so far, but I think that will be possible when I start earning money.

6. Present Perfect or Present Perfect Continuous?—Revision

Put in the right tenses. Use the Present Perfect Continuous where possible.

1. I (to live) here for three weeks, but (not to meet) any of my neighbours.
2. He (to work) in this factory for five years and (to earn) a lot of money in that time.
3. She (not to try) to read an English newspaper, although (to learn) English for several years.
4. Father (to look for) his glasses all day, but (not to find) them yet.
5. That letter (to lie) on my desk for weeks, but I (not to find) the time to answer it.
6. You already (to drink) three cups of coffee since you (to sit) here.
7. My friend (not to come) although I (to wait) for him for more than two hours.
8. The big tree (to stand) near our house since I was a boy. I'm glad they (not to cut) it down yet.
9. Look, that light (to burn) all night. I must (to forget) to switch it off.

7. Tenses Test

Put in the right tenses.

1. I (to try) to ring you up for a whole week. Where you (to be)? 2. It (to look) as if the radio (to be) on all night. I must (to forget) to switch it off before I (to go) to bed last night. 3. At last you (to come). I (to wait) here for more than

half an hour. 4. My brother has been staying in America since last year, so when he (to return) the month after next I (not to see) him for fourteen months. 5. If you (to tell) me that you already (to buy) that book, I (not to give) it to you as a birthday present, but now it (to be) too late. 6. I (to ring) the bell once more, but as the Millers (not to answer) it yet, I think they must (to go) out. I (not to come) all this way if I (to know) that. 7. I wish you (to tell) me last week that you (to come) to London. If I (to know) in time you (not to have) to stay in a hotel. 8. The manager (to talk) to an important customer at the moment, but he (to be) free for you soon. (to like) you to take a seat for a few minutes? 9. "Miss Smith (not to work) here for years. (to be) you sure that you (to get) the right name?" "Quite sure. She (to ring) me up yesterday, and I certainly (not to come) here if she (not to ask) me to."

8. Sentences with 'before' and 'after'

Join the following pairs of sentences using 'before' or 'after'.

Ex.: First Bill opened the window. Then he got into bed.
Before Bill **got** into bed he **opened** the window.
After Bill **had opened** the window he **got** into bed.

1. First Miss Jackson started learning English. Then she took up French. 2. First Mr. Davis ate a steak with peas. Then he had some ice-cream. 3. First Mr. Harrison missed his train. Then he took a taxi. 4. First Shirley worked as a secretary at the post-office. Then she got a post at the airport. 5. First Mr. Barton went for a walk with the dog. Then he answered his brother's letter. 6. First Mrs. Brown bought new shoes for the children. Then she looked for a new hat for herself. 7. First we did a test about tenses. Then we formed sentences with 'before' and 'after'.

<9. How to use your dictionary (III)>

Here is a section of a dictionary to show you how different it is from our English-German vocabulary at the end of this book:

nehmen *irr tr* to take (*etw von jdm* s.th. from s.o.); (*heraus-*) to take out; (*weg-*) to take away; (*fortbewegen*) to move; (*zurück-*) to take back; (*ergreifen*) to seize, to lay hold of; (*an-*) to accept; (*erhalten*) to receive, to get; (*kaufen*) to buy; (*in Besitz -*) to appropriate; (*gefangen-*) to capture; (*Hindernis*) to take, to clear; (*Graben*) to leap over; (*Eintrittskarte*) to book; (*unrechtmäßig*) to arrogate s.th. to o.s.; *Abschied -* to say good-by(e); to take leave; *sich in acht -* to be careful (*vor* of); *in Anspruch -* to lay claim (to); *unter Feuer -* to shell, to fire upon; to strafe; *alles in allem genommen* all things considered; *Anstoß -* to object; *auf sich -* to take s.th. upon o.s.; *kein Blatt vor den Mund -* to give s.o. a piece of o.'s mind; *ein Ende -* to come to an end; *es auf sich -* to take it upon o.s.; *es sich nicht - lassen* to insist on; *es genau -* to be very particular; to be pedantic; *sich etw zu Herzen -* to lay s.th. to heart; *sich das Leben -* to commit suicide; *leicht -* to treat lightly; *den Mund voll -* to talk big; *- wir den Fall* let us suppose; *Partei -* to take sides, to side with; *Platz -* to have (*od* take) a seat; *Schaden -* to suffer damage; *streng* (*od genau*)*genommen* strictly speaking; *Urlaub -* to get leave of absence; *wie man's nimmt!* that depends! *jdn beim Wort -* to take s.o. at his word; *zu sich -* (*Nahrung*) to eat, to have s.th., to take nourishment; (*Person*) to take in, to take to o.'s home.

Now translate the following story with the help of your dictionary:

1. Kapitän Smith wußte, daß er sich vor den Indianern *in acht nehmen* mußte.
2. Darum *nahm* er immer Geschenke *mit,* wenn er in den Teil des Landes kam, in dem die Indianer lebten.
3. Trotzdem wurde er eines Tages von den Indianern *gefangengenommen.*
4. Die Indianer wollten seine Geschenke nicht *annehmen.*
5. Statt dessen *nahmen* sie ihm alle Sachen *weg* und brachten ihn zu Powhatan, ihrem Häuptling.
6. Als die Indianer sich anschickten *(to prepare)*, Smith zu töten, *nahm* Pocahontas, Powhatans Lieblingstochter, *Partei* für ihn.
7. Sie *nahm an* (= dachte), daß sie das Leben des weißen Mannes retten könnte.
8. Schließlich *nahm* Powhatan seine erste Entscheidung *zurück.*
9. Einige Zeit später *nahm* das Indianermädchen *Abschied* von ihren Eltern. Sie ging mit Kapitän Smith nach Jamestown.

<10. Translation: Zwei Geschichten über Lincoln>

a) 1. Eines Morgens während des Bürgerkrieges sah ein Offizier Abraham Lincoln sich die Stiefel putzen. 2. „Herr Präsident“, rief der erstaunte Offizier aus, „meinen Sie, der Präsident der Vereinigten Staaten sollte seine eigenen Stiefel putzen?“ 3. Mit einem Lächeln antwortete Lincoln: „Wenn der Präsident nicht seine eigenen Stiefel putzt, wessen Stiefel sollte er [dann] putzen?“

b) 1. Als Abraham Lincoln einen seiner Freunde ärgerlich über jemanden sprechen hörte, riet er ihm, sich hinzusetzen und dem Mann einen zornigen Brief zu schreiben. 2. Als der Brief geschrieben war, las Lincolns Freund ihn dem Präsidenten vor, der davon *(by it)* sehr beeindruckt war. 3. Der Schreiber war sehr erfreut und fragte: „Wie würden Sie mir raten, den Brief zu schicken?“ 4. „Den Brief schicken?“ sagte Lincoln. „Ich würde ihn nicht schicken. 5. Ich schreibe manchmal Briefe wie diesen *(that)* — es tut mir gut; aber ich schicke sie niemals ab.“

8

1. Comprehension Test

1. Why did thousands of workers queue at the Ford factory one winter morning in 1914?
2. On what principles did the prosperity of the USA depend according to Henry Ford's ideas?
3. How was it possible for the Ford Motor Company to reduce the price of one car from $ 1,200 to $ 295 after 1914?
4. Tell the story of 'Tin Lizzy'.
5. What had to be done in the Ford plant after the death of 'Tin Lizzy' before a new model could be built?

6. Henry Ford wanted to make it possible for anybody with an average income to buy an automobile. Has this become possible for German workers, too? Say what you think.

<7.> As many people have cars today the traffic is often very heavy. Speak about the dangers for drivers and pedestrians. What can be done to prevent traffic accidents?

<2. Cars in England and America>

For several parts of the car different words are used in England and America. Here they are:

English:	**American:**
1 bonnet	hood
2 engine	motor
3 windscreen	windshield
4 tyre	tire
5 wing	fender
6 boot	trunk

3. From Henry Ford's Life—'that' after Superlatives

Complete the following sentences with the help of relative clauses and leave out 'that' where possible. Use the passive voice where necessary.

Ex.: When Henry Ford was a child he collected even the smallest bit of metal (to find) in the street.
When Henry Ford was a child he collected even the smallest bit of metal **(that) he found** in the street.

1. Tools were the best playthings young Henry (to have). 2. The first horseless coach (to see) was a steam engine on wheels. 3. For the first car (to build) he took the wheels of some old bicycles. 4. The most successful car (to make) was 'Tin Lizzy'. 5. The shortest time (to require) for the construction of 'Tin Lizzy' was 1 hour and 33 minutes. 6. Model T became the cheapest car (to find) in America. 7. The first car (to sell) cost $1,200. 8. The cheapest car (to buy) in America at that time was 'Tin Lizzy'. 9. The highest wages (to pay) in the United States at that time were those paid at the Ford plant in Detroit.

4. Prepositional Relative Clauses

Form relative clauses leaving out the relative pronoun and putting the preposition at the end.

Ex.: Everybody wanted to work for Henry Ford. (man)
Henry Ford was **the man everybody wanted to work for.**

1. People were impatiently waiting for Model A. (car)
2. All the newspapers wrote about Model A. (car)
3. Many people were hoping for a wage of five dollars a day. (wage)

4. 'Tin Lizzy' could not be accused of failure. (thing)
5. Many people were waiting for a position with the Ford Motor Company. (job)
6. All the Ford workers talked about the new assembly line. (thing)
7. All the other car builders were interested in the 'Tin Lizzy'. (car)
8. At first people laughed about the idea of the horseless coach. (thing)
9. Every worker trusted Henry Ford. (man)
10. Every American worker was proud of a position with the Ford Motor Company. (job)

<5. Train your Fantasy>

Every day in newspapers, on the radio and on TV you can read and hear publicity slogans like these:

This is the car all the world is speaking about.
This is the car millions are dreaming of.
This is the washing-machine every housewife is longing for.

Now try to find your own publicity slogans. You need not use relative clauses in every slogan. You need not only make up slogans about cars and their parts. What else can you make slogans about?

6. Relative Clauses in the Genitive

Make relative sentences in the genitive.

Ex.: As a second car many Americans use the 'Volkswagen'. Its import is growing from day to day.
As a second car many Americans use the 'Volkswagen' **the import of which** is growing from day to day.

Now connect the following sentences with the first sentence about the 'Volkswagen'.

1. Its smallness and cheapness is liked by many people.
2. Its shape is quite different from the big American cars.
3. Its rising sales surprise many people.
4. Its colour can be chosen according to people's wishes.
5. Its motor is small but efficient.

7. A Sentence Switchboard: 'that' in Relative Clauses

Form sentences and leave out 'that' where possible.

Everything Nothing Much Anything Little	(that)	appears in the newspapers we read in the newspapers can be read in the newspapers is printed in the newspapers	is true. is wrong. is interesting. is nonsense. is great fun.

Are all the sentences you have formed true? Which are the true ones?

<8. Who Gets the Arm-chair?—A Story in Pictures>

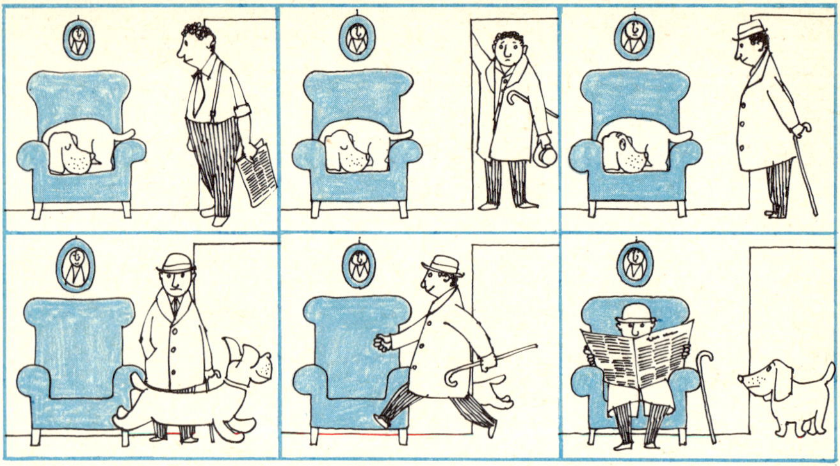

<9. How to use your dictionary (IV)>

Here again is a section of a dictionary:

take [teik] (took; taken) *tr* (weg-, ein-)nehmen; ergreifen, packen; bringen; begleiten; in Anspruch nehmen; erfordern; kosten; sich zuziehen; ermitteln; auswählen; verstehen; auffassen; halten (*for* für); *to ~ into account* in Betracht ziehen; *to ~ advantage of* sich zunutze machen; *to ~ the air* an die Luft gehen; *aero* aufsteigen; *to ~ alarm* ängstlich werden (*at* über); *to ~ the bearings* anpeilen; *to ~ breath* atmen; ausruhen; *to ~ care* sich in acht nehmen; sorgen (*of* für); to *~ a chair* sich setzen; *to ~ the chair* den Vorsitz übernehmen; *to ~ comfort* sich trösten; *to ~ compassion* Mitleid haben (*on* mit); *to ~ into consideration* in Betracht ziehen; *to ~ counsel* beratschlagen (*with* mit); *to ~ a drive* ausfahren; *to ~ effect* wirksam werden; gelingen; *to ~ exercise* sich Bewegung machen; *to ~ an examination* e-e Prüfung ablegen; *to ~ the fancy of s.o.* jdm gefallen; *to ~ a fancy to* eingenommen sein für; *to ~ fire* Feuer fangen; wütend werden (*at* über); *to ~ in hand* unternehmen; *to ~ heart* Mut fassen; *to ~ to heart* es sich zu Herzen nehmen; *to ~ a hint* einen Wink verstehen; *to ~ hold of* ergreifen; sich bemächtigen; *to ~ hold on* beeindrucken; *to ~ horse* aufsitzen; *to ~ one's leave* sich verabschieden (*of* von); *to ~ the liberty* sich erlauben; *to ~ s.o.'s measure* Maß nehmen; *to ~ a note of* aufschreiben; *to ~ notice of* beachten; *to ~ an oath* schwören; *to ~ offence at* beleidigt sein über; *to ~ pains* sich Mühe geben; *to ~ part in* teilnehmen; *to ~ pity* Mitleid haben (*on* mit); *to ~ the place of* ersetzen; *to ~ place* stattfinden; *to ~ pleasure* Vergnügen haben (*in* an); *to ~ possession of* Besitz ergreifen; *to ~ a pride* stolz sein (*in* auf); *to ~ a rest* sich ausruhen; *to ~ rise* entstehen; *to ~ a seat* sich setzen; *~ your seats!* einsteigen! *to ~ ship* sich einschiffen (*for* nach); *to ~ time* sich Zeit nehmen (*to* zu); *to ~ trouble* sich bemühen; *to ~ the trouble* sich die Mühe machen; *to ~ a turn* sich wenden; sich befassen (*at* mit); *to ~ a view of* prüfen; beurteilen; *to ~ views of* Aufnahmen machen; *to ~ a walk* spazierengehen; *to ~ the water* vom Stapel laufen; *to ~ s.o's word* glauben.

a) *Read this section carefully and look up the abbreviations.*

b) *Try to find good translations for the following sentences:*

1. Peter *took* the tea things to the kitchen. 2. Then he *took* the family album and

showed it to Robert. 3. Later on the boys *took* a bus and went to the harbour. 4. It *took* them about ten minutes to get there. 5. They *took* several pictures of ships lying in the harbour. 6. Next day they went to a football match which was *to take place* on the playing-field of Peter's school. 7. Peter had always *taken* an active *part* in sports at school. 8. He even joined in the match today, *taking the place* of a friend who had become ill.

Let's prepare the next exercise

a) We visited the farm **where** Henry Ford was born. ... auf der ...
Did you see the house **where** he once lived? ... in dem ...

b) It was a time **when** the car had not yet been invented. ... zu der ...

Relative clauses are often introduced
a) *by 'where'*
b) *by 'when'.*

<10. A Visit to the Ford Plant>

Translate the following sentences into English.

a) 1. Eine Gruppe von Touristen besucht die Fordfabrik in der Nähe von Detroit, in der alles hergestellt wird, was zu einem Auto gehört.
2. Die Fabrik hat einen eigenen Hafen, in dem Schiffe beladen *(to load)* und entladen *(to unload)* werden.
3. Hier sind die Fabrikanlagen, in denen Stahl produziert wird.
4. Dort sind die Gebäude, in denen Glas für die Wagenfenster hergestellt wird.
5. Dort drüben ist das Büro, in dem sich Männer und Frauen täglich um Stellungen bewerben.

b) 1. Zu der Zeit, in der Ford noch nicht seine eigene Fabrik gegründet hatte, baute er Autos in einem alten Schuppen *(shed)*.
2. [Der] 6. Juni 1903 war der Tag, an dem die Ford Motor Company gegründet wurde.
3. Während der Jahre, in denen Henry Ford Direktor der Ford Motor Company war, wurde die Fabrikanlage eine der modernsten der Welt.
4. Von 1946 an, dem Jahr, in dem Henry Ford seine Stellung als Direktor der Firma aufgab, war sein Enkel *(grandson)* Henry Ford II Direktor der Ford Motor Company.
5. Während der Jahre, in denen er Direktor der Firma war, wurde eine große Zahl von Ford-Werken in der ganzen Welt gebaut.
6. Im Jahre 1963, in dem Henry Ford hundert Jahre alt geworden wäre, sagte sein Enkel:
7. „Zu der Zeit, in der mein Großvater Direktor der FMC war, vollbrachte *(did)* er die folgenden wichtigen Dinge: Er baute das erste billige Auto, er benutzte das Fließband für Massenproduktion, und er war der erste, der einen Mindestlohn von fünf Dollar am Tag zahlte."

9

<1. Comprehension Test>

1. Who were the first settlers in the 'Southern Unknown Land'?
2. What conditions did they find in Australia?
3. Tell what you know about Australia's history from 1787 to the present time.
4. As you know, Australia is a Commonwealth country. What other countries belong to the Commonwealth?—Tell what you know about the Commonwealth today.

2. The Southern Unknown Land

Change the expressions in italics into verbal expressions.

Ex.: Let's *have a talk* about Australia, shall we?
Let's **talk** about Australia, shall we?

a) 1. When in the 17th century Spanish and Dutch sailors had explored the northern coast of Australia they *gave* the big island *the name of* 'New Holland'.
2. They *did not have* any *interest* in the country itself.
3. They *made no attempt* to found colonies in the newly-discovered country.
4. In 1770 Captain Cook *made a landing* on the eastern coast of Australia.
5. He *had been given the order to make a voyage* to the Pacific Ocean.
6. He *had formed a plan* to find the South Pole.
7. After his return to England he *made a report* to the king about the new country.

b) 1. The first *transportation* of convicts to Australia *was carried out* in 1787.
2. Captain Phillip *had been given the order* to accompany the transport.
3. In Australia the convicts *had a hard struggle* for existence.
4. *Supplies* of food for the settlers *came* after three years.
5. Gradually more people *became settlers* in Australia.

Let's prepare the next exercise

A nice **present** [ˈ——] was **presented** [—ˈ——] to the queen.

A number of words can be used as nouns and verbs.
Note: *Nouns have the stress on the first syllable, verbs on the second.*

3. Some Facts about Australia — Stresses Test

a) *Read the following text. Mind the stresses of the words in bold type.*

1. One day there was a talk about Australia in the evening classes of the London County Council. During the talk pictures were **projected** on the screen. Here are some facts the students learnt:

2. The eastern parts of Australia along the coast get enough rain. Their chief **produce** is wheat, which is **exported** to many countries.
3. Australia's main **exports** except wheat are wool, gold, meat, butter, skins, sugar, milk, cream, eggs, dried and fresh fruits. Her **imports** are arms, ammunition, oil, cotton, silk, tea, tobacco and paper.
4. In the large grass areas there is a continuous **increase** in the number of sheep farms.
5. As the distances are very great in Australia, animals are often **transported** in planes.
6. There is a great **contrast** between the areas near the coast and Central Australia. Central Australia is very dry and like a desert.
7. When after 1787 the number of settlers **increased,** there were some conflicts with the aborigines who tried to **protest** against the white men in their areas.
8. Sometimes aborigines who had **rebelled** against the white men were even killed.

b) *Now read the words in bold type as pairs.*
Ex.: project [ˈprɔdʒekt] — to project [prəˈdʒekt]
Check the spelling and pronunciation in your dictionary.

4. What Persons and Things are like

a) The aborigines are people who have a dark skin, long arms and long legs, big bones, dark hair, flat noses, thick lips and dark eyes.

Now describe the aborigines with adjectives:
They are **dark-skinned,** . . .

b) *Ex.:* What do you call a girl that looks beautiful?
She is called a **beautiful-looking** girl.

What do you call . . .

1. . . . a story that frightens you?
2. . . . news that worries you?
3. . . . a tour that disappoints you?
4. . . . a report that surprises you?
5. . . . a dress that looks nice?
6. . . . a noise that sounds funny?
7. . . . a man that looks angry?

c) *Ex.:* What do you call a wall that is painted green?
It is called a **green-painted** wall.

What do you call . . .

1. . . . a boy that has long arms?
2. . . . a girl that is dressed nicely?
3. . . . a door that is locked safely?
4. . . . a letter that is written well?
5. . . . a girl that has blue eyes?
6. . . . a woman that has a thin face?
7. . . . a girl that has long hair?

d) *Can you think of other adjectives that are formed like the ones above? Use them for describing persons and things.*

5. Word-families

Ex.: to live — to live on s.th. — lively — standard of living — living-room — living conditions — sign of life
to sleep — to go to sleep — sleep — sleeper — sleepy — sleeping-car

Now form similar word-families with the following verbs:
to walk, to sing, to help, to swim, to farm, to work, to save, to act
Look up these words in your dictionary.

6. Word-formation

a) *Form the opposites of verbs, nouns and adjectives by putting the prefix 'dis'- in front of them and give their German meaning. Use your dictionary if you cannot understand a newly-formed word.*

Ex.: to agree — **to disagree** = not agree *(nicht übereinstimmen)*
honest — **dishonest** = not honest *(unehrlich)*
approval— **disapproval** = *(Mißbilligung)*

to appear, to like, to please, to respect, to cover, to continue, to connect, to trust, to believe, to obey

interested, similar, pleased, united, used

advantage, honour, order, honesty

b) *Put the prefix re- in front of the verbs. It means that an action is repeated or done again.*

Ex.: to tell — to retell [ˈriːˈtel] *(= nacherzählen, wiedererzählen)*

to print, to appear, to play, to address, to admit, to arm, to build, to enter, to import, to open, to read, to take, to translate

c) *What adjectives or verbs do the following nouns come from?*
truth, warmth, height, depth, width, strength, length

<7. The Prefixes 'un-', 'in-', 'im-'>

Replace the words in bold type by others using prefixes.

a) **Prefix un-**

Ex.: This boy is **not able** to do his homework well.
This boy is **unable** to do his homework well.

1. The sun is shining. It is **not necessary** to take an umbrella.
2. Shirley Benson is **not happy** because she did not get the position she wanted in the export firm.
3. To be **not fortunate** means to be **not lucky.**
4. The old man was **not kind** to his dog.
5. If you do not play according to the rules you are **not fair.**
6. It is **not certain** whether Mr. Smith will come today.
7. This exercise is **not interesting,** is it?

b) **Prefix in- (im- before b, p, m)**

Ex.: The answer is **not correct.** It is **incorrect.**

1. It is **not possible** to swim across the ocean.
2. If you don't thank someone for a present you are **not polite.**
3. If you cannot wait until it is your turn you are **not patient.**
4. It is **not possible** to learn English in three weeks.

<8. Immigrants in Australia—An Interpreting Exercise>

Mr. Schneider, a joiner, and his wife are new immigrants in Sydney, Australia. One day they are invited by their neighbours, the Martins, and talk about life in Sydney. As Mrs. Schneider cannot yet speak English very well, her husband has to be the interpreter. *Find out what he says.*

1. *Mrs. Schneider:* Wir sind noch nicht lange in Sydney und kennen die Stadt noch nicht gut. Wie kann man sie am besten kennenlernen?
   Mr. Schneider: ...
2. *Mr. Martin:* You should join a Sydney Day Tour. There is one every day except Sunday. You'll be shown the beaches near Sydney, the famous Sydney Harbour Bridge, the University, the Zoo, the Australian Museum and other city sights.
   Mr. Schneider: ...
3. *Mrs. Schneider:* Ich denke, das wäre eine gute Idee. Vielleicht an einem Sonnabend. Ist es nötig, Plätze im voraus zu bestellen?
   Mr. Schneider: ...
4. *Mr. Martin:* I don't know exactly. But the Travel Agency in Martin Place will give you the necessary advice.
   Mr. Schneider: ...
5. *Mrs. Schneider:* Welche Städte kann man leicht an einem Tag erreichen, wenn man abends wieder in Sydney sein will? Sydney ist doch Endstation vieler Eisenbahnlinien, nicht wahr?
   Mr. Schneider: ...
6. *Mr. Martin:* Yes, it is. You could go to Newcastle, for example, the second largest city in New South Wales. The huge steelworks there can be visited daily.
   Mr. Schneider: ...
7. *Mrs. Schneider:* Ich interessiere mich nicht besonders für die Industrie. Wohin kann man sonst fahren?
   Mr. Schneider: ...
8. *Mr. Martin:* If you are interested in beautiful landscapes or even in mountain-climbing you can easily reach the Blue Mountains. If you want to make a week-end trip, go and see Canberra.
   Mr. Schneider: ...
9. *Mrs. Schneider:* Vielen Dank für Ihre Ratschläge, Mr. Martin.
   Mr. Schneider: ...

<9. Points for and against>

Write down three points for and three points against the following subjects and discuss them:
a boarding-school education; shopping at supermarkets; working mothers; pocket money for children; beards; living in a foreign country; travelling by car; being an only child; living in the country; staying at home in the summer holidays.

Which other subjects would you like to discuss?

<10. Translation: Der König, der ein Sträfling war>

1. Unter den Sträflingen in Australien war ein sehr großer und starker Mann von zwanzig [Jahren], William Buckley. 2. Sein einziges Verbrechen war gewesen, Brot zu stehlen, als er hungrig war. 3. Er entkam in den Busch. 4. Eines Tages, mehr tot als lebendig, fand er ein neues Eingeborenengrab mit einem zerbrochenen Speer *(spear)* obendrauf. 5. Es war das Grab eines toten Häuptlings. 6. Buckley nahm den Speer. 7. Er war nicht sehr weit gegangen, als er [auf] eine Gruppe von Eingeborenen traf, Mitgliedern aus dem Stamme des toten Mannes. 8. Sie erkannten den Speer wieder und dachten, daß ihr Häuptling in der Gestalt eines weißen Mannes aus der Welt der Toten zu ihnen zurückgekommen wäre. 9. Deshalb machten sie Buckley zu ihrem König, kleideten ihn in Känguruhhäute und lehrten ihn ihre Sprache. 10. Drei Jahre lang lebte Buckley als ihr König. 11. Eines Tages kamen einige der Eingeborenen mit Taschentüchern, die sie gestohlen hatten, zum Lager zurück. 12. Jetzt wußte Buckley, daß weiße Männer in der Nähe waren. 13. Er ging von seinen Eingeborenen weg und fand die weißen Männer. 14. Nachdem er zuerst Sträfling und dann Eingeborenenkönig gewesen war, kehrte Buckley zum Leben der Weißen zurück. 15. Man gab ihm die *(his)* Freiheit, und er lebte glücklich in seiner neuen Heimat.

10

<1. Comprehension Test>

1. How many per cent of the total population of the Commonwealth are coloured? Are all of them the original inhabitants of their countries? What are the others?
2. Why did tens of thousands of West Indian negroes immigrate into Britain in the 1950's and 1960's?
3. Explain the last sentence of our story. Why can we say that John Baker ended a journey that had been started four centuries before?
4. Talk about the problems John Baker met when he tried to find a suitable job in London.

<2. Choosing a Career>

After you have read the B-text 'Choosing a Career' write a letter of application for the position that you would like best among the ones offered. Write your age, which schools you have been to, which examinations you have passed, which special training you have had, whether you have worked for another firm, what your main hobbies are. Start the letter with 'Dear Sirs' and end it with 'Yours faithfully'.

3. The Infinitive with 'in order to' and 'so as to'

a) *Answer the following sentences using 'in order to' or 'so as to'.*

Ex.: Why did many people leave Jamaica? (good job, England)
Many people left Jamaica **so as to (in order to)** get a good job in England.

1. Why did John Baker go to England? (physics, London University)
2. Why did he study physics? (post, industry)
3. Why did he work as a liftboy in the evenings? (to pay, studies)
4. Why did plenty of negroes from the West Indies work as bus conductors, lorry drivers, porters or waiters in London? (better wages)
5. Why did John Baker sit in the waiting room of a big firm one day? (to be interviewed, staff manager)
6. Why did he write to a government department one day? (to ask, job)
7. Why did Nigeria urgently need qualified instructors? (to train, young workers)

<b)> *Complete the following sentences in a suitable way using 'in order to' or 'so as to'.*

1. The young lady went to England ...
2. I shall try to finish this piece of work today ...
3. The taxi is waiting ...
4. He has been working hard ...
5. He has searched all his pockets again and again ...
6. The Warners have gone to the seaside ...
7. She went all the way on foot ...

Let's prepare the next exercise: The Passive Infinitive

The book **is to be had.** ... ist zu haben.
Many negroes **are to be seen** at English universities. ... sind zu sehen ...
There **is** a lot of work **to be done.** ... muß getan werden.
Only the windows **remain to be cleaned.** ... müssen noch geputzt werden.

In English but not in German the infinitive of the passive is used after 'to be' and 'to remain'.
But: *There is no time to lose.* ... zu verlieren.

4. A Sentence Switchboard

Make sentences and translate them into German.

Ex.: Only some old houses remained to be painted.

Only	the kitchen furniture some old houses the garden chairs the bicycle	(to be) (to remain)	to be sold. to be repaired. to be painted. to be cleaned.

5. The Passive Infinitive

Change the words in italics into passive infinitives.

Ex.: If you are ill, there is nothing *you can do* but to stay in bed.
... there **is nothing to be done** ...

1. You are lying ill in bed; it is dark in the room, but *you can see* daylight through the curtains.
2. It must be about 9 o'clock because *you can hear* school children in the street.
3. But in your house everyone still seems to be asleep; *you can* only *hear* the ticking of the clock.
4. Suddenly you feel something hard under your arm. It is your sister's book. But what did she tell you? "*You must handle* this book carefully."
5. You sit up in bed and try to switch on the light; funny, *you cannot find* the bed-lamp.
6. "Well, why does the doctor say that *I must keep* my room dark until 9 o'clock in the morning?" you think.
7. There—crash! The lamp is on the floor! The house suddenly comes to life: *You can hear* quick steps and excited voices.
8. "Let them come," you think. "Fortunately I am ill and *they must treat* sick people nicely, mustn't they, even if they do break lamps?"

Let's prepare the next exercise: The Accusative with Infinitive with 'to'

a) I wish { that she would come. ↓ ↓ / — **her to come.** }	b) I expect { that he will do the work. ↓ ↓ / — **him to do the work.** }
a) *The infinitive with 'to' is used after verbs expressing a wish or its opposite:* *to want* *to wish* *I should like* *I should prefer* *to hate*	b) *The infinitive with 'to' is used after the following verbs:* *to advise* — *to expect* *to allow* — *to order* *to ask* — *to require* *to beg* — *to tell* *to cause* — *to warn*

6. A Porter's Work

After John Baker has worked as a lift-boy for quite a time he is offered the job of a hotel porter. He accepts it, of course, because that means more money for him. He has all kinds of things to do:

Ex.: A guest: "Call a taxi for me please." (to want)
A guest **wants him to call** a taxi.

1. *A lady:* "Carry my suit-case to my car please." (to ask)
2. *Hotel manager:* "Please work longer hours during the booksellers' meeting." (to expect)
3. *A businessman on the telephone:* "Please book two single rooms for me from Wednesday, February 13th, to Saturday, February 16th." (to ask)
4. *An old lady:* "Help me unlock my suit-case please." (to ask)
5. *Hotel manager:* "Ring up the doctor because a guest is ill." (to tell)
6. *Hotel manager:* "Show Mr. Miller his room please." (to order)

Let's prepare the next exercise: The Nominative with Infinitive

They expected him to look after poor negro families.

He was expected to look after poor negro families.

The infinitive after a verb in the passive voice must always have 'to'.

7. The Guest who Disappeared

An American of about forty has been staying at a London West End hotel for some days. One day he disappears with all his things but has not paid his bill. The police ask several people in the hotel about the man. This is what they tell the police:

1. Some people saw the American having supper with an unpleasant-looking man.
2. They saw him showing photographs to the other man.
3. A lady heard the men talking about a big sum of money.
4. Later they saw the American go upstairs to his room.
5. The person in the next room heard him walking to and fro and sighing from time to time.
6. Some hours later the lift-boy saw the unpleasant-looking man posting a big parcel at the post-office.
7. Nobody had seen the American leaving the hotel.

a) *Now say these sentences in the passive voice.*
Ex.: **The American was seen to have** supper with an unpleasant-looking man.

b) *Say the sentences of exercise 6 in the passive voice.*
Ex.: **John Baker is asked to carry** a suit-case to a lady's car.

8. Something about London's 9,000 Taxi Drivers

It is not easy to be a taxi driver in London.

Ex.: London taxi drivers must know 486 different routes across London. (to expect)
London taxi drivers **are expected to know** 486 different routes across London.

1. Taxi drivers have to wash their taxis every day, outside and inside. (to order)
2. They have their taxis overhauled once a year. (to expect)
3. Taxi drivers must not keep umbrellas and other things that people forget in taxis. (to warn)
4. They must take these things to the nearest police-station. (to tell)
5. They can accept a reward from the loser. (to allow)
6. As London has not enough taxi drivers, young men who like to drive should join the British School for Taxi Drivers. (to advise)
7. Visitors to London sometimes laugh about the odd shape of the taxis. (to see) But when they see how practical they are they soon begin to like the taxis and their drivers.

Let's prepare the next exercise: The German 'lassen'

1. a) A strange noise made him interrupt his work.
   b) They made the slaves work in the burning sun.
2. She had the servant prepare dinner for twelve persons.
3. Mr. Miller let us see his new house.

1. to make	=	a) lassen, verursachen
		b) lassen, jdn. zwingen
2. to have	=	lassen, veranlassen
3. to let	=	lassen, erlauben

9. The German 'lassen'

Translate the following sentences. Be careful with the German 'lassen'.

1. Mr. Walker ließ seine Sekretärin ihren Urlaub im August nehmen.
2. Der Verlust seines ganzen Geldes ließ Mr. Harrison seinen alten Beruf wieder aufnehmen.
3. Sie ließ den Hund immer in ihrem Zimmer schlafen.
4. Bitte, lassen Sie den Portier meinen Koffer zu meinem Wagen bringen und bringen Sie mir die Rechnung.
5. Seine Erkältung ließ ihn einige Tage im Bett bleiben.
6. Laß auch Mutter Peters Brief lesen.
7. Mrs. Brown ließ ihre Tochter die Zimmer für die Gäste vorbereiten.
8. Er ließ den Sklaven trotz seiner Krankheit schwer arbeiten.

Let's prepare the next exercise

a) It is important **for you to know** the rules of the road.
... daß du ... kennst.
b) Time is too short **for me to explain** them to you.
... als daß ich ... erklären könnte.
c) I'm waiting **for Father to explain** to you the most important traffic rules.
... bis Vater ... erklärt.

The expression 'for' + Noun (Pronoun) + Infinitive can be used after
a) it is difficult; it is important; it is possible; it is impossible; it is wrong; it is the custom; it is the rule; it is time;
b) adjectives with 'too' and 'enough'
c) to ask for; to long for; to wait for.

10. 'For' + Noun + Infinitive

Connect the following sentences.

Ex.: Nowadays girls learn a profession, too. That is the custom.
Nowadays **it is the custom for girls to learn** a profession, too.

1. You should introduce yourself to the staff manager. That is important. 2. Peter will finish this piece of work today. This should not be too difficult. 3. The bill should be sent to my firm. I have asked for that. 4. Everybody can save for a car nowadays. This is possible. 5. Father should go to the station. It is time. 6. I cannot tell you about my journey to Japan. Time is too short. 7. In England cars drive on the left. That is the rule. 8. Doris can understand this little English story. It is easy enough.

<11. Translation: William Wilberforce und der Sklavenhandel>

1. Die ersten afrikanischen Neger wurden 1563 gefangengenommen und als Sklaven nach den Westindischen [Inseln] verkauft. 2. Von dieser Zeit an wurde der Sklavenhandel mehr als 200 Jahre lang fortgesetzt und machte die englischen Sklavenhändler *(traders)* und Hafenstädte wohlhabend. 3. Die Leute in England und Amerika hatten schon lange gesagt, daß der Sklavenhandel eine schreckliche Sache sei, die eingestellt werden solle. 4. Aber William Wilberforce war der erste Staatsmann, der sein Leben der Frage der Sklaverei widmete. 5. Von 1787 an sprach er oft in der Öffentlichkeit über das harte Leben, das die Sklaven führten, und erwartete, daß [das] Parlament den Sklavenhandel abschaffen würde. 6. Aber die Vertreter des Sklavenhandels waren so stark und wohlhabend, daß Wilberforce zwanzig Jahre lang kämpfen mußte, bevor 1807 der Sklavenhandel im Britischen Weltreich abgeschafft wurde. 7. Dies jedoch war noch nicht das Ende der Sklavenprobleme. 8. Eine Menge Arbeit mußte noch getan werden. 9. Wilberforce wollte, daß die Sklaven frei sein und wie andere Menschen leben sollten. 10. Aber dieses Ziel war noch nicht erreicht, als er 1833 starb.

11

<1. Comprehension Test>

1. How was it possible that the newly-built Suez Canal was completely controlled by Britain and France?
2. Look at the map and explain why the Suez Canal was of such great importance for Britain before the First World War.
3. What are the main differences between the old concept of the British Empire and the new concept of the Commonwealth?

2. On a Big Ship — Participle Revision

a) *Use the verbs 'to stand, to sit, to lie, to stay, to go, to come' with participles and say what people were doing on a big passenger ship.*

Ex.: A Frenchman **lay sleeping** all day in his cabin.
A young lady **went singing** to the swimming-pool on the ship.
(to look into the grey water; to read magazines; to sun-bathe; to ...)

Go on.

b) *Use the verbs 'to be seen, to be heard, to be found' with participles and say what people were doing on the ship.*

Ex.: A little boy **was found watching** the engines.
An Italian **was heard singing** all day long.

What else were people seen, heard or found doing?

Let's prepare the next exercise

1. **Wanting** to finish the Canal as soon as possible, de Lesseps and his engineers **worked** day and night.	*Action at the same time.*
2. **Having finished** the Canal de Lesseps **made** plans for the future.	*One action after the other.*

3. Participial Constructions

Connect the following sentences using the right participles.

Ex.: Ferdinand de Lesseps had finished the construction of the Suez Canal. He wanted to celebrate the opening on November 17th, 1869.
Having finished the construction of the Suez Canal, Ferdinand de Lesseps **wanted** to celebrate the opening on November 17th, 1869.

1. Ferdinand de Lesseps wanted the opening of the Suez Canal to be a great feast. He had invitations written to all the sovereigns of Europe.
2. Many tourists had heard about the opening of the Canal. They streamed into Egypt.
3. The organizers of the feast expected about 6,000 guests. They had 1,000 servants and 500 cooks sent from other ports of the Mediterranean.

4. The organizers of the feast had been worried by rain for days. They were glad when the sun reappeared on the morning of November 16th.
5. The French Empress Eugénie looked at the many decorated ships at the entrance of the Suez Canal. She said that she had never seen anything so wonderful in all her life.
6. A few days before the opening Lesseps had sent some engineers to examine the Canal. He was told that a rock had been discovered that might be dangerous for the ships in the Canal.
7. The engineers and the workers worked day and night. They succeeded in removing the rock and thus preparing the Canal for the great day.

Let's prepare the next exercise

I **won't have** my rest **disturbed.**

I won't have I cannot have	} + Object + Past Participle =	Ich will nicht haben, daß ... Ich kann nicht zulassen, daß ...

4. 'to have' + Object + Past Participle

What the manager often says:

1. Don't drink tea too often during office hours.
2. Don't type private letters in the office.
3. Don't use the telephone for private calls.
4. Don't disturb my business conferences.
5. Don't read magazines during office hours.
6. Don't offer tea to visitors if I don't ask you to.
7. Don't show business letters to visitors.

When a new typist starts working at the office, another typist tells her:

1. He **won't have tea drunk** too often during office hours.
2. He won't have ...

Go on.

Let's prepare the next exercise: Participial Constructions with Conjunctions

While he was entertaining some friends at his home, Lionel Rothschild was visited by a government messenger.	→	**While entertaining** some friends at his home, Lionel Rothschild was visited by a government messenger.
Though it was registered under an Egyptian name, the Suez Canal was a French project.	→	**Though registered** under an Egyptian name, the Suez Canal was a French project.

Sometimes a conjunction is necessary to make the meaning of the participial construction clear: when, while, until, as if, thus, though, although, if.

5. Before the Opening of the Canal

Complete the sentences choosing the correct conjunctions from the following list: when, while, although, thus, if

Ex.: ... going to bed on the evening of November 16th, 1869, Ferdinand de Lesseps thought that nothing could hinder the opening of the Suez Canal now.
When going to bed on the evening ...

1. ... resting in his room de Lesseps was suddenly disturbed by some knocks at his door and was told the following news:
2. ... going through the Canal an Egyptian ship had sunk.
3. ... not removed by the following morning this ship would block the Canal.
4. ... working hard the engineers and workers did not succeed in removing the sunken ship.
5. ... being tired de Lesseps had a meeting with the engineers.
6. ... talking to the ruler of Egypt at 3 o'clock in the morning de Lesseps told him about the sunken ship.
7. The ruler gave him the order to blow up the ship, ... making the opening of the Canal possible.

6. Participial constructions with and without Conjunctions

Change the following sentences into participial constructions.
Remember: The participle must sometimes be in the first, sometimes in the second clause.

Ex.: Although we do not know exactly whether the weather will be fine tomorrow, we shall prepare our trip to the seaside.
Although not knowing exactly ...

1. The shop assistant discovered that he had a good voice and began to take singing-lessons.
2. One evening when Miss Brown was walking home from her office she saw a traffic accident.
3. While I was queueing for theatre tickets I heard that there were no more cheap tickets for the performance I wanted to see.
4. If you are well prepared for the examination you will not fail.
5. Until the patient is allowed to get up again he will have to stay in bed and take his medicine.
6. He refused to do the job and said that he would not work for so little money.
7. When I visit a city for the first time I always like to have a good street map with me.
8. Drivers who intend to take their cars with them to the Continent are advised to make early reservations.
9. He speaks excellent French because he lived in France for four years.
10. Our secretary left the office before closing-time and said that she had to go to the doctor's.

Let's prepare the next exercise

same subject

As **she** was ill **she** could not go to the party.
As **her husband** was ill **she** could not go to the party.

different subject

same subject

Being ill **she** could not go to the party.
Her husband being ill **she** could not go to the party.

different subjects

Usually the subject of the sentence is at the same time the subject of the participle. If not, the subject of the participle must be specially mentioned.

7. Participial Constructions with a Subject of their own

Connect the following sentences using participles. Don't forget: The participle must sometimes be in the first, sometimes in the second sentence.

Ex.: Peter is an Englishman. I asked him to help me translate a letter.
Peter being an Englishman I asked him to help me translate a letter.

1. The train was late. Mr. Potter could not reach his office in time.
2. The trams were full during the rush hour. Many people could not get in.
3. The manager entered the conference room first. His secretary followed him.
4. The whole family came to Mother's birthday. Uncle George arrived in a taxi.
5. The staff manager had entered the room. The conference began.
6. Mr. Jackson went alone to the theatre. His wife had caught flu.
7. Jack and George took part in the bicycle race. Jack won the first prize.

Let's prepare the next exercise

Considering he is British, he speaks German very well.
Generally speaking, Americans like big cars.
Strictly speaking, Big Ben is not the name of the clock tower of the Houses of Parliament but the name of the bell.
Judging from her dresses she can't have much money.

Some participial expressions have no subject. Often they are translated with the German 'man'.

considering	=	in Anbetracht
generally speaking	=	im allgemeinen
strictly speaking	=	strenggenommen; wenn man es genau nimmt
judging from	=	nach ... zu urteilen; wenn man nach ... geht

8. Participial Expressions with no Subject of their own

Complete the following sentences using one of the four expressions mentioned above.

1. ... she was in England for such a long time, her English is not too good.
2. ... his well-written letter, he must have had a good education.
3. ... the summer is usually colder and the winter warmer in England than in Germany.
4. ... the tomato is not a fruit but a vegetable.
5. ... his standard of living, he seems to earn quite a lot of money.
6. ... Germans are taller than Italians and Spaniards.
7. ... that it is almost autumn, I should not advise you to spend your holidays at the seaside.

<9. Translation: Der Suezkanal>

Use a participial construction in every sentence and as many different ones as possible.

1. Ferdinand de Lesseps begann den Kanal zu bauen, und die französische Regierung unterstützte seinen Plan. 2. Während er den Kanal baute, befreundete er sich mit Said Pascha, dem Sohn des ägyptischen Herrschers. 3. Da Ägypten nicht imstande war, für den Bau des Kanals zu zahlen, gründete de Lesseps eine Gesellschaft, die Aktien an verschiedene Länder verkaufte. 4. Schiffe, die von England nach Indien fuhren, konnten jetzt den Suezkanal benutzen und verkürzten auf diese Weise die Seereise um *(by)* 4563 Meilen. 5. Da der Kanal 103 Meilen lang ist, brauchen Schiffe ungefähr 13 Stunden, um ihn zu durchfahren. 6. Da der Kanal ursprünglich ziemlich schmal war, mußten die Schiffe oft warten, bevor sie ihn durchfahren konnten. 7. Nachdem die Aktionäre eine Menge Geld verdient hatten, reduzierten sie die Gebühr für die Benutzung des Kanals. 8. 1956 verstaatlichte Präsident Nasser den Suezkanal aus. 9. Nach dem 6-Tage-Krieg zwischen Israel und Ägypten wurde der Suezkanal gesperrt.

12

<1. Comprehension Test>

1. What was India's situation like at the end of the 19th century?
2. Why did Gandhi go to South Africa when he was a young man?
3. How was it possible for Gandhi to win the support of the masses for his plan of making India independent?
4. Why did Gandhi represent an insoluble problem to the British?
5. What great problem was Gandhi not able to solve after India had become independent?
6. Tell the story of Gandhi's death.

2. Gandhi in South Africa — Revision

Change the expressions in italics, using the following expressions with gerunds: to look forward to, to have the chance of, to succeed in, to decide on, to get tired of, to be interested in.

Ex.: After his law studies in London Gandhi *was glad that he could go back* to India.
After his law studies in London Gandhi **looked forward to going back** to India.

1. Unfortunately he *did not manage to become* a well-known lawyer in India.
2. After two years' working in India *it was possible for him to get* a job in South Africa.
3. *He wanted to work* among the Indian immigrants there.
4. *He was happy to be able to take up* the Indians' cause in the courts.
5. Later *he no longer wanted to work* as a lawyer.
6. *He made up his mind to lead* the coloured people in their struggle for better living conditions.

Let's prepare the next exercise

On reaching the age of 20 Gandhi travelled to London. Als ...
After qualifying he returned to India. Nachdem ...
He was put in prison **for breaking** the tax laws. ..., weil ...
Gandhi prevented a massacre **by going** fearlessly among the people. ...indem...

The construction preposition + gerund can be translated by a German subordinate clause beginning with a conjunction:

after	— nachdem	in spite of	— obwohl
before	— ehe; bevor	instead of	— statt
by	— dadurch, daß; indem	on	— wenn; als
for	— weil	without	— ohne daß
in	— indem; als		

Note: How / What } about going to the cinema? Wie wär's, wenn wir ins Kino gingen?

3. Unpleasant Shocks for Gandhi

Connect the following sentences using prepositions and gerunds.

Ex.: Gandhi stayed in South Africa for one week. Then he visited the court. *(after)*
After staying in South Africa for one week Gandhi visited the court.

1. He entered the court. He was not welcomed as a lawyer by the white judge but only asked to take off his ridiculous turban. *(on)*
2. He had not yet recovered from this shock. He had another unpleasant experience. *(before)*

3. He bought a first-class railway ticket. He hoped to have a comfortable journey. *(by)*
4. The white guard did not leave him in peace. He pushed him out of the compartment. *(instead of)*
5. Gandhi showed his first-class railway ticket. He was forced to leave the train. *(in spite of)*
6. He did not offer any resistance. He let people treat him in that way. *(without)*
7. He had these experiences. He made up his mind to fight for the rights of the coloured people. *(after)*
8. He practised his peaceful methods. He led India on her way to freedom. *(by)*

4. More Prepositions with Gerunds

Change the following sentences by prepositions and gerunds.

Ex.: If you read a guide-book you will find out that Folkestone is a very good place for a seaside holiday.
On reading a guide-book you will find out ...

1. Book a room at a hotel before you go there.
2. When you land at Dover you will have to show your passport and go through the customs.
3. You can reach Folkestone from Dover if you take a bus.
4. You should go to Folkestone in June and not in July or August.
5. When you have arrived in Dover you should take the next bus to Folkestone.
6. You can easily reach your hotel if you take a taxi.

5. Three Silly Beggars—Revision

Use the verbs in brackets as gerunds and where possible as infinitives.

1. One evening after a long day three beggars stopped (to beg) for food in the streets of Delhi and started (to walk) back to their hut. 2. They decided on (to prepare) their supper. 3. But each of them thought that there was little chance of (to get) a good supper, because the first beggar had only got a little meat, the second only a few vegetables and the third only some rice. 4. After some time they gave up (to argue) and agreed that they should put what they had into a pot and make a soup. 5. They at once started (to make) a fire. 6. The first beggar, however, hated (to share) his meat with the others. 7. So he intended (to play) a trick on them. 8. In the half dark room he only moved his hand towards the pot without (to throw) anything in. 9. He thought that he would get a nice supper and could enjoy (to eat) his meat afterwards. 10. But it happened that the second beggar thought the same about his vegetables and the third about his rice, and all of them were proud of (to have) hidden their food under their rags. 11. The three beggars had a very unpleasant shock when they lifted the pot off the fire and discovered that there was nothing in it except hot water.

Let's prepare the next exercise

1. *same subject*

She went to work though **she** was ill.
She went to work though **her child** was ill.

different subjects

same subject

She went to work in spite of being ill.
She went to work in spite of **her child('s)** being ill.

different subjects

2. I rely on **your (you) sending** back the book immediately.
Do you mind **my (me) using** the telephone?

1. *Usually the subject of the sentence is at the same time the subject of the gerund. If that is not so the subject of the gerund must be mentioned.*
2. *The subject of the gerund can be*
a) a noun (or pronoun) in the s-genitive or in the object case
b) a possessive adjective or a pronoun in the object case.

6. Using Gerunds (I)

Change the following sentences by further subjects.

Ex.: Do you mind coming to my party? (Fred)
Do you mind **Fred's coming** to my party?
Do you mind **Fred coming** to my party?

1. Mr. Barton was afraid of being late today. (his son)
2. Mrs. White was fond of wearing pretty dresses. (her daughter)
3. I don't mind saying I was wrong. (you)
4. I am looking forward to visiting London. (George)
5. George was proud of having won the first prize. (his sister)
6. Do you remember attending your (her) first dancing lesson? (Miss Black)

7. Using Gerunds (II)

Change the following sentences by using gerunds

a) *Ex.:* Would you mind if I open the window?
Would you mind **my opening** the window?
Would you mind **me opening** the window?

1. Do you remember that we met at a party last year?
2. Do you mind if I smoke a cigar?
3. Mr. Barton regretted that his son had broken the neighbour's window.

4. I cannot understand why John told you so many lies.
5. Do you remember that I told you about the dangers of smoking?
6. Mother hates it if we eat sweets between meals.
7. Can you imagine that Tom could swim the Channel?

b) *Ex.:* Father insisted that Robert should stay at home tonight.
Father **insisted on Robert's staying** at home tonight.
Father **insisted on Robert staying** at home tonight.

1. When staying alone in the house she locked all the doors for fear that a burglar might break in.
2. There is no danger that the lions will escape from the circus.
3. Barbara is proud that her brother has won a prize.
4. There is no chance that Mr. Miller would catch the early train, because he is still at the business conference.
5. The merchant lived in the hope that his daughter would marry a rich man one day.

8. Headings

Look at the following headings and try to give their meaning in good German:

Ex.: 'Looking for a Job' *Auf Stellungssuche*

'Letter-writing', 'Learning English', 'Going on a Bicycle Tour', 'Painting a Picture'. 'Waiting for Visitors', 'Leaving Home for the First Time', 'Beginning a New Life', 'Watching Animals', 'Buying a Car', 'Visiting London', 'Climbing a Mountain', 'Meeting People', 'Riding for Freedom', 'Travelling in England', 'Applying for a Job', 'Attacking the Enemy', 'Facing Death', 'Spreading the News'.

Try to find more headings.

<9. Translation: Der Protest gegen die Salzsteuer>

Use as many gerunds as possible.

1. Statt der britischen Regierung in Indien die neu eingeführte Salzsteuer zu zahlen, begannen Gandhi und seine Anhänger, Salz aus Seewasser zu gewinnen *(to make)*. 2. Dadurch liefen sie Gefahr, bestraft zu werden, weil es streng verboten war, Salz aus Seewasser zu machen. 3. Obwohl Gandhi am 4. Mai 1930 ins Gefängnis geworfen worden war, gingen 2500 Menschen am 22. Mai 1930 an die See, um ihr eigenes Salz zu gewinnen. 4. Hunderte von ihnen wurden von der Polizei geschlagen, aber nicht ein einziger schlug zurück, da alle an Gandhis friedliche Methoden glaubten. 5. Ohne einen Laut von sich zu geben *(to make a sound)* oder einen Arm zu *(in)* ihrer Verteidigung zu erheben, ertrugen *(to suffer)* sie die schrecklichen Schläge der Polizei. 6. Schließlich erwiesen sich Gandhis Ideen als richtig: Am 5. März 1931 wurde [es] von der Regierung erlaubt, Salz für persönlichen Gebrauch *(use)* zu gewinnen, und 100000 Gefangene wurden freigelassen.

13

<1. Comprehension Test>

1. Which other flights across the Atlantic Ocean had been carried out before Lindbergh's flight?
2. In which way was Lindbergh specially qualified for the New York—Paris flight?
3. What was the weather like during the flight? How did Lindbergh feel, when he saw the coast of Ireland?
4. What was his reception in Paris and later in New York like?
5. Compare the time Lindbergh needed for his flight New York—Paris with the time a modern plane would need. What other differences are there between Lindbergh's flight and flights today?

<2. Lindbergh's Flight>

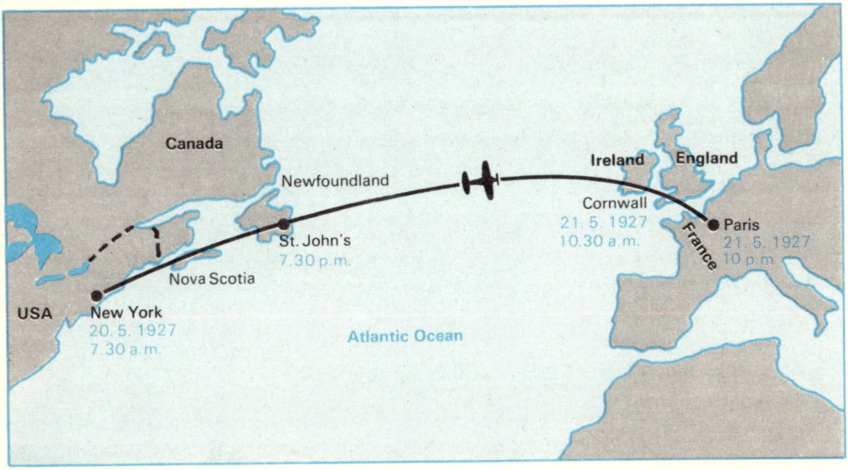

Look at the map and describe Lindbergh's flight. Which towns and landscapes did he see from the air?

3. Lindbergh's Landing in Paris—Revision

Read the following story and change the expressions in italics into the passive voice. Leave out the by-agent where possible.

1. When Lindbergh was flying over Paris he could recognize the Eiffel Tower and other famous buildings. 2. *Nobody* in America *had told him* exactly where the airport was. 3. He only knew that it was somewhere north-east of Paris. 4. Seeing that the airport was badly lit he made signs with his flashlight, but *they did not answer him.* 5. In America *people had advised him* not to fly

too low before landing on an unknown airfield. 6. After his landing *thousands of people approached him* from all sides. 7. Among the cheering crowd he lost his helmet, which was put on a reporter's head. 8. With a pilot's helmet on his head the reporter was thought to be Lindbergh. 9. *People did not believe his cries* 'I'm not Lindbergh'. 10. *They followed him* to the reception room. 11. There, of course, the mistake was discovered. 12. *People* who were at Paris airport on May 21st, 1927 *will never forget* Lindbergh's landing.

4. Preparations for the Flight to Paris — Revision

Change the expressions in italics into the passive voice. Leave out the by-agent where possible.

1. When Lindbergh decided to compete for the 25,000 dollar prize offered for the first flight from New York to Paris the great problem was how to get a suitable plane. 2. *One firm offered Lindbergh a plane* for $ 90,000, but that was much more than he could afford. 3. Again and again *people advised him* not to fly a single-engined plane. 4. But a single-engined plane was cheaper and less risky than a bigger plane. 5. *A friend of Lindbergh's promised him* $ 1,000 if he could find a suitable plane. 6. *A bank lent him the necessary money*. 7. One firm agreed to sell him a plane, but *they did not grant him the right* to fly it across the Atlantic. 8. They wanted him to test the plane, but another pilot chosen by them should fly it across the Atlantic. 9. Lindbergh's last hope was the Ryan Company in Detroit. 10. *The president of the company and the chief engineer showed Lindbergh their factory before they talked about business matters*. 11. They were willing to build a plane for about $ 10,000. 12. Lindbergh was filled with hope for his project.

<5. Things that happen on a plane>

Imagine you are in a plane. A young man **is offered** a glass of tomato juice. A restless boy **is told** stories by his mother. A . . .

Go on using the passive voice of the verbs to bring, to give, to hand, to offer, to pass, to pay, to promise, to sell, to show, to tell.

Let's prepare the next exercise

Subject	Active Verb + Preposition	Object
People	lost sight of	the plane.

Subject	Passive Verb
The plane	**was lost sight of.**

There are many English verbs and verbal expressions which are so closely connected with a preposition that the preposition remains with the verb when it is put into the passive voice.

6. Verbs + Prepositions in the Passive

Put the following sentences into the passive voice and leave out the by-agent where possible.

Ex.: People often spoke of Lindbergh as the 'flying fool'.
Lindbergh was often spoken of as the 'flying fool'.

1. There are people whose words you cannot rely on. 2. Wait here until they send for you. 3. In hospital they will look after you very well. 4. This girl always wants people to take notice of her. 5. They have thought of every detail for their trip. 6. They never heard of Mr. Black again.

Let's prepare the next exercise: The German 'es'

1. Who is this young man?	**He** is my teacher.	Es ist ...
And the young lady?	**She** is my cousin.	Es ist ...
And these girls?	**They** are my cousin's pupils.	Es sind ...
2. **There** were a few clouds in the sky.	Es waren ...	
There was no rain yesterday.	Es hat ...	
3. Is the weather going to be fine? I hope **so.**		Ich hoffe es.
It had been a wonderful day. Everybody said **so.**		Jeder sagte es.

The German 'es' is translated by different English constructions.

7. Two Switchboards

a) Is the weather going to be fine? Are your brothers coming tonight? Could Peter have missed the bus? Will the Bartons travel by train?	I We My parents	think so. believe so. expect so. suppose so.
b) Robert has broken a cup. Your aunt has sent a telegram. Tom's friend has had an accident.	So I notice. So I hear. So I see.	

8. The German 'es'

Translate the following sentences. Be careful with the German 'es'.

1. In der 28. Stunde seines Fluges sah Lindbergh plötzlich Hügel. Waren es die Hügel von Irland, Spanien oder Frankreich? 2. Könnte es Irland sein? Lindbergh hoffte es sehr. 3. Lindbergh sah nach unten und sah einen Mann. Es war ein Bauer, der auf dem Felde arbeitete. 4. Dann sah er eine Frau. Es war vielleicht die Frau des Bauern. 5. Hatten die zwei eine Ahnung *(any idea)*, daß er gerade den Atlantik überflogen hatte? Er glaubte es nicht. 6. In der 30. Stunde seines Fluges flog Lindbergh über die Felder von Cornwall. So kleine Felder gab es in Amerika nicht. 7. Wie war es möglich, dort genügend Getreide anzubauen? Lindbergh konnte es sich nicht vorstellen. 8. In der 33. Stunde sah Lindbergh Lichter: Es waren die Lichter von Paris.

<9. **The Pilot and his Friend. — A Story in Pictures**>

thief—a man who steals things

<10. **Translation: Der Tod einer Zeitung**>

1. Es gab nur eine Sache, über die am 8. und 9. Mai 1927 in Paris gesprochen wurde: der Versuch zweier Franzosen, ohne Unterbrechung von Paris nach New York zu fliegen. 2. Am 9. Mai war die französische Zeitung ‚La Presse' die erste, die die wunderbare Nachricht veröffentlichte, daß die Piloten sicher in New York angekommen seien:

3. „Lange Zeit, bevor das Flugzeug in der Nähe der Küste von Amerika gesichtet worden war, waren Tausende von Menschen zum New Yorker Hafen gekommen, wo sie ungeduldig auf den großen Augenblick warteten. 4. Der New Yorker Hafen war voll von Schiffen; es waren Kriegsschiffe und Passagierschiffe, bereit, die französischen Piloten zu begrüßen. 5. Endlich wurde das Flugzeug gesichtet: Langsam kreiste es herunter und machte eine perfekte Landung auf dem Wasser. 6. Sofort war das Flugzeug von Schiffen umgeben, und kleine amerikanische Flugzeuge kreisten über ihm. 7. Die beiden Franzosen hatten das Ziel erreicht, das von so vielen erträumt worden war. 8. Das Flugzeug wurde zum Kai gelotst *(guided)*, wo eine große [Menschen]menge die erfolgreichen Piloten begrüßte."

9. Jeder dachte, daß man sich auf diesen Zeitungsbericht verlassen könne. 10. Was man nicht wußte, war, daß die ganze Geschichte von einem Reporter erfunden worden war, der wollte, daß seine Zeitung die erste wäre, die diese Nachricht veröffentlichte. 11. Die Wahrheit ist, daß man das Flugzeug der beiden Franzosen über dem Atlantik aus den Augen verloren und daß man nie wieder [davon] gehört hat. 12. Der Artikel in ‚La Presse' verursachte einen öffentlichen Skandal in ganz Frankreich. 13. Die Zeitung erschien nie wieder.

14

<1. Comprehension Test>

1. What was the reason for the bus boycott in Montgomery?
2. What was the result of the bus boycott?
3. How did the negroes bring bus segregation to an end?
4. Compare Martin Luther King's methods with those of Gandhi in his struggle for freedom.
5. Say what you know about the colour problem in other parts of the world. Think of the Commonwealth and South Africa.

Let's prepare the next exercise

Do not use the following verbs in the continuous form:

a) *to hear, to notice, to see, to smell, to taste*

b) *to hate, to like, to love, to mind, to prefer*

c) *to want, to wish*

d) *to agree, to believe, to feel (in the sense of 'to think'), to know, to remember, to seem, to suppose, to think, to understand*

e) *to be, to belong, to contain, to exist, to have (= to possess), to know, to possess, to consist of, to fit*

2. The Bus Boycott in Montgomery

Put the verbs in brackets into the past tense. Use the continuous form where possible.

1. In the year 1955: 70.000 white and 50.000 coloured people (to live) in Montgomery. 2. 50% of the coloured women and 40% of the coloured men (to work) in the households of white people. 3. Normally they (to go) by bus to their work. The bus boycott began on the early morning of December 5th, 1955. 4. That morning Martin Luther King (to stand) at his window. 5. He (to feel) that the time had come for the coloured people to act. 6. He (to wish) that the bus boycott would be successful. 7. While he (to wait) impatiently for the first bus he (to smell) the coffee, that his wife (to prepare) in the kitchen. 8. Suddenly he (to hear) the noise of a motor and then (to see) the first bus passing through the street. 9. He (to notice) that it was quite empty. 10. 15 minutes later the second (to drive) past. 11. Martin Luther King (to see) that it was empty, too. 12. He (to know) that it would be a hard day for the coloured people. 13. He (not to want) to stay at home any longer, but (to decide) to drive through the streets instead. 14. He (to notice) that all the coloured people (to walk) to their work. 15. He (to hear) that coloured car owners (to give) coloured people lifts. 16. When he (to come) home his wife (to agree) with him: It was right to start the bus boycott.

3. The Beggar in the Park

Put the verbs in brackets in the present or past tense. Use the continuous form where possible.

A rich lady lived in a big hotel in London. One day when she (to look) out of the window, she (to see) a beggar in the park. He (to sit) on a chair and (to look) up at the windows of the hotel. The next day she (to notice) that the man (to be) still there. So she (to feel) she had better go down into the park and ask him why he (to sit) there. "Lady," he (to say), "I (to sit) here every day because I (to know) that some day I'll sleep in that hotel."—The lady well (to remember) the days before she (to become) rich and so she (to tell) the manager of the hotel to give the man a room.
The next morning the lady (to hear) a knock at the door. "I just (to want) to say good-bye," the man said. "What? (not to like) your bed?" the lady asked. "No, I (to think) my chair in the park was better. In the park I used to dream I (to be) in a warm bed in the hotel. But last night I (to dream) I (to be) back on the cold hard chair. So I (to believe) I'll go back to my chair in the park tonight."

Let's prepare the new exercise: The Continuous Form in the Passive

Look, today is spring cleaning day:

Carpets **are being beaten,**
clothes **are being washed,**
furniture **is being cleaned.**
When I visited you last spring, your house **was being painted.**

The continuous form of the passive is used for an action which is still continuing or was still continuing at a point of time in the past.

4. At New York Harbour

Two negro boys from Harlem, the negro quarter of New York, go to New York harbour to meet their father who has got a job there. While they are waiting for their father they watch the busy life around them:

a) *Ex.:* (lorries—to be driven up)—Lorries **are being driven up.**

(a heavy suit-case—to be lifted on to a boat); (furniture—to be carried over from a train); (parcels—to be weighed); (packages— to be put in vans); (passengers' luggage—to be brought to a boat); (immigrants—to be asked questions by the customs officers)

b) A car is being lifted on to a boat.
Suddenly two ropes break.

Ex.: First (the car—to be let down)—First the car **is let down** slowly.

Then (the old ropes—to be cut off quickly). Then (new ropes—to be tied round the car). At last (the car— to be lifted up and to be let down into the boat).

c) When the boys come home they tell their little sister what they have seen. "While we were waiting for Father, lorries were being driven up, a heavy suit-case . . .

Go on using the sentences under a) and b).

5. What People are going to do—Revision

During the bus boycott many coloured people want to help those that have to walk now instead of using a bus.

1. A taxi-driver wants to give people lifts for not more than the bus fare.
2. A private car owner wants to drive to town and back several times in order to take as many coloured people to town as possible.
3. A housewife wants to give other housewives lifts when they go shopping.
4. Another housewife wants to look after children whose parents need more time now to go to and from work.
5. A shop-owner wants to give shoes to people who need them urgently for their daily walk.
6. A third housewife wants to open her house for people that otherwise would have to wait in cold and rain for the next car or taxi.
7. A businessman wants to buy cars for the negroes.

a) The leader of a negroes' meeting asks several people what they are going to do during the bus boycott.

Ex.: "**How are you going to help** during the bus boycott?"
Taxi-driver: "**I'm going to** give people lifts for not more than the bus fare."

Go on using the sentences above.

b) What are you going to do next week-end? **I'm going to** give a party.
I'm going to . . .
Go on telling us your week-end plans.

Let's prepare the next exercise

I'm leaving for London tomorrow.
Is your brother **going** with you? No, he **is staying** at home.

As you have learned already you can use the continuous form of the present tense for a future action, when something is intended or planned. But an adverbial expression or the context must make it clear that the action will happen in the future.

I'll be leaving for my holiday tomorrow.
Will your brother be going with you?
No, **he'll be staying** at home.

The continuous form of the future can be used in the same sense. It is often used in polite questions.

6. A Teenagers' Party

Put the verbs in brackets into the continuous form of the future.

Ex.: I (to give) a party next Saturday. **I'll be giving** a party ...

Fred: I (to give) a party next Saturday. Would you like to come?
Harry: I'd love to. Susan (to come), too?
Fred: No, Susan (not to come), because she is going away for the week-end with her parents. But Susan's friend Mary (to come).
Harry: Robert (to join) us?
Fred: Yes, Robert (to join) us and his sister Ann, too.
Harry: Will your parents be at the party, too?
Fred: No, they won't, because they (to go) to the theatre that evening.
Harry: They (to join) us later?
Fred: O no, they don't like the kind of music we are going to hear.
Harry: You (to send) invitation cards?
Fred: I don't think that's necessary. I can ring up all my guests.
Harry: I'm looking forward to your party. Thank you for inviting me.

<7. Martin Luther King>

Martin Luther King was born in the southern city of Atlanta, Georgia, in 1929, the son of a Baptist preacher. Both his father and his grandfather had been pioneers in the negroes' struggle for civil rights, but little progress had been made up to that time. Racial segregation was still in force in Georgia and the other states of the 'Deep South'. The boy's world was governed by the signs 'White' and 'Coloured', and he had to learn to give up his seat to white people on buses and trains. Like his father and grandfather before him, King decided to become a preacher. While he was at college he discovered the books of Gandhi, who was leading the people of India to freedom and independence.

Gandhi's teaching of non-violent resistance made King decide to devote his life to the civil rights movement among the American negroes. By his example he showed his people how to organize themselves and fight for their rights by peaceful means—by strikes and protest marches instead of by riots and violence. But King's aim was not only to help the negroes; it was to show all Americans the need for reform. King's courage and energy made him a born leader of his people. Wherever racial conflict threatened to break out he was at once on the spot, organizing, controlling and preaching the lesson of non-violence. He ignored danger. Many times he was put in prison for leading protest marches against racial discrimination in the South; bombs were thrown at his house; several times he was attacked in the streets. Yet his movement gained strength and reached a climax in the summer of 1963, when 200,000 people, whites and blacks of all ages, marched through Washington to demand equal rights for negroes. In 1964 Martin Luther King was awarded the Nobel peace prize. He was shot dead in a Memphis motel on April 4th, 1968, but his ideas live on.

Now write a summary of this piece, about one half to one third of the original text in length. Don't leave out anything important. The following points will help you:

a) boyhood under segregation in the South
b) training to be a preacher
c) influence of Gandhi
d) King's message to his people
e) his courage and energy
f) march on Washington 1963
h) Killed in 1968

<8. Translation: Eine Frage der Farbe>

1. Mary Jackson war ein farbiges Mädchen in einer gemischten Schule des amerikanischen mittleren Westen. 2. Sie konnte hervorragend zeichnen und wollte die Kunsthochschule *(Art School)* besuchen. 3. Ihre Lehrerin hatte ihr geraten, sich um *(for)* ein Stipendium zu bewerben. 4. Deshalb schickte Mary ein Bild ein und wartete ungeduldig, während die Bilder auf der Kunsthochschule geprüft wurden. 5. Eines Tages teilte ihr der Direktor mit *(to tell)*, daß sie mit ihrem Bild das Stipendium gewonnen habe. 6. Mary war hocherfreut: Ein Stipendium würde ihr sehr helfen, denn ihre Eltern waren keine reichen Leute. 7. Während [der] Versammlung [am] nächsten Freitag würde die ganze Schule von ihrem Erfolg hören, und man erwartete von ihr, daß sie eine kleine Rede hielte. 8. [Der] Freitagmorgen kam. 9. Als der Direktor Mary die Schule betreten sah, rief er sie in sein Zimmer. 10. Er sah besorgt aus, als er sagte: „Ich habe eine schlechte Nachricht für Sie, Mary. 11. Ich habe einen Brief von der Kunsthochschule bekommen, in dem man schreibt, daß Sie das Stipendium nicht bekommen können, weil Sie farbig sind. 12. Man wußte das nicht, als Sie Ihr Bild einschickten. 13. Es hat niemals einen farbigen Studenten *(student)* an der Kunsthochschule gegeben, und man fürchtet, daß es Schwierigkeiten mit den weißen Studenten und ihren Eltern geben wird." 14. Als Mary dies hörte, war sie sehr enttäuscht, aber sie gab [die] Hoffnung nicht auf. 15. „Es gibt andere Schulen in anderen Städten", dachte sie. 16. „Irgendwie werde ich einen Weg finden, Kunst zu studieren. 17. Aber später werde ich für die Rechte der Farbigen kämpfen."

15

<1. Comprehension Test>

1. Tell the story of Sputnik I.
2. What did American scientists do after the challenge of Sputnik I?
3. What happened in September and October 1959?
4. How are astronauts trained?
5. Describe the effects of weightlessness in space.
6. What were Russian and American astronauts able to do in the years between 1961 and 1965?
7. Say what you know about the latest space flights.

Let's prepare the next exercise: Inversion

Here are the Harrisons.
First comes Mr. Harrison.
Then comes his wife.

The subject of a sentence can be put after the predicate in short sentences with verbs like 'to be, to stand, to lie, to come, to follow' especially if the sentences are introduced by 'here, there, first, then, next, last of all, in, out, down, off' or similar adverbials.

Inversion is not possible in short sentences if the subject of a sentence is a pronoun:

Here are the Harrisons.—Here they are.

2. The First Rocket

Put the adverbs and adverbial phrases in italics at the beginning of the sentences.

Ex.: A man came *out of the car.*
Out of the car came a man.

1. The year was 1926, the place an American farm. 2. A car approached and stopped near a small hill. 3. A man came *out of the car.* 4. He was the scientist Dr. Goddard. 5. Two other men came *next.* 6. Dr. Goddard's wife came *last of all.* 7. The men were carrying a small rocket, one of the first rockets ever launched. 8. Together they climbed the hill. 9. The men worked for quite a time and then all was ready. 10. The rocket stood *there* on the hill, ready to be launched. 11. One of Dr. Goddard's assistants lit a torch, and the rocket went *off.* 12. It shot *up* into the sky. 13. The men's eyes followed the rocket's flight, until it came back to earth. 14. It had reached a speed of sixty miles an hour and travelled 184 feet. 15. That is not much, of course, compared with the rockets of today. 16. But in 1926 the launching of that rocket was a great success.

Let's prepare the next exercise

1. **Scarcely had I closed** my eyes, when the telephone rang.
   Seldom had I seen so beautiful a landscape.
   Never shall I forget that day.
2. **Rarely did the sun come out** during those December days.
   Never did they forget the dangers of that journey.
   Seldom did they meet any people during their trip.

1. *If a sentence is introduced by 'hardly, scarcely ... when, never, no sooner ... than, rarely' or 'seldom', the subject is put between the auxiliary and the verb.*
2. *If there is no auxiliary a form of 'to do' must be used.*

3. Poor People

Use 'rarely', 'seldom' and 'never' with the following sentences.

a) Mr. Penniless has always been very poor. **Never has he** had lunch in a restaurant, **seldom has he** ... (to go on holiday, to invite guests, to go to the theatre, to ...). *Go on.*

b) Mr. Penniless's father was very poor, too. **Never did he** have lunch in a restaurant, **seldom did he** .... *Go on.*

4. An Open Switchboard

I Aunt Mary The young lady Dr. Fisher	had hardly had scarcely	closed my (his, her) eyes entered the room ordered the meal started my (his, her) walk	when ... when ... when ... when ...

Complete the sentences of the switchboard and say them in this way:
Hardly had I closed my eyes when the telephone rang.

5. The First American in Space

Put the adverbials in italics at the beginning of the sentences.

1. On May 5th, 1961, Alan Shepard entered his Mercury capsule at Cape Kennedy. It was a great moment for the United States. An American had *never before* flown into space.
2. All over the country people were sitting round their radios and television sets. There had *seldom* been such excitement.
3. The rocket had *hardly* left the ground when Shepard felt several hard shocks in the capsule.
4. Shepard could have returned to earth by pressing a button, but he flew on and the rocket rose steadily into space. The astronaut did *not for a moment* think of giving up the flight.
5. The capsule was *no sooner* separated from the rocket than Shepard became weightless.
6. When Shepard had reached a height of 115 miles he saw the earth spread out like a map below him. He had *never* seen such a wonderful sight.
7. Fifteen minutes after the start Shepard came down into the sea, knowing that his flight had been a success. He had *never in his life* felt so happy.

6. Inversion after 'nor, neither, so' — Revision

Robert and Richard are talking about men in space.
Fill in what Richard said using 'nor, neither' or 'so'.

Robert:	*Richard:*
I read the report about the latest space flight yesterday.	... I.
I think it must be a great feeling to be so far away from the earth.	... I.

I should like to be an astronaut myself when I'm older.	... I.
But my mother doesn't like the idea at all.	... mine.
She would be worried about me.	... mine.
But I wouldn't be afraid a bit.	... I.
My father says space flying is something for adventurers and fools.	... mine.
He can't imagine that it is much use.	... mine.
But I hope to persuade my parents one day.	... I.
I don't know how to become an astronaut.	... I.
I must ask someone.	... I.

Let's prepare the next exercise

A strike had been threatening for many months, but **it was the metal workers** who began it.

It was not only higher wages that they demanded but better working conditions, too.

It was not before the end of March that the strike ended.

Parts of sentences can be emphasized by 'it is ...' or 'it was ...'.

Don't forget: *'It is (was) ...' is always used in the singular, even if the emphasized word is in the plural.*

7. The Use of 'it is ...' and 'it was ...'

a) *Join the following sentences using 'it was ...'.*

Ex.: Both the Americans and the Russians tried to launch a satellite.
The Russians succeeded in doing so first.
Both the Americans and the Russians tried to launch a satellite, **but it was the Russians who** succeeded in doing so first.

1. Three locomotives took part in the Rainhill race in 1829. Stephenson's 'Rocket' won the prize of £500. 2. Many car builders had dreamed of producing cheap cars for the masses. Henry Ford made it possible by using the assembly line. 3. There had been many plans for a waterway between the Mediterranean and the Red Sea. The French finally built the Suez Canal. 4. Many American pilots thought of flying from New York to Paris in 1927. Charles Lindbergh made the flight and won the prize of $25,000. 5. Many countries knew about the big southern island, Australia. The English began to settle there in 1788.

b) *Emphasize the words in italics by using 'it is ...', 'it was ...'.*

Ex.: The Californian gold-diggers did *not only* find *gold* in California, but hardship and disease, too.
It was not only gold that the Californian gold-seekers found in California, but hardship and disease, too.

1. The workers in the Ford plant did *not only* like *the higher wages* but also the shorter working hours.
2. Columbus hoped to find *the sea-route to India* and not that to America.

3. Gandhi wanted to win freedom for his people *by peaceful means* and not by fighting and killing.
4. The coloured people do *not only* want to end *segregation on buses* but in schools and restaurants, too.
5. Today's astronauts do *not only* want to reach *the moon*, but Mars and Venus and other planets, too.

c) *Emphasize the words in italics by using 'it was ...'.*

Ex.: In the year 1926 Goddard launched the first rocket.
It was in the year 1926 that Goddard launched the first rocket.

1. *The years after 1961* were very important for the exploration of space by men.
2. Men did *not* fly into space *before 1961*.
3. *In the years after the Second World War* the old concept of the British Empire began to change.
4. *In 1947* India became a free republic in the Commonwealth.
5. *In 1957* the Russians sent the first Sputnik into space.

<8. Translation: Wie die ersten Astronauten ausgewählt wurden>

1. Am Nachmittag des 9. April 1959 wurde ein Projekt bekanntgegeben, das bis zu diesem Tag streng geheim gewesen war. 2. Bei einer Pressekonferenz *(press)* in Washington wurden sieben Männer der Öffentlichkeit vorgestellt. 3. Sie sollten Amerikas erste Astronauten sein. 4. Wie sind diese sieben Männer ausgewählt worden? 5. Die Auswahl begann 1958, kurze Zeit nachdem die amerikanische Regierung ihre Einwilligung zu Weltraumflügen gegeben hatte. 6. Zuerst wurden 69 hochqualifizierte Testpiloten ausgewählt, die Tausende von Stunden in der Luft gewesen waren. 7. In einem Interview in Washington fragte man sie, ob sie bereit seien, als Astronauten ausgebildet zu werden. 8. 54 der 69 Männer nahmen das ungewöhnliche Angebot *(offer)* an. 9. Diese 54 Männer wurden sorgfältig von Ärzten untersucht, und ihr Allgemeinwissen und ihr technisches Wissen wurde getestet. 10. Nach diesen Tests blieben sieben Männer übrig, die für Flüge in den Weltraum ausgebildet werden sollten. 11. Sie lernten, der plötzlichen Beschleunigung standzuhalten, [die] nötig [ist] für [das] Abschießen der Raketen in [den] Weltraum, sie gewöhnten sich daran, hin- und hergeschleudert zu werden und die Instrumente zu lesen. 12. Überdies lernten sie das Gefühl der Schwerelosigkeit kennen. 13. Jeder der sieben Männer hoffte, der erste Mann im Weltraum zu sein, aber es war Alan B. Shepard, der schließlich gewählt wurde.

A Story for Discussion

The Cigarette Lighter

"Nice of you to come and see me off, Henry," said Uncle James as they stood on the Southampton platform at Waterloo Station. Uncle James had been in England for ten years, and was going back to Australia for good. He took a small package out of his pocket and handed it to his nephew.

"Just something for you to remember me by," he said. "Don't open it now. The train's due to go in two minutes."

When the train had disappeared, Henry opened the package, and found a handsome cigarette lighter. He was very surprised. Uncle James was not usually so generous.

The next day, when Uncle James was already on the high seas, Henry was looking round a big London store. He saw on a counter several lighters exactly like the one Uncle James had given him.

"H'm," he said to himself, "I'd like to know how much the old chap paid for my lighter."

There was no assistant at the counter, and he began to finger one of the lighters. Just as he was putting it back on the counter, the price tag dropped on to the floor. He stopped to pick it up, and his own lighter fell out of his pocket. He was just putting it back in his pocket when a man came up and stopped him.

"Not so quick, young man," he said. "I'm the store detective. Shoplifting isn't so easy as you think."

Henry protested that he wasn't shoplifting. He explained that the lighter had been given him by his uncle the day before, and that he had not started to use it. The detective asked him for his uncle's name and address and telephone number.

"He's on his way to Australia," said Henry.

"You can't expect me to believe that," answered the detective.

How would you have dealt with this situation?

1. *If you had been in Henry's place, what would you have said to the detective? Suggest three different ways of proving that the lighter had not been stolen.*
2. *Suppose that Henry was not able to prove, to the detective's satisfaction, that the lighter was his own, and was therefore charged with theft at a Magistrates' Court. Try to act the trial. The clerk will read the charge, the detective will give evidence, and, as Henry is not quite eighteen, his father will appear to say a word or two on his behalf.*

P. M. Richard and Wendy Hall

Wörterverzeichnis

1. Dieses Wörterverzeichnis setzt den verbindlichen Wortschatz von Teil 1, 2, 3 und 4 als bekannt voraus.
2. Die Wörter der verbindlichen Lesestücke und Übungen sind **fett** gedruckt.
3. Abkürzungen: s.o. = someone, s.th. = something, jdn., jdm. = jemanden, jemandem.
4. Die Jahreszahlen hinter Personennamen geben die Lebenszeit an.

1 A. Magna Carta—The First Step to Freedom

Magna Carta = the Great Charter [ˈmægnə ˈkɑ:tə] [ˈtʃɑ:tə]	der große Freibrief, die große Urkunde
1. neither ... nor [ˈnaiðə ... ˈnɔ:]	weder ... noch
Richard the Lionheart	Richard Löwenherz *(König von England, 1157—99)*
crusade [kru:ˈseid]	Kreuzzug
at that time	zu dieser Zeit
bad, worse, worst [wə:s, wə:st]	schlimm
to fear for s.th.	um etwas bangen
to murder [ˈmə:də]	ermorden
nephew [ˈnevju:]	Neffe
baron [ˈbærən]	Baron
sum [sʌm]	Summe
townspeople *(pl.)*	Stadtbewohner
merchant [ˈmə:tʃənt]	Händler
goods *(pl.)*	Waren
to hinder [ˈhində]	hindern
everybody else	alle anderen
trial [ˈtraiəl]	Gerichtsverfahren, Prozeß
jail [dʒeil]	Gefängnis
to put an end to s.th.	einer Sache ein Ende bereiten
archbishop [ˈɑ:tʃbiʃəp]	Erzbischof
to draw up, drew, drawn	aufstellen, abfassen
consent [kənˈsent]	Einverständnis
bishop [ˈbiʃəp]	Bischof
fair	fair, gerecht
to change colour	die Farbe wechseln
to make s.o. a slave	jemanden zum Sklaven machen
rage [ˈreidʒ]	Wut(anfall)
2. Runnymede [ˈrʌnimi:d]	*(Feld an der Themse in der Nähe von Windsor)*
inwardly [ˈinwədli]	innerlich, im Innern
fury [ˈfjuəri]	Wut
to boil with fury	vor Wut kochen
to unroll [ʌnˈrəul]	aufrollen
parchment [ˈpɑ:tʃmənt]	Pergament
to fix [fiks]	festmachen
seal [si:l]	Siegel
to fix the seal	das Siegel aufdrücken
enemy [ˈenimi]	Feind
to arm [ɑ:m]	bewaffnen
just	*hier:* einfach
to put to	befestigen an
3. revenge [riˈvendʒ]	Rache
from abroad [əˈbrɔ:d]	aus dem Ausland
whirlwind [ˈwə:lwind]	Wirbelwind
to sweep, swept, swept [swept]	fegen
resistance [riˈzistəns]	Widerstand
to meet	treffen auf
immediately [iˈmi:djətli]	sofort, unverzüglich
campaign [kæmˈpein]	Feldzug
to strike down	niederwerfen
to believe [biˈli:v]	glauben
to poison [ˈpɔizn]	vergiften
Henry III [ˈhenri]	Heinrich III. *(König von England, 1207—72)*

to confirm [kən'fə:m]	bestätigen
living ['liviŋ]	lebendig
document ['dɔkjument]	Dokument, *hier:* Zeugnis
to be seen	zu sehen
museum [mju:'ziəm]	Museum

<Picture Text>

foundation [faun'deiʃən]	Grund

<B. London Through the Ages>

age	Zeitalter
south-eastern ['i:stən]	südöstlich
Anglo-Saxon ['æŋglou'sæksən]	angelsächsisch
Winchester ['wintʃistə]	*(Stadt im Süden Englands)*
important	bedeutend
Europe ['juərəp]	Europa
flanked ['flæŋkt]	seitlich begrenzt
mighty ['maiti]	mächtig
to the south-west	im Südwesten
in comparison [kəm'pærisn]	im Vergleich
Whitehall ['wait'hɔ:l]	*(Name eines ehemaligen Königspalastes)*
courtier ['kɔ:tjə]	Höfling
past	an ... vorbei
Charing Cross ['tʃæriŋ 'krɔs]	*(heute: Distrikt im Zentrum Londons)*
to have a drink	etwas trinken
ant-hill ['ænthil]	Ameisenhaufen
Greater London	Groß-London
ancient ['einʃənt]	alt, ehemalig
exports ['ekspɔ:ts]	Gesamtexport
dock [dɔk]	Dock
Londoner ['lʌndənə]	Londoner
suburban [sə'bə:bən]	vorstädtisch, Vorstadt-
the Underground	*(Untergrundbahn in London)*
to lunch	Lunch einnehmen
crowded ['kraudid]	überfüllt
canteen [kæn'ti:n]	Kantine
cathedral [kə'θi:drəl]	Kathedrale
discipline ['disiplin]	Disziplin
striking ['straikiŋ]	auffallend
feature ['fi:tʃə]	Merkmal, Erscheinung

<Anecdotes>

anecdote ['ænikdəut]	Anekdote
1. Politeness [pə'laitnis]	Höflichkeit
opposite ['ɔpəzit]	entgegengesetzt
direction [di'rekʃən]	Richtung
to pass [pɑ:s]	aneinander vorbeikommen
neither ['naiðə]	kein(er, e, es) (von beiden)
to give way	Platz machen
silence ['sailəns]	Schweigen
unbroken	ungebrochen
2. choice [tʃɔis]	Wahl
voter ['vəutə]	Wähler
blessing ['blesiŋ]	Segen
House of Commons ['kɔmənz]	Unterhaus
3. conscience ['kɔnʃəns]	Gewissen
in court [kɔ:t]	vor Gericht
to be charged with s.th. [tʃɑ:dʒd]	einer Sache beschuldigt werden
vote [vəut]	Wahlstimme
both ... and [bəuθ]	sowohl ... als (auch)
Conservative candidate [kən'sə:vətiv 'kændidit]	Kandidat der Konservativen Partei
Labour candidate ['leibə]	Kandidat der Labour Partei
how on earth [ə:θ]	wie in aller Welt
to vote [vəut]	wählen
4. compromise ['kɔmprəmaiz]	Kompromiß, Vergleich
once upon a time there were	es waren einmal
diplomat ['dipləmæt]	Diplomat
to dispute [dis'pju:t]	disputieren, streiten (über)
recently ['ri:sntli]	kürzlich, vor kurzem
colleague ['kɔli:g]	Kollege

aside [ə'said]	beiseite
5. dismissal [dis'misəl]	Entlassung
head	Leiter, Chef
store [stɔ:]	Kauf-, Warenhaus
a week's money	Geld für eine Woche
clear out! [kliər‿aut]	verschwinde!
to hire ['haiə]	an-, einstellen
boss [bɔs]	Chef *(am.)*
departmental manager [ˌdi:pɑ:t'mentl 'mænidʒə]	Abteilungsleiter

Exercises

1. either ['aiðə]	eine(r, s) von beiden
neither	auch nicht
2. subject	Thema
4. to emphasize ['emfəsaiz]	betonen, hervorheben
6. to interpret [in'tə:prit]	verdolmetschen
interpreter [in'tə:pritə]	Dolmetscher(in)

2 A. The Railway Story

1. ridiculous [ri'dikjuləs]	lächerlich
quarterly ['kwɔ:təli]	Vierteljahresschrift, vierteljährlich
review [ri'vju:]	Rundschau, Zeitschrift
Quarterly Review	*(Name einer englischen Zeitschrift)*
locomotive ['ləukəˌməutiv]	Lokomotive
to travel	*hier:* fahren
to fix (at)	*hier:* festlegen (auf)
to consider [kən'sidə]	betrachten (als), halten für
Rainhill ['rein'hil]	*(Ort in der Grafschaft Lancashire)*
Lancashire ['læŋkəʃiə]	*(Grafschaft im NW Englands)*
director [di'rektə]	Direktor
Liverpool ['livəpu:l]	*(Industrie- und Hafenstadt an der Westküste Englands)*
to race [reis]	(um die Wette) rennen, fahren
to offer	aussetzen
stove-pipe ['stəuvpaip]	Ofenrohr
funnel ['fʌnl]	Schornstein
Rocket ['rɔkit]	Rakete *(hier: Name der Lokomotive)*
builder	Erbauer, Konstrukteur
George Stephenson ['sti:vnsn]	*(engl. Eisenbahningenieur, 1781—1848)*
to appoint [ə'pɔint]	ernennen (zu)
Planet ['plænit]	Planet *(hier: Name der Lokomotive)*
at an average speed	mit einer Durchschnittsgeschwindigkeit
m.p.h. = miles per hour	Meilen pro Stunde
2. public	Öffentlichkeit
Queen Victoria [vik'tɔ:riə]	*(engl. Königin, 1819—1901)*
immediate [i'mi:djət]	augenblicklich, unverzüglich
outcry	Aufschrei, Schrei der Entrüstung
to risk [risk]	wagen, riskieren
to risk one's life	sein Leben aufs Spiel setzen
Briton ['britn]	*(hist.-poet. Form für „Brite")*
indifferent (to) [in'difrənt]	gleichgültig (gegenüber)
Paddington Station ['pædiŋtən]	*(Bahnhof in London)*
attitude ['ætitju:d]	Haltung, Einstellung
towards	gegen(über)
fever ['fi:və]	Fieber
to shoot up	emporschießen
to die down	erlöschen
to take s.th. for	etwas halten für
gold mine ['gəuldmain]	Goldmine, -grube
to ruin [ruin]	ruinieren, zugrunderichten
to divide up [di'vaid]	aufteilen

region [ˈriːdʒən]	Bezirk, Gegend
terminus [ˈtəːminəs]	Endstation
Southern Railway [ˈsʌðən]	*(frühere engl. Eisenbahngesellschaft)*
Great Western (Railway)	*(frühere engl. Eisenbahngesellschaft)*
to cross	durchqueren
Underground	Untergrundbahn *(in London)*
line	Eisenbahnlinie
bitter [ˈbitə]	bitter, erbittert
month after month	Monat für Monat
to reduce (to) [riˈdjuːs]	verringern (auf)
3. magic [ˈmædʒik]	magisch, Zauber-
to achieve [əˈtʃiːv]	erreichen
to thunder [ˈθʌndə]	donnern
Somerset [ˈsʌməsit]	*(Grafschaft im SW Englands)*
record [ˈrekɔːd]	Rekord
at the record of	mit dem Rekord von
safe	*hier:* unangetastet
Diesel [ˈdiːzəl]	*(dt. Ingenieur, 1858—1913)*
to take over	(die Führung) übernehmen
to run at	fahren
to need	müssen
to modernize [ˈmɔdənaiz]	modernisieren
to set up	aufstellen
rank [ræŋk]	Reihe
to electrify [iˈlektrifai]	elektrifizieren
rivalry [ˈraivəlri]	Wetteifer, Rivalität
not any more	nicht mehr
to nationalize [ˈnæʃnəlaiz]	verstaatlichen
British Railways	*(Name der staatlichen engl. Eisenbahn)*
field	Gebiet
transportation [ˌtrænspɔːˈteiʃən]	Beförderung, Transport
motor-car	Auto
aeroplane [ˈɛərəplein]	Flugzeug
competitor (to) [kəmˈpetitə]	Konkurrent (für)
both . . . and	sowohl . . . als (auch)

<Picture Text>

turning point [ˈtəːniŋpɔint]	Wendepunkt

B. Going by Train

vacant [ˈveikənt]	frei
Hyde Park Corner [ˈhaid ˈpɑːk]	*(U-Bahn-Station in London)*
in the nick of time [nik]	gerade im rechten Augenblick
the train is due to start . . . [djuː]	der Zug soll . . . abfahren
to be bound for [baund]	fahren nach
non-stop train	D-Zug
Leamington Spa [ˈlemiŋtən ˈspɑː]	*(Ort in der Grafschaft Warwickshire, Mittelengland)*
connection [kəˈnekʃən]	Anschluß, Verbindung
to consult [kənˈsʌlt]	nachsehen in
a.m. = ante meridiem [ˈæntiməˈridiən]	vormittags
an hour's wait	eine Stunde Aufenthalt
matinée [ˈmætinei]	Nachmittagsvorstellung
p.m. = post meridiem [ˈpəust]	nachmittags
do you mind?	haben Sie etwas dagegen?
stuffy [ˈstʌfi]	schwül, stickig
compartment [kəmˈpɑːtmənt]	(Zug)Abteil
quite [kwait]	recht
close [kləus]	eng
dining car [ˈdainiŋ]	Speisewagen
in the front	vorn
in the rear [riə]	hinten
non-smoker [ˈnɔn ˈsməukə]	Nichtraucher(abteil)
penalty [ˈpenlti]	(Geld)Strafe
communication cord [kəˌmjuːniˈkeiʃən ˈkɔːd]	Notbremse
heavy	*hier:* hoch
to draw	*hier:* lenken
attention [əˈtenʃən]	Aufmerksamkeit

<Stephenson and his Opponents>

foolish [ˈfu:liʃ]	töricht
to stray [strei]	sich verlaufen
line [lain]	Schiene
awkward [ˈɔ:kwəd]	unangenehm, gefährlich

<Night Mail—an extract>

postal order [ˈpəustəl]	Postanweisung
next door	nebenan
to pull up	sich hinaufarbeiten
Beattock [ˈbi:tɔk]	*(Name einer Steigung zwischen England und Schottland)*
steady [ˈstedi]	gleichmäßig
climb [klaim]	Aufstieg
gradient [ˈgreidjənt]	Steigung, Gefälle
on time	pünktlich
dawn [dɔ:n]	Morgendämmerung
to freshen [ˈfreʃn]	*hier:* anbrechen
done [dʌn]	*hier:* bewältigt
toward [təˈwɔ:d]	nach ... hin, auf ... zu
to descend [diˈsend]	hinunterfahren
tug [tʌg]	Schlepper, Schleppdampfer
to yelp [jelp]	kläffen
glade [gleid]	Hain
crane [krein]	Kran
apparatus [ˌæpəˈreitəs]	technische Anlagen
furnace [ˈfə:nis]	(Hoch)Ofen
gigantic [dʒaiˈgæntik]	riesig, gigantisch
chessman [ˈtʃesmæn]	Schachfigur
glen [e]	enges Tal
loch [lɔk]	See *(schott.)*
bank [bæŋk]	Bank(haus)
to receipt [riˈsi:t]	quittieren
to inspect [inˈspekt]	besichtigen, prüfen
stock	Vieh(bestand)
application for [ˌæpliˈkeiʃən]	Bewerbung (um)
situation [ˌsitjuˈeiʃən]	Stellung
timid [ˈtimid]	schüchtern
lovers' declaration [ˌdekləˈreiʃən]	Liebeserklärung
gossip [ˈgɔsip]	Klatsch
news circumstantial [ˌsə:kəmˈstænʃəl]	belanglose alltägliche Nachrichten
financial [faiˈnænʃəl]	finanziell, Finanz-
hue [hju:]	(Farb)Ton
pink [piŋk]	rosa
violet [ˈvaiəlit]	violett
spelt [e]	geschrieben *(orthographisch)*
well-set	wohlgebaut
granite [ˈgrænit]	fest, aus Granit gebaut
Aberdeen [ˌæbəˈdi:n]	*(Stadt im nordöstlichen Schottland)*
to wake [weik]	erwachen
none [nʌn]	kein(er, e, es)
to quicken [ˈkwikən]	schneller schlagen *(Herz)*
for	denn
Wystan Hugh Auden [ˈwistən ˈhju: ˈɔ:dən]	*(in Amerika lebender engl. Dichter, geb. 1907)*

Exercises

1. fact [fækt]	Tatsache
2. line	Schiene *(engl.)*
track [træk]	Schiene *(am.)*
luggage van [ˈlʌgidʒ ˈvæn]	Gepäckwagen *(engl.)*
baggage car [ˈbægidʒ]	Gepäckwagen *(am.)*
passenger coach [ˈpæsindʒə]	Personenwagen *(engl.)*
passenger car	Personenwagen *(am.)*
3. to keep hold of	festhalten
5. to possess [pəˈzes]	besitzen
8. to make haste [heist]	(sich be)eilen
to invent [inˈvent]	erfinden
blind [blaind]	blind

Vocabulary Revision: Railways

to have a look at the time-table	auf den Fahrplan sehen
to board a train / **to get on a train**	in einen Zug einsteigen
to get off a train	aus einem Zug aussteigen
to go by train	mit dem Zug fahren
to pass through a town	durch eine Stadt fahren
to be on the train	im Zug sein
to pull the communication cord	die Notbremse ziehen
to book a couchette	einen (Platz im) Liegewagen buchen
to reach one's destination	seinen Bestimmungsort erreichen
non-smoker	Nichtraucherabteil
non-stop train	D-Zug
express	Eilzug, Schnellzug
sleeper	Schlafwagen
platform	Bahnsteig
rack	Gepäcknetz
terminus	Endstation
engine driver	Lokomotivführer
station-master	Stationsvorsteher
passenger	Reisender
How long does it take me to get to the station?	Wie lange brauche ich bis zum Bahnhof?
What is the fare?	Wie hoch ist das Fahrgeld?
The train is late.	Der Zug hat Verspätung.
The train is leaving.	Der Zug fährt ab.
The train goes at an average speed of 70 m.p.h.	Der Zug hat eine Durchschnittsgeschwindigkeit von 70 Meilen in der Stunde.
Is there a good connection from Oxford?	Habe ich in Oxford guten Anschluß?
Is there a dining car on the train?	Hat der Zug einen Speisewagen?

3 A. From the Cradle to the Grave

cradle [ˈkreidl]	Wiege
grave [ˈgreiv]	Grab
1. to hoot [hu:t]	tuten
siren [ˈsaiərin]	Sirene
Oldham [ˈəuldəm]	*(Stadt in der Grafschaft Lancashire)*
Nancy [ˈnænsi]	*(weibl. Vorname)*
Robinson [ˈrɔbinsn]	*(Familienname)*
fitter [ˈfitə]	Monteur
packer [ˈpækə]	Packer(in)
Derek [ˈderik]	*(männl. Vorname)*
Kevin [ˈkevin]	*(männl. Vorname)*
to sit for an examination	eine Prüfung machen
school-leaving examination	Abschlußprüfung an einer Schule
general [ˈdʒenərəl]	allgemein
certificate [səˈtifikit]	Zeugnis, Bescheinigung
ordinary [ˈɔ:dnri]	gewöhnlich
level [levl]	Niveau, Maßstab
General Certificate of Education at Ordinary Level	*(Prüfung am Ende der Mittelstufe)*

scientific [ˌsaiənˈtifik]	(natur)wissenschaftlich
assistant [əˈsistənt]	Assistent
Harwell [ˈhɑːwəl]	*(kleiner Ort im S Englands)*
atomic [əˈtɔmik]	Atom-
energy [ˈenədʒi]	Energie
grim [grim]	grimmig, hart
pretty grim	*hier:* ziemlich „wacklig“
to make it	*hier:* es schaffen
I should be all right in maths	„Mathe“ müßte ich eigentlich schaffen
to attend [əˈtend]	besuchen
2. washing-machine	Waschmaschine
purchase [ˈpəːtʃəs]	Kauf
hire-purchase [ˈhaiə]	Abzahlungskauf
to buy by hire-purchase	auf Abzahlung kaufen
Red Lion	*(Name einer Gastwirtschaft)*
including [inˈkluːdiŋ]	einschließlich
Blackpool [ˈblækpuːl]	*(Badeort an der NW-Küste Englands)*
to enjoy s.th.	etwas genießen
sandy [ˈsændi]	sandig, Sand-
luck [lʌk]	Glück
anywhere else	irgendwoanders
slot [slɔt]	Schlitz
slot-machine	Spielautomat
pier [ˈpiə]	Pier, Hafendamm
attraction [əˈtrækʃən]	Reiz, Anziehungskraft
3. illness [ˈilnis]	Krankheit
unemployment [ˈʌnimˈplɔiment]	Arbeitslosigkeit
income [ˈinkəm]	Einkommen
in income tax [tæks]	an Einkommensteuer, Lohnsteuer
contribution [ˌkɔntriˈbjuːʃən]	Beitrag
health [helθ]	Gesundheit
service [ˈsəːvis]	Dienst(leistung)
National Health Service	staatlicher Gesundheitsdienst
insurance [inˈʃuərəns]	Versicherung
National Insurance	staatliche Sozialversicherung
social [ˈsəuʃəl]	sozial
security [siˈkjuəriti]	Sicherheit
to be well	sich wohl, gesund fühlen
sick [sik]	krank
to feel sick	sich krank fühlen
at half past five	um halb sechs
to diagnose [ˈdaiəgnəuz]	feststellen *(eine Krankheit)*
pneumonia [njuːˈməunjə]	Lungenentzündung
the same night	am gleichen Abend
thanks to	dank
accommodation [əˌkɔməˈdeiʃən]	Unterbringung, Unterkunft
state	staatlich, Staats-
birth [bəːθ]	Geburt
new-born	neugeboren
allowance [əˈlauəns]	Zuschuß
old age	(hohes) Alter
to be obliged to [əˈblaidʒd]	müssen, zu etwas gezwungen sein
won't = will not [wəunt]	
to starve [stɑːv]	verhungern, Hungers sterben
pension [ˈpenʃən]	Rente, Pension
funeral [ˈfjuːnərəl]	Beerdigung
costs [kɔsts]	Kosten
welfare state [ˈwelfɛə ˈsteit]	Wohlfahrtsstaat
to look after	sehen nach, sich kümmern um

<B. A Sunday in Harlech>

Harlech [ˈhɑːlek]	*(Ort in Nordwales)*
to the west	westlich, im Westen
to face	gegenüberliegen
Irish Sea	Irische See *(zwischen England und Irland)*
Snowdonia [snəuˈdəunjə]	*(Gebiet um den Snowdon, Nordwales)*
community [kəˈmjuːniti]	Gemeinde, Gemeinschaft
Anglican [ˈæŋglikən]	Anglikaner(in), anglikanisch
direction [diˈrekʃən]	Richtung
insistent [inˈsistənt]	eindringlich

opposite [ˈɔpəzit]	gegenüber
High Street	Hauptstraße
Baptist [ˈbæptist]	Baptist(in), Baptisten-
Methodist [ˈmeθədist]	Methodist(in), Methodisten-
minister [ˈministə]	Pfarrer, Geistlicher
congregation [ˌkɔŋgriˈgeiʃən]	Gemeinde *(religiös)*
Congregationalists [ˌkɔŋgriˈgeiʃnəlists]	Kongregationalisten *(freikirchliche Gemeinschaft)*
row [rəu]	Reihe
David [ˈdeivid]	David
chapel [ˈtʃæpəl]	Kapelle *(Kirche)*
Catholic [ˈkæθəlik]	Katholik(in), katholisch
Presbyterian [ˌprezbiˈtiəriən]	Presbyterianer(in), presbyterianisch
decoration [ˌdekəˈreiʃən]	Schmuck, Verzierung
to depict [diˈpikt]	*(bildl.)* darstellen
Bible [ˈbaibl]	Bibel
eternal [iˈtə:nl]	ewig
altar [ˈɔ:ltə]	Altar
font	Taufbecken
to date from [deit]	stammen aus
plain [plein]	schlicht, einfach
just	nur
organ [ˈɔ:gən]	Orgel
service	Gottesdienst
hymn [him]	Kirchenlied
activity [ækˈtiviti]	Tätigkeit
diversity [daiˈvə:siti]	Mannigfaltigkeit
Christian [ˈkristjən]	christlich
worship [ˈwə:ʃip]	Kult(us), Verehrung

The Case for the Defence

called	namens
Adams [ˈædəmz]	*(Familienname)*
for	wegen
murder of [ˈmə:də]	Mord an
Salmon [ˈsæmən]	*(Familienname)*
evidence [ˈevidəns]	Zeugnis, Aussage *(Gericht)*
to give evidence	als Zeuge aussagen
counsel [ˈkaunsəl]	Anwalt
counsel for the Crown [kraun]	Staatsanwalt
to bring out	vorbringen
gently [ˈdʒentli]	vorsichtig
firm [ə:]	bestimmt
downstairs [ˈdaunˈstεəz]	die Treppe hinunter
court [ɔ:]	Gericht(shof), Gerichtssaal
in court	vor Gericht
across [əˈkrɔs]	hinüber
in the dock	auf der Anklagebank
certain [ˈsə:tn]	sicher
to be mistaken [misˈteikən]	sich irren
counsel for the defence [diˈfens]	Verteidiger
to cross-examine [ˈkrɔsigˈzæmin]	ein Kreuzverhör vornehmen
to depend on [diˈpend]	abhängen von
eyesight [ˈaisait]	Sehkraft, Augenlicht
spectacles *(pl.)* [ˈspektəklz]	Brille
remarkable [riˈmɑ:kəbl]	bemerkenswert, außerordentlich (gut)
doubt [daut]	Zweifel
none whatever [ˈnʌn wɔtˈevə]	überhaupt keine, gar keine
to take a look round	umherschauen
to examine [igˈzæmin]	genau ansehen, prüfen
at the back	hinten
image [ˈimidʒ]	Ebenbild
the same [ei]	gleich, genauso
striped [ai]	gestreift
to think	überlegen
to swear, swore, sworn [εə, ɔ:]	(be)schwören
twin	Zwilling (s-)
witness [ˈwitnis]	Zeuge
alibi [ˈælibai]	Alibi
to acquit [əˈkwit]	freisprechen
for lack of evidence [ˈlæk‿əv ˈevidəns]	wegen Mangels an Beweisen
extraordinary [iksˈtrɔ:dnri]	außergewöhnlich
to wedge [wedʒ]	(ein)zwängen
twins [i]	Zwillinge
to get s.o. to do s.th.	jemanden dazu bringen, etwas zu tun
back way	Hinterausgang

front [ʌ]	Vorder-
squeal [iː]	schriller Schrei
divine [diˈvain]	göttlich
vengeance [ˈvendʒəns]	Vergeltung, Strafe
to get on one's feet	aufstehen, sich erheben
over	hinüber
to cry	weinen
innocent [ˈinəsnt]	unschuldig
at night	nachts
Graham Greene [ˈgreiəm ˈgriːn]	*(engl. Schriftsteller, geb. 1904)*
abridged [əˈbridʒd]	gekürzt

Exercises

1. to compare [kəmˈpɛə]	vergleichen
worker [ˈwəːkə]	Arbeiter(in)
tens of thousands	Zehntausende
coal [kəul]	Kohle
carriage [ˈkæridʒ]	Wagen
passage [ˈpæsidʒ]	Gang
pump [pʌmp]	Pumpe
3. might [mait]	könnte
5. to spend (on)	ausgeben (für)
alcohol [ˈælkəhɔl]	Alkohol

4 A. The Tunnel Project

project [ˈprɔdʒekt]	Plan, Projekt
school magazine [ˌmægəˈziːn]	Schülerzeitung
Folkestone [ˈfəukstən]	*(Stadt an der Südostküste Englands)*
article [ˈɑːtikl]	Artikel, Aufsatz *(Zeitung)*
discussion [disˈkʌʃən]	Diskussion, Erörterung
subject	Gegenstand, Thema
resident [ˈrezidənt]	Einwohner, Ortsansässiger
Folkstone residents	Einwohner von Folkstone
to introduce a subject	in ein Thema einführen, ein Thema zur Sprache bringen
statesman [ˈsteitsmən]	Staatsmann
reality [riːˈæliti]	Wirklichkeit
under	unter ... durch
no longer	nicht mehr, nicht länger
to isolate [ˈaisəleit]	absondern, isolieren
"Continent Isolated"	„Das europäische Festland ist abgeschnitten"
unhappy [ʌnˈhæpi]	unbehaglich
seasick	seekrank
to rage [reidʒ]	wüten
to carry	tragen, bringen, *hier:* befördern
double-deck train [ˈdʌblˈdek]	zweistöckiger Zug
vehicle [ˈviːikl]	Fahrzeug
every five minutes	alle fünf Minuten
practical [ˈpræktikəl]	praktisch
motorway	Autobahn
instead of	statt
to transport [trænsˈpɔːt]	befördern, transportieren
exhaust [igˈzɔːst]	Auspuff
fume [fjuːm]	Dampf, Rauch
exhaust fumes	Auspuffgase
ventilation [ˌventiˈleiʃən]	(Ent)Lüftung
to invest [inˈvest]	anlegen, investieren
economic [ˌiːkəˈnɔmik]	wirtschaftlich
enormous [iˈnɔːməs]	ungeheuer
freight [freit]	Fracht
imports [ˈimpɔːts]	Importwaren
European Common Market	EWG = Europäische Wirtschaftsgemeinschaft
gateway	*hier:* Tor
absolutely [ˈæbsəluːtli]	vollkommen, durchaus
to become of	werden aus
ferry [ˈferi]	Fähre
furthermore [ˈfəːðəˈmɔː]	überdies
what's the use of ...?	welchen Zweck hat ...?
to destroy [disˈtrɔi]	zerstören, vernichten
to prevent s.o. from doing s.th.	jemanden hindern, etwas zu tun

waste [weist]	Verschwendung
retired [ri'taiəd]	pensioniert
supply [sə'plai]	Nachschub
situation [ˌsitju'eiʃən]	Lage, Situation
pessimistic [ˌpesi'mistik]	pessimistisch
to object [əb'dʒekt]	einwenden
as well	ebensogut, genausogut
enterprise ['entəpraiz]	Unternehmung, Unternehmen
skyscraper ['skaiˌskreipə]	Wolkenkratzer
standstill	Stillstand
to continue	fortfahren *(in einer Rede)*
risky ['riski]	gewagt, riskant
tributary ['tribjutəri]	Nebenfluß
to come into being	entstehen
earthquake ['ə:θkweik]	Erdbeben
Portsmouth ['pɔ:tsməθ]	*(Hafenstadt an der Südküste Englands)*
to stand s.th.	etwas aushalten
unstable ['ʌn'steibl]	nicht fest, unbeständig
crack [kræk]	Riß
catastrophe [kə'tæstrəfi]	Katastrophe
lively ['laivli]	lebhaft
unfortunately [ʌn'fɔ:tʃnitli]	unglücklicherweise, leider
space [speis]	Raum, Platz
a report on [ri'pɔ:t]	ein Bericht über
majority [mə'dʒɔriti]	Mehrheit
those present (= those that were present)	die Anwesenden
favour ['feivə]	Gunst
to be in favour of s.th.	für etwas sein
doubt [daut]	Zweifel
share [ʃɛə]	Aktie
stock [stɔk]	Kapital
exchange [iks'tʃeindʒ]	Austausch
stock exchange	Börse

<Picture Text>

model ['mɔdl]	Modell
really ['riəli]	in Wirklichkeit
lane [ei]	Spur

<B. Some English Traits>

trait [trei]	(Charakter)Zug
1. self-control ['selfkən'trəul]	Selbstbeherrschung
explorer [iks'plɔ:rə]	Forscher, Forschungsreisender
missionary ['miʃnəri]	Missionar
David Livingstone ['liviŋstən]	*(schott. Missionar und Afrikaforscher, 1813—73)*
H.M. Stanley ['stænli]	*(engl. Afrikaforscher, 1841—1904)*
hardship ['hɑ:dʃip]	Mühsal
to stand face to face with s.o.	jemandem von Angesicht zu Angesicht gegenüberstehen
missing	vermißt
to fall on each other's necks	einander um den Hals fallen
to presume [pri'zju:m]	annehmen
to address [ə'dres]	ansprechen
2. fan [fæn]	begeisterter Anhänger, „Narr“
to maintain [men'tein]	beibehalten, (be)wahren
playing-field	Sportplatz
ever since	seitdem
praise [preiz]	Lob
loser ['lu:zə]	Verlierer
pastime ['pɑ:staim]	Zeitvertreib
passion ['pæʃən]	Leidenschaft
scientist ['saiəntist]	(Natur)Wissenschaftler
professional [prə'feʃənl]	Berufs-, professionell
footballer ['futbɔ:lə]	Fußballspieler
boxer ['bɔksə]	Boxer
jockey ['dʒɔki]	Jockei
cricketer ['krikitə]	Kricketspieler
Sir Gordon Richards ['gɔ:dn]	*(berühmter engl. Jockei)*
Sir Stanley Matthews ['stænli 'mæθju:z]	*(berühmter engl. Fußballspieler)*
to knight [nait]	zum Ritter schlagen
to make	*hier:* leisten
3. love of animals	Tierliebe

scarcely [ˈskɛəsli]	kaum
Fluffy [ˈflʌfi]	*(Hundename)*
Whisky [ˈwiski]	*(Katzenname)*
cemetery [ˈsemitri]	Friedhof
Kensington Gardens	*(Park in London)*
darling [ˈdɑːliŋ]	Liebling
familiar [fəˈmiljə]	(wohl)bekannt
space [speis]	Weltraum
bitterly [ˈbitəli]	bitterlich
to be ashamed of s.th. [əˈʃeimd]	sich einer Sache schämen
affection for [əˈfekʃən]	Liebe, Zuneigung zu

<A Prospect of the Sea>

prospect [ˈprɔspekt]	Vorstellung
corn [ɔː]	Korn, Getreide
to sway [ei]	schwanken, sich wiegen
from side to side	hin und her
branch [ɑː]	Zweig
to hide, hid, hidden [ai, i, i]	verbergen
unbroken	*hier:* ungetrübt
edge [edʒ]	Rand, Saum
noon [uː]	Mittag
to smell of [e]	riechen nach
cattle [ˈkætl]	Vieh
to stretch [e]	(sich) (aus)strecken
wave [ei]	Welle, Woge
to glide [ai]	gleiten
heavens [ˈhevnz]	Himmelsgewölbe
seven-league boots [liːg]	Siebenmeilenstiefel
nest	Nest
tousled [ˈtauzld]	zerzaust
to rise to one's feet	aufstehen, sich erheben
lazy [ei]	träge
to wander [ɔ]	wandern
strip [i]	Streifen
hillside [ˈhilˈsaid]	Abhang
mock [ɔ]	scheinbar, unecht
to roll over [rəul]	herumrollen
weeds [iː]	*hier:* Wasserpflanzen
to stand up	sich erheben
pillar [ˈpilə]	Pfeiler, Säule
to magnify [ˈmægnifai]	vergrößern
to lash [æ]	peitschen
tail [ei]	Schwanz
as	während
pebble [ˈpebl]	Kiesel(stein)
bed	Flußbett
drowned [au]	ertrunken
princess [prinˈses]	Prinzessin
pigtail [ˈpigteil]	Zopf
string	Saite
fiddle [ˈfidl]	Geige, Fiedel
net	Netz
to pluck [ʌ]	ausreißen, zupfen
mermaid [ˈməːmeid]	Meerjungfrau
prince [i]	Prinz
to tauten [ˈtɔːtən]	straff anspannen
to bend, bent, bent	biegen
harp [ɑː]	Harfe
tune [tjuːn]	Melodie
to skid [i]	*hier:* hüpfen, schlittern
to scuttle [ʌ]	rennen, dahintrippeln
at	*hier:* nach
gnat [næt]	Mücke
lark [ɑː]	Lerche
to dart [ɑː]	schießen
distance [ˈdistəns]	Ferne
wood-pigeon [ˈpidʒin]	Ringeltaube

Exercises

1. disadvantage [ˌdisədˈvɑːntidʒ]	Nachteil
point [pɔint]	Punkt
3. fantasy [ˈfæntəsi]	Phantasie
5. guide-book	Führer *(Buch)*
7. prefix [ˈpriːfiks]	Vorsilbe
meaning [ˈmiːniŋ]	Bedeutung
8. happiness [ˈhæpinis]	Glück(seligkeit)
lucky	glücklich
better luck	mehr Glück
lucky day	Glückstag
lucky fellow	Glückspilz
lucky penny	Glückspfennig
9. to suit [sjuːt]	passen
description [disˈkripʃən]	Beschreibung

Vocabulary Revision: Discussing

The discussion is about to begin.	Die Diskussion wird gleich beginnen.
to be appointed leader of a discussion group	zum Leiter einer Diskussionsgruppe ernannt werden
to introduce a subject	ein Thema zur Sprache bringen
to report on Commonwealth countries	über Commonwealth-Länder berichten
to talk about education	über Erziehung sprechen
to interrupt the speech	die Rede unterbrechen
to continue the speech	die Rede fortsetzen
to agree with the speaker	mit dem Redner übereinstimmen
to agree to a plan	mit einem Plan einverstanden sein
to be in favour of a plan	einen Plan begünstigen
to ask about s.th.	nach etwas fragen
to answer questions	Fragen beantworten
to argue about s.th.	über etwas streiten
to think about a question	über eine Frage nachdenken
to discuss the question	die Frage diskutieren
to bring the discussion to an end	die Diskussion beenden

<Britain and the British>

The Face of Britain

to mean [i:]	*hier:* bezeichnen
as	als
republic [riˈpʌblik]	Republik
to recognize [ˈrekəgnaiz]	anerkennen
official [əˈfiʃəl]	offiziell
by the grace of God	von Gottes Gnaden
realm [relm]	(König)Reich
to include [inˈklu:d]	umfassen
from the earliest times	seit frühester Zeit
foreigner [ˈfɔrinə]	Ausländer

The Britons

A seafaring nation

seafaring [ˈsi:ˌfɛəriŋ]	seefahrend
to separate [ˈsepəreit]	trennen
to conquer [ˈkɔŋkə]	erobern
islander [ˈailəndə]	Inselbewohner
from	von . . . entfernt
musician [mjuˈziʃən]	Musiker
Captain Cook [kuk]	*(engl. Weltumsegler, 1728—79)*
Nelson [ˈnelsn]	*(brit. Admiral, 1758—1805)*
to enable [iˈneibl]	in den Stand setzen, befähigen
empire [ˈempaiə]	(Welt)Reich
influence [ˈinfluəns]	Einfluß
way of life	Lebensweise

A nation of town-dwellers

town-dweller [ˈdwelə]	Stadtbewohner
in size [saiz]	der Größe nach
agriculture [ˈægrikʌltʃə]	Landwirtschaft
industrialisation [inˌdʌstriəlaiˈzeiʃən]	Industrialisierung
Greater London	Groß-London
within [wiˈðin]	innerhalb
Leeds [i:]	*(Industriestadt in Mittelengland)*
Newcastle-on-Tyne [ˈnju: kɑ:sl‿ən ˈtain]	*(Hafenstadt an der Nordostküste Englands)*

Cardiff [ˈkɑːdif]	*(Hafenstadt an der Südostküste von Wales)*
density [ˈdensiti]	Dichte

An industrial nation

first and foremost [ˈfɔːməust]	in erster Linie
to centre [ˈsentə]	konzentrieren
coal-field [kəul]	Kohlenrevier
works [əː]	Betrieb, Fabrik
needle [iː]	Nadel
to mass-produce [ˈmæsprəˌdjuːs]	serienmäßig herstellen
shipbuilding	Schiffbau
coal mining	Kohlenbergbau
gas [æ]	Gas
electricity [ilekˈtrisiti]	Elektrizität
development [diˈveləpmənt]	Entwicklung
to neglect [niˈglekt]	vernachlässigen
effect [iˈfekt]	(Aus)Wirkung
of that	davon
self-supporting [ˈselfsəˈpɔːtiŋ]	autark, sich selbst versorgend
to import [imˈpɔːt]	einführen, importieren
to pay for	bezahlen
manufactured goods [ˌmænjuˈfæktʃəd]	Fertigwaren

Population and Industry

miscellaneous [ˌmisiˈleinjəs]	gemischt, verschieden

Politics and the State

politics [ˈpɔlitiks]	Politik

The oldest Parliament

past [ɑː]	vergangen
institution [ˌinstiˈtjuːʃən]	Einrichtung
especially [isˈpeʃəli]	besonders
House of Lords [lɔːdz]	Oberhaus
House of Commons [ˈkɔmənz]	Unterhaus
to elect [iˈlekt]	wählen
election [iˈlekʃən]	Wahl
to hold	abhalten
by right of birth [bəːθ]	auf Grund der (adligen) Herkunft
nomination [ˌnɔmiˈneiʃən]	Berufung
party [ˈpɑːti]	Partei
Conservative Party [kənˈsəːvətiv]	konservative Partei
Labour Party [ˈleibə]	Labour Party *(brit. Arbeiterpartei)*
Liberal Party [ˈlibərəl]	liberale Partei
Prime Minister [ˈpraim ˈministə]	Premierminister
cabinet minister [ˈkæbinit]	Kabinettminister
minority [maiˈnɔriti]	Minderheit
opposition [ˌɔpəˈziʃən]	Opposition *(polit.)*
official [əˈfiʃəl]	Beamter
speaker	Sprecher
debate [diˈbeit]	Debatte
rare [rɛə]	selten
experience of Parliament [iksˈpiəriəns]	Parlamentserfahrung
reputation [ˌrepjuˈteiʃən]	(guter) Ruf
fairness [ˈfɛənis]	Gerechtigkeit, Unparteilichkeit

The British monarchy

monarchy [ˈmɔnəki]	Monarchie
to trace back to [treis]	zurückverfolgen bis in
descent [diˈsent]	Herkunft
monarch [ˈmɔnək]	Monarch(in), König(in)
to hold	innehaben
supreme [sjuˈpriːm]	höchst(er, e, es)
growth [grəuθ]	Erstarken
to decrease [diːˈkriːs]	abnehmen, sich verringern
active [ˈæktiv]	aktiv
to reign [rein]	herrschen
political [pəˈlitikəl]	politisch
to take	fällen, vornehmen
personal [ˈpəːsnl]	persönlich
present [ˈpreznt]	gegenwärtig, jetzig
to symbolize [ˈsimbəlaiz]	symbolisieren

Important People

important [imˈpɔ:tənt] bedeutend
importance [imˈpɔ:təns] Bedeutung
to control [kənˈtrəul] kontrollieren
place Stelle
association [əˌsəusiˈeiʃən] Vereinigung, Bund
affair [əˈfɛə] Angelegenheit
pride [ai] Stolz

Queen Elizabeth I

Elizabeth [iˈlizəbəθ] *(Königin von England, 1533—1603)*
reign [rein] Regierung(szeit)
"Sea Dog" Seebär
Raleigh [ˈrɔ:li] *(engl. Seefahrer und Schriftsteller, 1552—1618)*
to challenge [ˈtʃælindʒ] herausfordern
to avoid [əˈvɔid] vermeiden
fearless [ˈfiəlis] furchtlos
emergency [iˈmə:dʒənsi] (plötzlich eintretende) Notlage
may mag
defeat [diˈfi:t] Niederlage, Besiegung
traders [ei] Kaufleute
explorer [iksˈplɔ:rə] Forscher, Forschungsreisender
increasingly [inˈkri:siŋli] zunehmend, in steigendem Maße
prosperous [ˈprɔspərəs] wohlhabend

William Shakespeare

age [eidʒ] Zeitalter
literature [ˈlitəritʃə] Literatur
dominant [ˈdɔminənt] überragend
dramatist [ˈdræmətist] Dramatiker
Elizabethan [iˌlizəˈbi:θən] elisabethanisch
as wie
Hamlet [ˈhæmlit] *(Drama von Shakespeare)*
Macbeth [məkˈbeθ] *(Drama von Shakespeare)*
Julius Caesar [ˈdʒu:ljəs ˈsi:zə] *(Drama von Shakespeare)*
As You Like it *(Lustspiel von Shakespeare)*
A Midsummer Night's Dream *(Lustspiel von Shakespeare)*
Romeo and Juliet [ˈrəumiəu‿ənˈdʒu:ljət] *(Drama von Shakespeare)*
The Merchant of Venice [ˈmə:tʃənt‿əv ˈvenis] *(Drama von Shakespeare)*

Oliver Cromwell

Oliver Cromwell [ˈɔlivə ˈkrɔmwəl] *(engl. Staatsmann, 1599—1658)*
conflict [ˈkɔnflikt] Ringen, Streit
James I [dʒeimz] *(König von England, 1566—1625)*
Charles I [tʃɑ:lz] *(König von England, 1600—1649)*
to rule [u:] herrschen, regieren
Puritan [ˈpjuəritən] Puritaner(in)
sect [e] Sekte
to persecute [ˈpə:sikju:t] verfolgen
belief [biˈli:f] Glaube
devout [diˈvaut] fromm
supporter [səˈpɔ:tə] Anhänger
to revolt [riˈvəlt] sich empören
Civil War [ˈsivl] *(der engl. Bürgerkrieg 1642—49)*
virtuous [ˈvə:tjuəs] tugendhaft
by *hier:* mit
to ban [æ] verbieten
to forbid, forbade, forbidden [fəˈbid, ei, i] verbieten, untersagen
sports Sport(veranstaltung)

Queen Victoria

uninterrupted [ˈʌnˌintəˈrʌptid] ununterbrochen
material [məˈtiəriəl] materiell
rapid [ˈræpid] schnell, rasch
growth [əu] Wachstum
empress [ˈempris] Kaiserin
India [ˈindjə] Indien
greatness [ˈgreitnis] Größe
prince [i] Prinz
Albert of Saxe-Coburg-Gotha [ˈælbət‿əv ˈsæks ˈkəubə:g ˈgəuθə] Albert von Sachsen-Coburg-Gotha *(Gemahl der Königin Victoria, 1819—61)*

to withdraw, withdrew, withdrawn [wiðˈdrɔ:, u:, ɔ:]	(sich) zurückziehen
threshold [ˈθreʃhəuld]	Schwelle

Charles Dickens

Charles Dickens [ˈtʃɑ:lz ˈdikinz]	*(engl. Romanschriftsteller, 1812—70)*
Victorian [vikˈtɔ:riən]	viktorianisch
wealth [e]	Reichtum, Wohlstand
poverty [ˈpɔvəti]	Armut
mansion [ˈmænʃən]	Villa
industrialist [inˈdʌstriəlist]	Industrieller
worker	Arbeiter
to raise [ei]	(sich) erheben
inequality [ˌiniˈkwɔliti]	Ungerechtigkeit
to make s.o. aware [əˈwɛə] of s.th.	jemanden etwas gewahr werden lassen, jemanden zur Erkenntnis einer Sache bringen
fellow-countryman	Landsmann
need [i:]	Notwendigkeit
reform [riˈfɔ:m]	Reform
novelist [ˈnɔvəlist]	Romanschriftsteller
to imprison for [imˈprizn]	einsperren wegen
debt [det]	Schuld *(finanziell)*
childhood [ˈtʃaildhud]	Kindheit
to be reflected in [riˈflektid]	sich widerspiegeln in
novel [ˈnɔvəl]	Roman
fame [ei]	Ruhm
Oliver Twist [ˈɔlivə ˈtwist]	*(Roman von Dickens)*
David Copperfield [ˈdeivid ˈkɔpəfi:ld]	*(Roman von Dickens)*
unforgettable [ˈʌnfəˈgetəbl]	unvergeßlich
injustice [inˈdʒʌstis]	Ungerechtigkeit
to warm [ɔ:]	(er)wärmen
humour [ˈhju:mə]	Humor
humanity [hjuˈmæniti]	Menschlichkeit
quality [ˈkwɔliti]	Eigenschaft, Qualität
to appear [əˈpiə]	sich zeigen
clearly [iə]	deutlich
The Pickwick Papers [ˈpikwik]	Die Pickwickier *(Roman von Dickens)*
story	Erzählung
carol [ˈkærəl]	Lied
A Christmas Carol	*(Weihnachtserzählung von Dickens)*

Sir Winston Churchill

Sir Winston Churchill [ˈwinstən ˈtʃə:tʃil]	*(Brit. Staatsmann und Premierminister, 1874–1965)*
change [tʃeindʒ]	Veränderung
to hasten [ˈheisn]	beschleunigen
to emerge [iˈmə:dʒ]	sich erheben
adventurous [ədˈventʃərəs]	abenteuerlich
the 1930s [ˈnainti:nˈθə:tiz]	die dreißiger Jahre (des 20. Jhdt.)
to be out of favour [ˈfeivə]	in Ungnade gefallen sein
to warn of [ɔ:]	warnen vor
to listen to	hören auf
to be called to power [ˈpauə]	an die Macht gerufen werden
but	außer
toil [ɔi]	Mühe, Plage
tear [iə]	Träne
sweat [e]	Schweiß
determination [diˌtə:miˈneiʃən]	Entschlossenheit
sincerity [sinˈseriti]	Aufrichtigkeit
leadership [ˈli:dəʃip]	Führung
to contribute [kənˈtribjut]	beitragen
towards [təˈwɔ:dz]	zu
allied [ˈælaid]	alliiert *(Alliierte: Gegner Deutschlands im 2. Weltkrieg)*

Important Dates

corner-stone	Grundstein
Charles II	*(König von England, 1630–85)*
War of Independence [ˌindiˈpendəns]	Unabhängigkeitskrieg
Napoleonic [nəˌpəuliˈɔnik]	napoleonisch
coronation [ˌkɔrəˈneiʃən]	Krönung

A Warning to Beginners

beginner	Anfänger
the other way round	umgekehrt
respectable [risˈpektəbl]	ehrbar
gay [ei]	lustig, fröhlich
cheerful [ˈtʃiəful]	heiter, fröhlich
peer [piə]	Adliger
motor-manufacturer [ˈməutəˌmænjuˈfæktʃərə]	Automobilfabrikant
peculiar [piˈkju:ljə]	absonderlich, komisch
rag [æ]	„Fetzen“
dull [ʌ]	langweilig, fade
dreary [ˈdriəri]	trübselig, öde
topic [ˈtɔpik]	Thema
phrase [ei]	Phrase, Redensart
as though [ðəu]	als ob
shovel [ˈʃʌvl]	Schaufel
upside down	verkehrt herum
food [fu:d]	Essen
manners [ˈmænəz]	Sitten, Manieren
openly	öffentlich
to declare [diˈklɛə]	erklären
at one time or another	irgendwann, irgendeinmal
to be superior to s.o. [sju:ˈpiəriə]	jemandem überlegen sein
to fight wars	Kriege führen
heroic [hiˈrəuik]	heroisch
to combat [ˈkɔmbət]	bekämpfen
to mention [ˈmenʃən]	erwähnen
sensitive [ˈsensitiv]	feinfühlig
touchy [ˈtʌtʃi]	leicht gekränkt
exquisite [ˈekskwizit]	ausgesucht, äußerst fein
sense [sens]	Sinn
to offend [əˈfend]	beleidigen
to lie [ai]	lügen
Continental [ˌkɔntiˈnentl]	Bewohner des europ. Festlandes
George Mikes [ˈdʒɔ:dʒ ˈmikeʃ]	*(engl. Schriftsteller ungar. Herkunft)*
alien [ˈeiljən]	Fremder, Ausländer

5 A. The Watchword is 'Attack'

watchword [ˈwɔtʃwə:d]	Losung
episode [ˈepisəud]	Episode, Vorfall
War of Independence	Unabhängigkeitskrieg
1. dull [dʌl]	trübe
Delaware River [ˈdeləwɛə]	*(Fluß im NO der USA)*
Trenton [ˈtrentən]	*(Stadt im NO der USA)*
quarter [ˈkwɔ:tə]	Quartier
opposite [ˈɔpəzit]	gegenüberliegend
command [kəˈmɑ:nd]	Kommando, Befehl
to advance [ədˈvɑ:ns]	vorrücken
rag	Lumpen
to run short of s.th.	etwas wird knapp, geht zu Ende
demoralized [diˈmɔrəlaizd]	demoralisiert, zucht- und mutlos
to believe in s.th.	an etwas glauben
final [ˈfainl]	endgültig, End-
to forbid, forbade, forbidden [fəˈbid, fəˈbeid, fəˈbidn]	verbieten
to row [rəu]	rudern
contact [ˈkɔntækt]	Kontakt, Berührung
rebel [ˈrebl]	Rebell, Aufrührer
2. Kenneth Strawn [ˈkeniθ ˈstrɔ:n]	*(Eigenname)*
faint [feint]	schwach
tap [tæp]	Pochen
pane [pein]	(Fenster)Scheibe
in a low voice	leise, gedämpft
to come across s.o.	auf jemanden stoßen
lieutenant [lefˈtenənt]	Leutnant
he's my father, you know	er ist nämlich mein Vater
since	seitdem
regiment [ˈredʒimənt]	Regiment
Pennsylvania [ˌpensilˈveinjə]	*(Staat im NO der USA)*
to knock	(an)klopfen
loudly	laut, vernehmlich
3. to throw over	umwerfen
unfriendly [ʌnˈfrendli]	unfreundlich
here	hierher

to play fair	ehrlich sein
beast [bi:st]	Biest
spy [spai]	Spion
dear	teuer
to catch s.o. by the shoulder	jemanden bei der Schulter ergreifen
hard	*hier:* heftig
to leap [li:p]	springen
to throw s.o. to the ground	jemanden zu Boden werfen
in a moment	augenblicklich
to get the better of s.o.	jemanden besiegen, unterkriegen
to strike	schlagen
butt [bʌt]	(Gewehr)Kolben
to loosen [ˈlu:sn]	(sich) lockern, lösen
grip [grip]	Griff
unconscious [ʌnˈkɔnʃəs]	bewußtlos
he is likely to recover soon	er wird sich wahrscheinlich bald erholen
to hasten [ˈheisn]	hasten, (sich) beeilen
they hastened to get the boat out	sie holten eilig (schleunigst) das Boot heraus
you had better come	es wäre besser, wenn du kämst; du kommst besser ...
fairly	ziemlich, ganz
to launch [lɔ:ntʃ]	aussetzen *(Boot)*, vom Stapel lassen
to go into	*hier:* eintauchen in
oar [ɔ:]	Ruder
to move	*hier:* (dahin)treiben
ice-floe [ˈaisˌfləu]	Eisscholle
to the safety	in die Sicherheit
4. force	*hier:* Heeresmacht
to take s.o. by surprise	jemanden überrumpeln
American [əˈmerikən]	Amerikaner
to take s.o. prisoner	jemanden gefangennehmen
with hardly any losses ...	und hatten kaum irgendwelche eigenen Verluste
Philadelphia [ˌfiləˈdelfjə]	*(Stadt im NO der USA)*
to turn the tables	den Spieß umkehren
additional [əˈdiʃənl]	zusätzlich
strength	*hier:* Heeresstärke, Heeresmacht
terms [tə:mz]	Bedingungen

<Picture Text>

forces [ˈfɔ:sis]	Truppen

<B. The Declaration of Independence>

Declaration of Independence [ˌdekləˈreiʃən]	Unabhängigkeitserklärung
once	sobald
to insist on [inˈsist]	bestehen auf
separation [ˌsepəˈreiʃən]	Trennung
unanimous [ju:ˈnænimәs]	einmütig
self-evident [ˈselfˈevidənt]	selbstverständlich, offensichtlich
we hold ... self-evident	wir halten ... für selbstverständlich
to endow [inˈdau]	ausstatten
Creator [kri:ˈeitə]	Schöpfer *(Gott)*
certain [ˈsə:tn]	bestimmt
inalienable [inˈeiljənəbl]	unveräußerlich
pursuit (of) [pəˈsju:t]	Streben (nach)
happiness [ˈhæpinis]	Glück(seligkeit)
to secure [siˈkjuə]	sichern
to institute [ˈinstitju:t]	einsetzen
man	Mensch
to derive [diˈraiv]	herleiten
just	gerecht
powers	(Macht)Befugnisse
whenever	immer wenn
destructive [disˈtrʌktiv]	verderblich
end	Ziel
to alter [ˈɔ:ltə]	ändern
to abolish [əˈbɔliʃ]	abschaffen
proclamation	Verkündigung
encouragement [inˈkʌridʒmənt]	Ermutigung
Thomas Jefferson [ˈtɔməs ˈdʒefəsn]	*(3. Präsident der USA, 1743–1826)*

<The First Day in America>

immigrant [ˈimigrənt]	Einwanderer
unsuccessful [ˌʌnsəkˈsesful]	erfolglos
to come on	angehen
patch [æ]	Stelle, Fleck
rock [ɔ]	Felsen
to roll up [əu]	zusammenrollen
pillow [ˈpiləu]	Kopfkissen
to flash [æ]	leuchten, blitzen
to sit up	sich aufrichten
head lamp	Scheinwerfer
to cough [kɔf]	*hier:* stottern, spucken
to die [ai]	*hier:* stehenbleiben
more than an hour	über eine Stunde
to knock [nɔk]	*hier:* herumhantieren
hood [u]	Motorhaube
to close [kləuz]	schließen
to slide, slid, slid [ai, i, i]	rutschen
bench [bentʃ]	Bank
in between [biˈtwi:n]	dazwischen
to crank [kræŋk]	(Motor) anwerfen
to curse [kə:s]	verwünschen
to kick	(mit dem Fuß) treten, Fußtritte versetzen
radiator [ˈreidieitə]	Kühler
Model T [ˈmɔdl ˈti:]	*(bekanntes Ford-modell)*
snort [ɔ:]	Schnauben
to run up	herbeilaufen
headlight [ˈhedlait]	Scheinwerfer
to thumb (through) [θʌm]	durchblättern
to turn to s.th. [ə:]	sich etwas zuwenden
it took him quite a time . . .	es kostete ihn eine ganze Menge Zeit
automobile [ˈɔ:təməbi:l]	Auto(mobil)
Georgian [ˈdʒɔ:dʒən]	georgisch, grusinisch
to get in	einsteigen
to take s.o. through the streets	jemanden durch die Straßen fahren
for that	dafür
to fall asleep [əˈsli:p]	einschlafen
to think to oneself	bei sich denken
about this	darüber
to change one's mind [ai]	seine Meinung ändern
Papashvily [ˌpʌpʌʃˈvili]	*(Familienname)*

Exercises

2. Fredericksburg [ˈfredriksbə:g]	*(Stadt in Virginia, USA)*
certainly	bestimmt
auxiliary [ɔ:gˈziljəri]	Hilfsverb
compound [ˈkɔmpaund]	zusammengesetzt
4. bookseller [ˈbukselə]	Buchhändler
7. hen [hen]	Huhn, Henne

6 A. The Gold Rush

1. Roberts [ˈrɔbəts]	*(Familienname)*
barber [ˈbɑ:bə]	Barbier
to wave [weiv]	*hier:* schwenken
listen to this!	hör dir das an!
to unfold [ˈʌnfəuld]	entfalten
American River	*(Nebenfluß des Sacramento in Kalifornien)*
sawmill [ˈsɔ:ˌmil]	Sägewerk
to deepen [ˈdi:pən]	ausschachten, vertiefen
carpenter [ˈkɑ:pintə]	Zimmermann
to abandon [əˈbændən]	verlassen, aufgeben
to desert [diˈzət]	verlassen, im Stich lassen
westward [ˈwestwəd]	westwärts, nach Westen
round	um . . . herum
to go overland	auf dem Landweg reisen
to be on	in Gang sein, *hier:* ausgebrochen sein
fortune [ˈfɔ:tʃən]	Vermögen
beard [ˈbiəd]	Bart
at two cents a beard	den Bart zu zwei Cent
Sally [ˈsæli]	*(weibl. Vorname)*

to that	dazu
counter	Ladentisch
(to be going) to be married	heiraten (wollen)
2. St. Joseph [ˈdʒəuzif]	*(Stadt am Missouri im Staate Missouri)*
early in March	Anfang März
to provide [prəˈvaid]	liefern
sufficient [səˈfiʃənt]	genügend, ausreichend
to rain cats and dogs	in Strömen gießen, „Bindfäden" regnen
to drench (to) [drentʃ]	durchnässen (bis auf)
skin [skin]	Haut
wet	feucht
disease [diˈzi:z]	Krankheit
fellow-traveller	Reisegefährte
half, *pl.* **halves**	die Hälfte
party	*hier:* Reisegesellschaft
to follow	verfolgen
unseen	unsichtbar
by	*hier:* bei
to aim [eim]	zielen
to sweat [swet]	schwitzen
Great Salt Lake [sɔ:lt]	*(Großer Salzsee, im W der USA)*
trap [træp]	Falle
pioneer [ˌpaiəˈniə]	Pionier
to struggle on	sich vorwärtskämpfen, sich weiterschleppen
sand [sænd]	Sand
wheel [wi:l]	(Wagen)Rad
dust [dʌst]	Staub, *hier:* feiner Sand
Sierra Mountains [ˈsiərə ˈmauntinz]	*(Gebirgszug im W der USA)*
to break down	zusammenbrechen
on leaving	bei der Abreise von
hardship [ˈha:dʃip]	Mühsal
3. lucky	glücklich
to be born lucky	als Glückspilz geboren sein
to dig (for) [dig]	graben (nach)
to strike a goldfield	auf Gold stoßen
claim [kleim]	Anrecht, *hier:* Landanteil
to settle [setl]	sich niederlassen
ideal [aiˈdiəl]	ideal
cattle [kætl]	Vieh
fruit growing	Obstanbau
corn [kɔ:n]	Getreide, (*am.* Mais)
to be filled with	wimmeln von
adventurer [ədˈventʃərə]	Abenteurer
to shrink (from) [ʃriŋk]	zurückschrecken (vor)
murder [ˈmə:də]	Mord
to leave home	von zu Hause fortgehen
straight away	sofort, auf der Stelle
Cape Horn [ˈkeip ˈhɔ:n]	Kap Hoorn *(Südspitze Südamerikas)*
rich	*hier:* fruchtbar
farmland [ˈfa:mlænd]	Ackerboden

<Picture Text>

gold-digger [ˈgəuldˌdigə]	Goldgräber

<B. The Great Migration>

migration [maiˈgreiʃən]	Wanderung
besides [biˈsaidz]	außer
colonization [ˌkɔlənaiˈzeiʃən]	Kolonisation
to include [inˈklu:d]	umfassen
Dutch *(pl.)*	Holländer
Scandinavian [ˌskændiˈneivjən]	Skandinavier
to take place	stattfinden
immigrant [ˈimigrənt]	Einwanderer
wave [weiv]	Welle
peak [pi:k]	Gipfel, Höhepunkt
1860's	die sechziger Jahre des 19. Jh.
arrival [əˈraivəl]	Ankömmling
immigration [imiˈgreiʃən]	Einwanderung
to dwindle [dwindl]	sinken, schrumpfen
considerable [kənˈsidərəbl]	beträchtlich
Italian [iˈtæljən]	Italiener
Finn [fin]	Finne
Wendy Hall [ˈwendi ˈhɔ:l]	*(Eigenname)*

<A Fight with a Bear>

fight [ai]	Kampf
to bed down	sich niederlegen, sich lagern
Cleve [kli:v]	*(männl. Vorname)*
awake [əˈweik]	wach
cover [ˈkʌvə]	Dach
lit [i]	erleuchtet
Lilith [ˈliliθ]	*(weibl. Vorname)*
to stretch out [stretʃ]	(sich) ausstrecken
sigh [sai]	Seufzer
breathing [ˈbri:ðiŋ]	Atmen
to turn over [ə:]	(sich) herumdrehen; umwerfen
to seek [i:]	suchen
comfortable [ˈkʌmfətəbl]	bequem
position [pəˈziʃən]	Lage
sound [au]	Geräusch
snort [ɔ:]	Schnauben
rifle [ai]	Gewehr
to continue [kənˈtinju]	andauern
to struggle [ʌ]	zappeln
picket pin [ˈpikit]	Pflock
to listen	horchen
instant [ˈinstənt]	Augenblick
stillness [ˈstilnis]	Stille
to rattle [æ]	klappern
to rear [riə]	sich aufbäumen
to plunge [plʌndʒ]	sich nach vorn werfen
to fight [ai]	sich herumschlagen mit
to roll out [əu]	hervorrollen
to rear up [riə]	sich aufrichten
rapid [ˈræpid]	schnell
to blind [ai]	blenden
flash [æ]	Mündungsfeuer
to lunge at [lʌndʒ]	losstürzen auf
paw [pɔ:]	Tatze
blow [əu]	Schlag
to tear off [tɛə]	abreißen
to knock down [nɔk]	zu Boden schlagen
lunge [lʌndʒ]	Stoß
to roll over	am Boden entlangrollen
to cling to [kliŋ]	festhalten
to crash [æ]	krachen
upward [ˈʌpwəd]	nach oben
belly [ˈbeli]	Bauch
to scramble to one's feet [ˈskræmbl]	sich aufrappeln
level [ˈlevl]	waagerecht
trigger [ˈtrigə]	Abzug *(Feuerwaffe)*
to click [i]	knacken
to miss fire [ˈfaiə]	versagen *(Gewehr)*
cartridge [ˈka:tridʒ]	Patrone
to back away	zurückweichen
to strain one's eyes [strein]	krampfhaft blicken
toward [təˈwɔ:d]	auf . . . hin
front [ʌ]	Vorder-
branch [a:]	Zweig, Ast
to blaze up [ei]	auflodern
weapon [ˈwepən]	Waffe
bullet [ˈbulit]	Gewehr-, Pistolenkugel
chest [tʃest]	Brust
centre [ˈsentə]	Mitte
for	denn
stomach [ˈstʌmək]	Magen
spine [ai]	Rückgrat
despite [disˈpait]	trotz
killing [ˈkiliŋ]	tödlich
. . . had it not been for that.	. . . wenn der (4. Schuß) nicht gewesen wäre.
Louis l'Amour [ˈlu:i laˈmuə]	*(Eigenname)*

Exercises

2. guitar [giˈta:]	Gitarre
tune [tju:n]	Melodie
Frisco = San Francisco [ˈfriskəu]	
lump [lʌmp]	Klumpen
washbowl [ˈwɔʃbəul]	Waschschüssel
4. determinative [diˈtə:minətiv]	determinativ, bestimmend
ox, *pl.* **oxen** [ɔks, ˈɔksən]	Ochse
7. predicate [ˈpredikit]	Prädikat
8. to interpret [inˈtə:prit]	verdolmetschen
interpreter [inˈtə:pritə]	Dolmetscher(in)

Vocabulary Revision: Money and Business

to earn money	Geld verdienen
to send s.o. a bill	jemandem eine Rechnung schicken
to pay a bill	eine Rechnung bezahlen
to be broke	„pleite“ sein
to owe s.o. money	jemandem Geld schulden
to borrow money	sich Geld borgen
to lend money to s.o.	jemandem Geld leihen
to go on a business trip	eine Geschäftsreise machen
to dictate a business letter	einen Geschäftsbrief diktieren
to receive a rise in salary	eine Gehaltserhöhung bekommen
to apply for a post	sich um eine Stellung bewerben
to be introduced to the director of the firm	dem Direktor der Firma vorgestellt werden
We are short of money.	Wir sind „knapp bei Kasse“.
He visited me on business.	Er besuchte mich geschäftlich.
a five-dollar job	Stellung mit 5 Dollar Tageslohn

7 A. Death of a President

1. to elect s.o. [iˈlekt]	jemanden wählen (zu)
anti-slavery [ˈænti]	gegen die Sklaverei eingestellt
to enter	*hier:* betreten
for a long time	lange Zeit
quarrel [ˈkwɔrəl]	Streit
to go on	(an)dauern
election [iˈlekʃən]	Wahl
strong	*hier:* entschieden
to act [ækt]	handeln
secession [siˈseʃən]	Lossagung, Abfall *(Sezession)*
Confederate States [kənˈfedərit]	Staatenbund, „die Konföderation“
Richmond [ˈritʃmənd]	*(Hauptstadt von Virginia, USA)*
to renounce [riˈnauns]	verzichten (auf)
abolition [ˌæbəˈliʃən]	Abschaffung
to separate from [ˈsepəreit]	(sich) trennen von
Confederate armies	die Truppen der Konföderation
from	von ... entfernt
turning point	Wendepunkt
Gettysburg [ˈgetizbə:g]	*(Stadt in Pennsylvania, USA)*
to abolish [əˈbɔliʃ]	abschaffen
2. to awaken to [əˈweikən]	erwachen von, bei
cannon-fire [ˈkænən]	Kanonendonner
Lee [li:]	*(General der Südstaaten im am. Sezessionskrieg)*
Grant [grɑ:nt]	*(General der Nordstaaten im am. Sezessionskrieg)*
reunification [ˌri:ju:nifiˈkeiʃən]	Wiedervereinigung
right of voting [ˈvəutiŋ]	Wahlrecht
John Wilkes Booth [ˈwilks ˈbu:ð]	*(Eigenname)*
Lewis Paine [ˈlu:is ˈpein]	*(Eigenname)*
to make a speech	eine Rede halten
fanatical [fəˈnætikəl]	fanatisch
supporter [səˈpɔ:tə]	Vertreter, Verfechter
born to be	geboren sein zu
mind	Gedanken *(pl.)*, Herz
to carry in one's mind	(in Gedanken) mit sich herumtragen
3. box	Loge

state box	Ehrenloge
knob [nɔb]	Knopf, Griff
facing	zugewandt
rocking chair [ˈrɔkiŋ]	Schaukelstuhl
two other	noch zwei
bodyguard [ˈbɔdigɑ:d]	Leibwache
major [ˈmeidʒə]	Major
Rathbone [ˈræθbəun]	*(Familienname)*
fiancée [fiˈɔŋsei]	Verlobte *(sg.)*
joke [dʒəuk]	Witz, Spaß
trigger [ˈtrigə]	Abzug *(Feuerwaffe)*
to pull the trigger	abdrücken
sound [saund]	Geräusch, Klang
to break	*hier:* zerplatzen lassen
paper bag	Papiertüte
in the midst of [midst]	inmitten
laughter [ˈlɑ:ftə]	Gelächter
towards	auf
chest [tʃest]	Brust
to rock [rɔk]	schaukeln
to grapple with [ˈgræpl]	kämpfen, ringen mit
edge [edʒ]	Rand
wing [wiŋ]	Seitenkulisse
to stop	aufhalten
to pierce [ˈpiəs]	durchdringen
scream [skri:m]	Schrei
to shoot, shot, shot	erschießen
filled with	erfüllt von
fright [frait]	Schrecken, Entsetzen
wound [wu:nd]	Verletzung, Wunde
mortal [ˈmɔ:tl]	tödlich
it is impossible for him ...	er kann unmöglich ...
to meet	*hier:* finden
murderer [ˈmə:dərə]	Mörder
to corner s.o.	jemanden stellen
Virginian [vəˈdʒinjən]	virginisch
to carry on	weiter-, fortführen
class	(Gesellschafts) Schicht
uneducated	ungebildet
citizen [ˈsitizn]	(Staats)Bürger
to continue	(fort)dauern, weitergehen

<Picture Text>

assassination [əˌsæsiˈneiʃən]	Ermordung

<B. What is New York>

Dutch *(pl.)*	Holländer
trading post	Handelsniederlassung
celestial [siˈlestjəl]	himmlisch
burial [ˈberiəl]	Begräbnis
New Amsterdam [ˈæmstəˈdæm]	Neu-Amsterdam *(ursprüngl. Name von New York)*
to rename [ˈri:ˈneim]	umbenennen
federal [ˈfedərəl]	Bundes-
cosmopolitan [ˌkɔzməˈpɔlitən]	Welt-
to include [inˈklu:d]	umfassen
numerous [ˈnju:mərəs]	zahlreich
Italian	Italiener
Pole [pəul]	Pole
food	Speise
daily newspaper	Tageszeitung
financial [faiˈnænʃəl]	Geld-, Finanz-
Wall Street	*(Banken- und Börsenstraße in New York)*
banking house [ˈbæŋkiŋ]	Bank(haus)
to be situated [ˈsitjueitid]	liegen
to dominate [ˈdɔmineit]	beherrschen
home	*hier:* Sitz
permanent [ˈpə:mənənt]	ständig
headquarters [ˈhedˈkwɔ:təz]	Hauptquartier
to design [diˈzain]	entwerfen
Le Corbusier [kərbüˈzje]	*(berühmter franz. Architekt, 1887–1965)*
acre [ˈeikə]	*(engl. Flächenmaß, 4047 qm)*
to overlook	überblicken
East River	*(Wasserstraße zwischen Long Island und Manhattan)*

<Night Movement – New York>

night	nächtlich, Nacht
to cool [u:]	kühlen
noon [u:]	Mittag
skyline	Horizont, Silhouette
a long way off	weit entfernt
dancer [ˈdɑ:nsə]	Tänzer
singer [ˈsiŋə]	Sänger
Carl Sandburg [ˈkɑ:l ˈsænbə:g]	*(am. Dichter, 1878–1967)*

<Carl Sandburg: My First Payday>

Illinois [ˌiliˈnɔi]	*(Staat im Mittelwesten der USA)*
Swedish [ˈswi:diʃ]	schwedisch
immigrant [ˈimigrənt]	Einwanderer
job [dʒɔb]	Stelle
pants [æ]	lange (Herren)Hose
Callender & Rodine [ˈkælindər‿ən ˈrəudain]	*(Firmenname)*
to guess [ges]	schätzen
moustache [məsˈtɑ:ʃ]	Schnurrbart
wide [ai]	breit
stomach [ˈstʌmək]	Magen
bay-window [ˈbeiwindəu]	Erkerfenster, *hier:* dicker Bauch
rosy [ˈrəuzi]	rosig
through [θru:]	bis einschließlich
to dig in [i]	sich energisch an die Arbeit machen
board [ɔ:]	Brett
dirt [ə:]	Schmutz
sidewalk [ˈsaidwɔ:k]	Gehweg *(am.)*
basketful [ˈbɑ:skitful]	Korb(voll)
to join [dʒɔin]	sich gesellen zu
sweepings [ˈswi:piŋz]	Kehricht
layer [ˈleiə]	Schicht
to blow [əu]	wehen
look [u]	Ausdruck
as though [ðəu]	als ob
thanks	danke

Exercises

2. Kentucky [kenˈtʌki]	*(Staat im O der USA)*
Indiana [ˌindiˈænə]	*(Staat im Mittelwesten der USA)*
New Salem [ˈseilem]	*(kleine Stadt im Staate Indiana)*
4. consecration [ˌkɔnsiˈkreiʃən]	Weihe
cemetery [ˈsemitri]	Friedhof
blind [blaind]	blind
to replace (by) [riˈpleis]	ersetzen (durch)
period [ˈpiəriəd]	Zeitraum

8 A. The Man who put America on Wheels

as	als
minimum [ˈminiməm]	Minimum, Mindest-
day's work	tägliche Arbeitszeit
from . . . to	von . . . auf
industrialist [inˈdʌstriəlist]	Industrieller
present	gegenwärtig, jetzig
rate [reit]	(Lohn)Satz
to queue [kju:]	anstehen, Schlange stehen
Detroit [dəˈtrɔit]	*(Stadt im Staate Michigan im NO der USA)*
freight train	Güterzug
to cling to [kliŋ]	sich (an)klammern an
buffer [ˈbʌfə]	Puffer *(Zug)*
in the hope of	in der Hoffnung auf
five-dollar job	„fünf-Dollar-Stellung" *(Stellung mit 5 Dollar Tageslohn)*
to close	schließen
there were	es gab
vacancy [ˈveikənsi]	freie (Arbeits)Stelle
police	Polizei
crowds	Menschenmassen
hose [həuz]	Spritzenschlauch
fire hose	Feuerwehrschlauch
Henry Ford	*(am. Großindustrieller, 1863–1947)*
to roll [rəul]	rollen
to set the ball rolling	den Stein ins Rollen bringen

selling price	Verkaufspreis
buying power	Kaufkraft
to depend on [di'pend]	abhängig sein von
principle ['prinsəpl]	Grundsatz, Prinzip
2. horseless	ohne Pferde, nicht von Pferden gezogen
Gottlieb Daimler	*(dt. Ingenieur, 1834–1900)*
Carl Friedrich Benz	*(dt. Ingenieur, 1844–1929)*
inventor [in'ventə]	Erfinder
anybody	jeder(mann)
automobile ['ɔ:təməbi:l]	Auto(mobil)
car	*hier:* Wagentyp
model ['mɔdl]	Modell, Konstruktion
to fulfil [ful'fil]	erfüllen
assembly line [ə'sembli]	Fließband
to move on	sich weiterbewegen, vorrücken
to assemble [ə'sembl]	versammeln, *hier:* bereitstellen
screw [skru:]	Schraube
as	während
to cut	kürzen
to require [ri'kwaiə]	erfordern, brauchen
construction [kən'strʌkʃən]	Bau, Konstruktion
3. affectionate [ə'fekʃnit]	liebevoll
tin [tin]	Blech-
Lizzy ['lizi]	*(Kurzform für Elizabeth)*
Tin Lizzy	„Blechliesel"
to compare	sich vergleichen (lassen)
sunshine ['sʌnʃain]	Sonnenschein
provided	vorausgesetzt
ugly ['ʌgli]	häßlich
speedometer [spi'dɔmitə]	Geschwindigkeitsmesser, Tachometer
cushion ['kuʃən]	Kissen
cap	Verschluß, Kappe
to poke [pəuk]	stecken
to accuse (of) [ə'kju:z]	(einer Sache) beschuldigen
failure ['feiljə]	Versagen
bathtub ['bɑ:θtʌb]	Badewanne
maker	Hersteller, Fabrikant
above all	vor allem
General Motors	*(berühmte am. Automobilfirma)*
attractive [ə'træktiv]	anziehend, *hier:* ansprechend
4. outmoded ['aut'məudid]	veraltet, überholt
sales	*hier:* Verkaufsziffern
plant [plɑ:nt]	(Fabrik)Anlage
to remake ['ri:'meik]	erneuern, *hier:* umstellen
to invent [in'vent]	erfinden
brake [breik]	Bremse
windscreen ['windskri:n]	Windschutzscheibe
windscreen wiper	Scheibenwischer
buyer	Käufer
empire	(Welt)Reich
to march on	fortschreiten
to adopt [ə'dɔpt]	*hier:* übernehmen

<Picture Text>

Edsel Ford ['edsəl 'fɔ:d]	*(Sohn von Henry Ford, gest. 1943)*

B. On a Motor Trip

to give s.o. a lift	jemanden (im Auto) mitnehmen
to drop s.o.	jemanden absetzen
to pick s.o. up	jemanden mitnehmen, abholen
to ride in the back	hinten sitzen
make	Marke
second-hand	gebraucht
top speed	Höchstgeschwindigkeit
gear [giə]	Gang *(Auto)*
to change gear	den Gang schalten
to put on the brakes	die Bremsen anziehen, bremsen
tyre ['taiə]	Reifen
flat tyre	Reifenpanne
to be out of petrol	kein Benzin (mehr) haben
gallon ['gælən]	*(engl. Raummaß, 4,55 l)*

oil	Ölstand
pint [paint]	*(engl. Raummaß, 0,568 l)*
pressure [ˈpreʃə]	Druck
the other day	neulich
smash [smæʃ]	Zusammenstoß
to bump into [bʌmp]	zusammenstoßen mit
bend [bend]	Kurve
to fine for [fain]	bestrafen, verurteilen wegen
speeding	Geschwindigkeits-übertretung

<American and British English>

stress [e]	Betonung
next to last	vorletzt(er, e, es)
syllable [ˈsiləbl]	Silbe
laboratory [ləˈbɔrətəri]	Laboratorium
spelling [ˈspeliŋ]	Rechtschreibung
to civilize [ˈsivilaiz]	zivilisieren
to organize [ˈɔ:gənaiz]	organisieren
to simplify [ˈsimplifai]	vereinfachen
to mean [i:]	bezeichnen
common [ˈkɔmən]	(allgemein) gebräuchlich
baggage [ˈbægidʒ]	Gepäck *(am.)*
truck [ʌ]	Lastkraftwagen *(am.)*
sidewalk [ˈsaidwɔ:k]	Gehsteig *(am.)*
gas [æ]	Benzin *(am.)*
cookie [u]	Keks *(am.)*
vacation [vəˈkeiʃən]	(Schul)Ferien, Urlaub *(am.)*
fall [ɔ:]	Herbst *(am.)*
streetcar [ˈstri:tkɑ:]	Straßenbahn(wagen) *(am.)*
guy [gai]	Bursche *(am.)*
doorman [ˈdɔ:mæn]	Pförtner, Portier *(am.)*
flat [æ]	Wohnung *(engl.)*
apartment [əˈpɑ:tmənt]	Wohnung *(am.)*
chemist's [ˈkemists]	Apotheke *(engl.)*
drug store [ˈdrʌgstɔ:]	Apotheke *(am.)*
bill [i]	(Geld)Schein *(am.)*
check [e]	Rechnung *(am.)* [*(am.)*
candies [ˈkændiz]	Süßigkeiten, Bonbons
elevator [ˈeliveitə]	Fahrstuhl, Aufzug *(am.)*
closet [ˈklɔzit]	Schrank *(am.)*
mailman [ˈmeilmæn]	Postbote, Briefträger *(am.)*

Exercises

1. heavy	*hier:* dicht
2. bonnet [ˈbɔnit]	Motorhaube *(engl.)*
hood [hud]	Motorhaube *(am.)*
windshield [ˈwindʃi:ld]	Windschutzscheibe *(am.)*
tire [ˈtaiə]	Reifen *(am.)*
wing [wiŋ]	Kotflügel *(engl.)*
fender [ˈfendə]	Kotflügel *(am.)*
boot [bu:t]	Kofferraum *(engl.)*
trunk [trʌŋk]	Kofferraum *(am.)*
4. prepositional [ˌprepəˈziʃnl]	präpositional
5. publicity [pʌbˈlisiti]	Reklame
slogan [ˈsləugən]	Werbespruch

Vocabulary Revision: Cars

to buy a car on hire-purchase	einen Wagen auf Abzahlung kaufen
to buy a second-hand car	einen Gebrauchtwagen kaufen
to take driving-lessons	Fahrstunden nehmen
to take s.o. for a ride	jemanden zu einer Spazierfahrt mitnehmen
to sit (ride) in the front	vorn sitzen
to sit (ride) in the back	hinten sitzen
to pick s.o. up with the car	jemanden mit dem Wagen abholen
to obey the traffic rules	sich nach den Verkehrsregeln richten
to drop s.o.	jemanden absetzen
to use a seat-belt	einen Sicherheitsgurt benutzen
to change gear	den Gang schalten

to drive at top speed	mit Höchstgeschwindigkeit fahren
to bump into a lorry	mit einem Lastwagen zusammenstoßen
to be fined for speeding	wegen Geschwindigkeitsübertretung bestraft werden
to look at the speedometer	auf den Geschwindigkeitsmesser sehen
to be out of petrol	kein Benzin mehr haben
to put on the brakes	die Bremsen anziehen
to stop the car	den Wagen anhalten
to have a flat tyre	eine Reifenpanne haben
The windscreen wiper is out of order.	Der Scheibenwischer ist nicht in Ordnung.
to look at the car body	sich die Karosserie ansehen
to offer a car for sale	einen Wagen zum Verkauf anbieten
The selling-price was too high.	Der Verkaufspreis war zu hoch.
Which make do you prefer?	Welche Automarke bevorzugen Sie?
car maker	Autofabrikant
exhaust fumes	Auspuffgase
motorway	Autobahn

<America and the Americans>

The Many Faces of America

joined together [dʒɔind]	verbunden
Mexico [ˈmeksikəu]	Mexiko
to range [reindʒ]	reichen
arctic [ˈɑ:ktik]	arktisch
Florida [ˈflɔridə]	*(Staat im SO der USA)*
snowy [əu]	schneebedeckt
abundance [əˈbʌndəns]	Überfluß
industrialized [inˈdʌstriəlaizd]	industrialisiert
automation [ˌɔ:təˈmeiʃən]	Automation
entirely [inˈtaiəli]	völlig
automatic [ˌɔ:təˈmætik]	automatisch
human labour [ˈhju:mən ˈleibə]	menschliche Arbeit
advanced [ədˈvɑ:nst]	fortgeschritten
pushbutton [ˈpuʃˌbʌtn]	(Druck)Knopf
Michigan [ˈmiʃigən]	*(Staat im N der USA)*
process [ˈprəuses]	Arbeitsgang
human [ˈhju:mən]	Mensch
to employ [imˈplɔi]	beschäftigen
to supervise [ˈsju:pəvaiz]	überwachen
machinery *(pl.)* [məˈʃi:nəri]	Maschinen
remote control [riˈmount kənˈtrəul]	Fernsteuerung
immigration [ˌimiˈgreiʃən]	Einwanderung
wave [ei]	Welle
total [ˈtəutl]	Gesamt-
is	*hier:* beträgt
melting pot [ˈmeltiŋpɔt]	Schmelztiegel
immigrant [ˈimigrənt]	Einwanderer

The Americans

The Melting Pot

Dutch [ʌ]	Holländer
to establish [isˈtæbliʃ]	gründen
trading post [ˈtreidiŋpəust]	Handelsniederlassung
New Amsterdam [ˈnju: ˈæmstəˈdæm]	Neu Amsterdam *(ursprünglicher Name von New York)*
Swedish [ˈswi:diʃ]	schwedisch
Delaware [ˈdeləwɛə]	*(Staat im O der USA)*

Huguenot [ˈhju:gənɔt]	Hugenotte
South Carolina [ˌkærəˈlainə]	*(Staat im SO der USA)*
to make up	ausmachen
Italian [iˈtæljən]	Italiener
Scandinavian [ˌskændiˈneivjən]	Skandinavier
Finn [fin]	Finne
fugitive [ˈfju:dʒitiv]	Flüchtling
political [pəˈlitikəl]	politisch
oppression [əˈpreʃən]	Unterdrückung
to overcome [ˌəuvəˈkʌm]	überwinden
to solve [ɔ]	lösen
factor [ˈfæktə]	Faktor, Umstand
to fuse [fju:z]	verschmelzen
New Englander [ˈiŋgləndə]	Neuengländer *(Bewohner einer der nordöstlichen Staaten der USA)*
Virginian [vəˈdʒinjən]	Virginier
rapid [ˈræpid]	schnell, rasch

The Indians and the Negroes

racial [ˈreiʃəl]	rassisch
minority [maiˈnɔriti]	Minderheit
to integrate [ˈintigreit]	eingliedern
to shrink to [i]	zusammenschrumpfen auf
desperate [ˈdesparit]	verzweifelt
way of life	Lebensweise
to keep to oneself	für sich bleiben
reservation [ˌrezəˈveiʃən]	Reservat, Schutzgebiet
to provide [prəˈvaid]	zur Verfügung stellen
to vote [əu]	wählen
talented [ˈtæləntid]	begabt
job [dʒɔb]	Stellung
to put up with	sich abfinden mit
poor [puə]	schlecht, unzulänglich
housing accomodation [ˈhauziŋ əˌkɔməˈdeiʃən]	Wohnverhältnisse
Federal Government [ˈfedərəl ˈgʌvənmənt]	Bundesregierung
to show oneself to ...	zeigen, daß
racial discrimination [ˈreiʃəl disˌkrimiˈneiʃən]	Rassendiskriminierung

Politics and the State

politics [ˈpɔlitiks]	Politik
commander-in-chief [kəˈmɑ:ndərinˈtʃi:f]	Oberbefehlshaber
powers [ˈpauəz]	Machtbefugnisse
considerable [kənˈsidərəbl]	beträchtlich
to negotiate [nɪˈgəuʃieit]	verhandeln über
to recommend [ˌrekəˈmend]	vorschlagen
to veto [ˈvi:təu]	Zustimmung verweigern für
bill [i]	Gesetz(entwurf)
presidency [ˈprezidənsi]	Präsidentenamt
party [ˈpɑ:ti]	Partei
Republicans [riˈpʌblikənz]	Republikaner *(am. Partei)*
Democrats [ˈdeməkræts]	Demokraten *(am. Partei)*
presidential [ˌpreziˈdenʃəl]	Präsidentschafts-
election campaign [iˈlekʃən kæmˈpein]	Wahlkampf
battle [æ]	Kampf
personality [ˌpə:səˈnæliti]	Persönlichkeit
policy, policies [ˈpɔlisi]	Politik
Senate [ˈsenət]	Senat
House of Representatives [ˌrepriˈzentətivz]	Repräsentantenhaus
to be made up of	sich zusammensetzen aus
to approve [əˈpru:v]	billigen
to reject [riˈdʒekt]	ablehnen
appointment [əˈpɔintmənt]	Beschluß
to suggest [səˈdʒest]	vorschlagen
taxation law [tækˈseiʃən]	Steuergesetz
to originate [əˈridʒineit]	seinen Ursprung haben
to be bound [au]	verpflichtet sein
to observe [əbˈzə:v]	einhalten
Federal [ˈfedərəl]	Bundes-
to manage [ˈmænidʒ]	führen
affair [əˈfɛə]	Angelegenheit

public health [ˈpʌblik ˈhelθ]	öffentliche Gesundheitspflege
punishment [ˈpʌniʃmənt]	Bestrafung
criminal [ˈkriminəl]	Verbrecher

Power and Responsibility

to grow [əu]	emporwachsen
interference [ˌintəˈfiərəns]	Einmischung
slogan [ˈsləugən]	Wahlspruch
isolationism [ˌaisəˈleiʃənizm]	Isolationismus
to avoid [əˈvɔid]	vermeiden
alliance [əˈlaiəns]	Bündnis
to take [ei]	vornehmen, ergreifen
measure [ˈmeʒə]	Maßnahme
interest [ˈintrist]	Interesse
Philippines [ˈfilipi:nz]	Philippinen *(Inselgruppe im Pazifik)*
to occupy [ˈɔkjupai]	besetzen
Hawaiian Islands [hɑ:ˈwaiiən ˈailəndz]	Hawaii-Inseln *(im nördlichen Pazifischen Ozean)*
Panama Canal [ˈpænəmɑ: kəˈnæl]	Panamakanal
decisive [diˈsaisiv]	entscheidend
to withdraw [wiðˈdrɔ:]	(sich) zurückziehen
event [iˈvent]	Ereignis, Geschehnis
Asia [ˈeiʃə]	Asien
concept [ˈkɔnsept]	Vorstellung, Gedanke
ruins [ˈruinz]	Trümmer
leadership [ˈli:dəʃip]	Führung
to pass to [ɑ:]	übergehen auf
to turn one's back on s.th.	einer Sache den Rükken kehren
characteristically [ˌkæriktəˈristikəli]	charakteristischerweise
to adapt oneself to [əˈdæpt]	sich anpassen an
Marshall Aid Plan [ˈmɑ:ʃəl ˈeid ˈplæn]	Marshallplan *(am. Wirtschaftshilfe für Westeuropa)*
shattered [æ]	zerrüttet
economy [iˈkɔnəmi]	Wirtschaft
burden [ə:]	Bürde, Last
to confine to [kənˈfain]	beschränken auf
material [məˈtiəriəl]	materiell
post-war [ˈpəust]	Nachkriegs-
reconstruction [ˈri:kənsˈtrʌkʃən]	Wiederaufbau-
to group [u:]	gruppieren
rival [ˈraivəl]	rivalisierend
Communist [ˈkɔmjunist]	kommunistisch
Soviet Union [ˈsəuviət ˈju:njən]	Sowjetunion

Important Dates

Columbus [kəˈlʌmbəs]	Kolumbus
Declaration of Independence [ˌdekləˈreiʃən‿əv‿indiˈpendəns]	Unabhängigkeitserklärung
drive [ai]	Vorstoß, Zug
Wright brothers [rait]	Gebrüder Wright
World Economic Depression [ˌi:kəˈnɔmik diˈpreʃən]	Weltwirtschaftskrise
atom bomb [ˈætəm ˈbɔm]	Atombombe
to drop [ɔ]	abwerfen
Hiroshima [ˌhirɔˈʃi:mə]	*(Stadt in Japan)*
John F. Kennedy [ˈkenidi]	*(Präsident der USA, 1917–1963)*

Important People

important [imˈpɔ:tənt]	bedeutend

George Washington

planter [ɑ:]	Pflanzer
to emigrate [ˈemigreit]	auswandern
to serve [ə:]	dienen
wisdom [ˈwizdəm]	Weisheit
character [ˈkæriktə]	Charakter
respect [risˈpekt]	Achtung
countryman [ˈkʌntrimæn]	Landsmann

Abraham Lincoln

to study law [lɔ:]	Jura studieren
spare time [εə]	Freizeit
lawyer [ˈlɔ:jə]	Rechtsanwalt

plantation [plænˈteiʃən]	Plantage, Pflanzung
to rebel [riˈbel]	sich empören
to re-unite [ˈriːjuːˈnait]	wiedervereinigen
to set free	freilassen

Walt Whitman

Walt Whitman [wɔːlt ˈwitmən]	*(am. Dichter, 1819–1892)*
literature [ˈlitəritʃə]	Literatur
style [ai]	Stil
to influence [ˈinfluəns]	beeinflussen
writer [ˈraitə]	Schriftsteller
to draw [ɔː]	beziehen
inspiration [ˌinspiˈreiʃən]	Inspiration
to reflect [riˈflekt]	widerspiegeln
restless [ˈrestlis]	ruhelos
vision [ˈviʒən]	Vision
youthful [ˈjuːθful]	jugendlich
sinewy [ˈsinjui]	kraftvoll

Thomas A. Edison

Thomas A. Edison [ˈtɔməs ˈedisn]	*(am. Erfinder, 1847–1931)*
long-distance-train [ˈlɔŋ ˌdistəns ˈtrein]	Fernschnellzug
telegraph operator [ˈteligrɑːf ˈɔpəreitə]	Telegraphist
to set up	gründen
electrical apparatus [iˈlektrikəl ˌæpəˈreitəs]	elektrische Geräte
series [ˈsiəriːz]	Reihe
invention [inˈvenʃən]	Erfindung
to take out	erwirken *(Patent)*
patent [ˈpeitənt]	Patent
electric light bulb [iˈlektrik ˈlait ˈbʌlb]	Glühbirne
gramophone [ˈgræməfəun]	Grammophon

John D. Rockefeller

John D. Rockefeller [ˈrɔkifelə]	*(am. Ölmillionär, 1839–1937)*
professional [prəˈfeʃənl]	beruflich
assistant [əˈsistənt]	Hilfs-
book-keeper	Buchhalter
multi-millionaire [ˈmʌltimiljəˈnɛə]	vielfacher Millionär
ruthless [ˈruːθlis]	rücksichtslos
method [ˈmeθəd]	Methode
competition [ˌkɔmpiˈtiʃən]	Konkurrenz
Standard Oil Company [ˈstændəd ˈɔil ˈkʌmpəni]	*(größter Erdölkonzern der Welt)*
refinery [riˈfainəri]	Raffinerie
to form [ɔː]	*hier:* umwandeln
trust [ʌ]	Trust, Konzern
association [əˌsəusiˈeiʃən]	Verband
to compete [kəmˈpiːt]	konkurrieren
to dissolve [diˈzɔlv]	auflösen
to retire [riˈtaiə]	sich zurückziehen
vast [ɑː]	gewaltig
to own [əu]	besitzen
ore-fields [ɔː]	Erzvorkommen
coal-fields [əu]	Kohlevorkommen
bank [æ]	Bank(haus)
to make into	machen zu
popularity [ˌpɔpjuˈlæriti]	Beliebtheit
gift [i]	Zuwendung, Schenkung
research [riˈsəːtʃ]	Forschung
to establish [isˈtæbliʃ]	gründen
foundation [faunˈdeiʃən]	Stiftung
benefit [ˈbenifit]	Nutzen
to fight [ai]	bekämpfen
plague [pleig]	Plage

John F. Kennedy

navy [ˈneivi]	Kriegsmarine
ability [əˈbiliti]	Fähigkeit
ambition [æmˈbiʃən]	Ehrgeiz
to the front [ʌ]	in den Vordergrund
political [pəˈlitikəl]	politisch
Democratic Party [ˌdeməˈkrætik]	Demokratische Partei *(am. Partei)*
narrow [ˈnærəu]	knapp
to secure [siˈkjuə]	sichern
civil right [ˈsivl]	Bürgerrecht
to ban [æ]	verbieten
use [juːs]	Gebrauch

nuclear weapon ['nju:kliə 'wepən]	Kernwaffe
to raise [ei]	erwecken
relation [ri'leiʃən]	Beziehung
to realize ['riəlaiz]	verwirklichen
in office ['ɔfis]	im Amt
assassin [ə'sæsin]	Meuchelmörder
Dallas ['dæləs]	*(Stadt in Texas, USA)*

Anecdotes

1. anecdote ['ænikdəut]	Anekdote
Christopher Columbus ['kristəfə kə'lʌmbəs]	*(Entdecker Amerikas, 1436–1506)*
Red Indian	Indianer
2. in fact [æ]	tatsächlich
how is ... getting on?	wie geht es ... ?

9 A. From Prison Camp to Sovereign State

prison camp	Gefangenenlager
sovereign ['sɔvrin]	souverän
1. from earliest times	seit frühester Zeit
legendary ['ledʒəndəri]	sagenhaft, legendär
unknown	unbekannt
shore [ʃɔ:]	Küste, Strand
not until	erst, *hier:* nicht bis zu
they found it a wilderness	sie fanden es als Wildnis vor
black-skinned [skind]	dunkelhäutig
aborigines *(pl.)* [,æbə'ridʒini:z]	Ureinwohner
primitive ['primitiv]	primitiv
Dutch *(pl.)*	Holländer
little to interest them	wenig, was sie interessierte
Captain Cook	*(brit. Weltumsegler, 1728–79)*
bound for [baund]	unterwegs nach, *hier:* mit Kurs auf
convict ['kɔnvikt]	Sträfling
criminal ['kriminl]	Verbrecher
to sentence ['sentəns]	verurteilen
transportation [,trænspɔ:'teiʃən]	Verbannung, Deportation
for life	lebenslänglich
penal ['pi:nl]	Straf-
harsh [hɑ:ʃ]	hart, streng
overcrowded	überfüllt
common	üblich, alltäglich
crime [kraim]	Verbrechen, strafbare Handlung
theft [θeft]	Diebstahl
2. Phillip ['filip]	*(Familienname)*
expedition	Expedition, Unternehmen
illusion [i'lu:ʒən]	Illusion, falsche Vorstellung
to lie ahead	bevorstehen
to be determined [di'tə:mind]	entschlossen sein
to carry out	aus-, durchführen
to maintain [men'tein]	behaupten, erhalten
existence [ig'zistəns]	Leben, Existenz
struggle for existence	Kampf ums Dasein
guard [gɑ:d]	Wache, Bewacher
experienced [iks'piəriənst]	erfahren
to be lost	verlorengehen
scarce [skɛəs]	knapp
crop [krɔp]	Feldfrucht, Getreide
food	Nahrung
plant [plɑ:nt]	Pflanze
curious ['kjuəriəs]	seltsam, merkwürdig
for the first few years	während der ersten paar Jahre
nothing more	nichts weiter
to be better off	besser dran sein
supply [sə'plai]	Vorrat
two years' supply	Vorrat für zwei Jahre
to save from	retten vor
starvation [stɑ:'veiʃən]	Hungertod, Verhungern
3. sentence	Strafe, Urteil
to have finished one's sentence	seine Strafe verbüßt haben
to grow up	entstehen
explorer [iks'plɔ:rə]	Forscher, Forschungsreisender

Blue Mountains	Blaue Berge *(Gebirgszug an der SO-Küste Australiens)*
to establish [is'tæbliʃ]	gründen, errichten
to stop	*hier:* einstellen
to turn to	sich richten auf
in full swing [swiŋ]	in vollem Gang, Schwung
fantastic [fæn'tæstik]	phantastisch
nugget ['nʌgit]	Goldklumpen
man	Mensch
they waited for men to come	sie warteten darauf, daß Menschen kämen
worth of gold	Gold im Werte von
to take from the earth	aus der Erde holen
4. from that time	*hier:* mit dieser Zeit
telegraph ['teligrɑ:f]	Telegraph
widely-separated	weitverstreut, weit auseinanderliegend
close [kləus]	nahe
to put behind one	hinter sich lassen
to take to	sich verlegen auf
to unite [ju:'nait]	sich zusammenschließen, vereinigen
to take one's place with	seinen Platz einnehmen neben
self-governing	selbständig, sich selbst regierend
member	Glied

<Picture Text>

King George III [dʒɔ:dʒ]	*(König von England, 1738–1820)*

B. Paying a Visit

to pay a visit	einen Besuch machen
Gordon ['gɔ:dn]	*(Familienname)*
may I see ...?	kann ich ... sprechen?
to call	vorsprechen, einen kurzen Besuch machen
to intrude [in'tru:d]	stören
how do you do?	*(allgem. Begrüßungsformel in England)*
we are glad ...	wir freuen uns, wir sind erfreut, ...
will you have ...,	nehmen Sie ...?
I love it	ich bin begeistert davon
fascinating ['fæsineitiŋ]	faszinierend, hinreißend
I hope so	ich hoffe es
would you care ...?	möchten Sie gern, interessiert es Sie ...?
to wash one's hands	*(wird gebraucht für:* zur Toilette gehen)
whenever	wann immer, immer wenn

<A Ship Sails up to Bideford>

Bideford ['bidifəd]	*(kl. Hafenstadt in Devon)*
breeze [bri:z]	Brise
mast [ɑ:]	Mast
seas [i:]	Wellen(berge)
Devon ['devn]	*(Grafschaft im südwestlichen England)*
misty ['misti]	neblig
hold [əu]	Schiffs-, Laderaum
Jaffa ['dʒæfə]	*(Hafenstadt in Israel)*
date [deit]	Dattel
China ['tʃainə]	China
bale [ei]	Ballen
dye [dai]	*hier:* gefärbte Stoffe
to sparkle [ɑ:]	funkeln
feather ['feðə]	Feder
snake [ei]	Schlange
to glide [ai]	gleiten
gull [ʌ]	Möwe
hull [ʌ]	Rumpf *(Schiff)*
Herbert Asquith ['hə:bət 'æskwiθ]	*(engl. Dichter)*

<The Lights on the Islands>

to hump [hʌmp]	sich buckelartig erheben
to reflect [ri'flekt]	widerspiegeln
steady ['stedi]	gleichbleibend
gleam [i:]	Schimmer
Laura ['lɔ:rə]	*(weibl. Vorname)*
to slide, slid, slid [ai, i]	gleiten

hump [ʌ]	kl. Hügel, Buckel
to recede [riˈsi:d]	zurückweichen
to obscure [əbˈskjuə]	verdunkeln
secret [ˈsi:krit]	verschwiegen
self-contained [ˈselfkənˈteind]	eigenständig, unabhängig
off duty [ˈdju:ti]	dienstfrei
gaze [geiz]	(starrender) Blick
leper colony [ˈlepə]	Aussätzigen-, Leprakolonie
penal settlement [ˈpi:nl]	Strafkolonie
sin [i]	Sünde
V. Sackville-West [ˈsækvil ˈwest]	*(engl. Schriftstellerin, 1892–1962)*
signpost [ˈsainpəust]	Wegweiser

Exercises

2. verbal [ˈvə:bəl]	verbal
to present [priˈzent]	schenken, überreichen
stress [stres]	Betonung
syllable [ˈsiləbl]	Silbe
3. to project [prəˈdʒekt]	projizieren
produce [ˈprɔdju:s]	Erzeugnis
increase [ˈinkri:s]	Zunahme
to rebel [riˈbel]	rebellieren, sich empören
6. prefix [ˈpri:fiks]	Vorsilbe
7. to be not fortunate [ˈfɔ:tʃnit]	kein Glück haben
8. Canberra [ˈkænbərə]	*(Bundeshauptstadt von Australien)*

10 A. Journey's End

1. total [təutl]	Gesamt-
is	*hier:* beträgt
of these	davon
coloured people	Farbige
original [əˈridʒənl]	Ur-, ursprünglich
the West Indies [ˈindiz]	Westindien *(die Inseln Mittelamerikas)*
plantation [plænˈteiʃən]	Pflanzung, Plantage
Jamaica [dʒəˈmeikə]	Jamaika
to set free	freilassen
no matter	gleichgültig, ganz gleich
may	mag
standard of living	Lebensstandard
to cause	veranlassen
to immigrate [ˈimigreit]	einwandern
the 1950s	die fünfziger Jahre *(des 20. Jhd.)*
living conditions	Lebensbedingungen
2. immigrant [ˈimigrənt]	Einwanderer
great-grandson [ˈgrænsʌn]	Urenkel
to do well	Erfolg haben, gut vorwärts kommen
Kingston [ˈkiŋstən]	*(Hauptstadt von Jamaika)*
to study [ˈstʌdi]	studieren
physics [ˈfiziks]	Physik
to take a post	eine Stellung annehmen
physicist [ˈfizisist]	Physiker
to pay for	bezahlen
study	Studium
lift-boy	Fahrstuhlführer
West End	*(vornehmer Stadtteil Londons)*
it seemed to him	ihm schien, es schien ihm
qualified [ˈkwɔlifaid]	befähigt, qualifiziert, ausgebildet
chance of a job	(gute) Aussicht auf eine Stellung
rare [rɛə]	selten
higher profession	gehobener Beruf
3. to apply for [əˈplai]	sich bewerben um
research [riˈsə:tʃ]	Forschung
manufacturer [ˌmænjuˈfæktʃərə]	Hersteller
firm of plastic manufacturers	Kunststoffwerk
to appear for	erscheinen zu
interview [ˈintəvju:]	Unterredung
waiting room	Wartezimmer
applicant [ˈæplikənt]	Bewerber

graduate [ˈgrædjuit]	Akademiker
the only negro present = . . . who was present	
curious [ˈkjuəriəs]	neugierig
qualification [ˌkwɔlifiˈkeiʃən]	Befähigung, Qualifikation
staff [stɑ:f]	Personal
staff manager	Personalchef
vague [veig]	unbestimmt
scarcely [ˈskɛəsli]	kaum
we regret to inform you [riˈgret; inˈfɔ:m]	wir bedauern, Ihnen mitteilen zu müssen
filled	*hier:* besetzt
reason	Begründung
lack of [læk]	Mangel an, mangelnd
barrier [ˈbæriə]	Schranke
in despair	voll Verzweiflung
government department	Regierungsstelle
to ask	bitten, ersuchen
to be successful	Erfolg haben
welfare officer	Fürsorger
he is expected	man erwartet von ihm, es wird von ihm erwartet
to make	*hier:* lassen
to hesitate [ˈheziteit]	zögern
4. instructor (to) [inˈstrʌktə]	Ausbilder (für)
science graduate	*(akademisch gebildeter Naturwissenschaftler)*
language difficulty	Sprachschwierigkeit
refusal [riˈfju:zəl]	Ablehnung, Absage
scientist [ˈsaiəntist]	(Natur)Wissenschaftler
so as to	um zu
educated	gebildet
ancestor [ˈænsistə]	Vorfahr

<B. Choosing a Career>

career [kəˈriə]	Laufbahn, Beruf
to pass an examination	ein Examen bestehen
choice [tʃɔis]	(Aus)Wahl
employment [imˈplɔimənt]	(An)Stellung, Beschäftigung
offer	Angebot
special training	Fachausbildung
bank	Bank(haus)
first class	erstklassig
Ltd. = Limited [ˈlimitid]	mit beschränkter Haftung
book-keeper	Buchhalter
in own handwriting	handschriftlich
frosted foods [ˈfrɔstid]	Tiefkühlkost
High Wycombe [ˈwikəm]	*(Kleinstadt in Buckinghamshire)*
saleswoman	Verkäuferin
fine	vornehm, elegant
store	Kaufhaus
Harrods [ˈhærədz]	*(großes elegantes Kaufhaus in London)*
exporter [iksˈpɔ:tə]	Exporteur
Dagenham [ˈdægənəm]	*(Vorstadt von London, in Essex)*
mechanic [miˈkænik]	Mechaniker
expense [iksˈpens]	Ausgabe, Auslage
residential expenses [ˌreziˈdenʃəl]	Ausgaben für Unterbringung
management [ˈmænidʒmənt]	Geschäftsleitung
management post	leitende Stellung
Cardiff [ˈkɑ:dif]	*(Hafenstadt im südwestlichen Wales)*

<The Queen's First Christmas TV Talk>

talk [ɔ:]	Ansprache
to broadcast [ˈbrɔ:dkɑ:st]	(im Rundfunk) senden
landmark [ˈlændmɑ:k]	Markstein
to gather round [ˈgæðə]	sich rundum versammeln
as they are at this moment	so wie sie es in diesem Augenblick tun
that is how	so
medium [ˈmi:djəm]	Medium, Mittel
personal [ˈpə:snl]	persönlich
inevitable [inˈevitəbl]	unvermeidlich
remote [riˈməut]	unbestimmt, vage
successor to s.o. [səkˈsesə]	jemandes Nachfolger
familiar [fəˈmiljə]	bekannt, vertraut
all	überall
change [tʃeindʒ]	Veränderung

unable [ʌnˈeibl]	unfähig
to decide [diˈsaid]	entscheiden
to discard [disˈkɑ:d]	fallenlassen
to take advantage of s.th. [ədˈvɑ:ntidʒ]	aus etwas Vorteil ziehen
invention [inˈvenʃən]	Erfindung
trouble [ˈtrʌbl]	Unruhe, Verwirrung
unthinking [ˈʌnˈθiŋkiŋ]	gedankenlos
ageless [ˈeidʒlis]	zeitlos
outworn [ˈautwɔ:n]	abgenützt
machinery [məˈʃi:nəri]	Maschinen
religion [riˈlidʒən]	Religion
aside [əˈsaid]	weg
morality [məˈræliti]	Moral, Sittlichkeit
meaningless [ˈmi:niŋlis]	bedeutungslos
to count [au]	betrachten
foolishness [ˈfu:liʃnis]	Dummheit
self-interest [ˈselfˈintrist]	Eigennutz, eigener Vorteil
self-restraint [ˈselfriˈstreint]	Selbstbeherrschung, Selbstbeschränkung
critical [ˈkritikəl]	kritisch
respect [risˈpekt]	Ansehen
to stand up for	eintreten für
honest [ˈɔnist]	rechtschaffen
to withstand [wiðˈstænd]	widerstehen
subtle [ˈsʌtl]	schleichend
corruption [kəˈrʌpʃən]	verderblicher Einfluß
cynic [ˈsinik]	Zyniker
to cherish [ˈtʃeriʃ]	hegen
to take (a) pride [ai] in	stolz sein auf
quality [ˈkwɔliti]	Fähigkeit
to set an example to s.o. [igˈzɑ:mpl]	jemandem ein Beispiel geben
to encourage [inˈkʌridʒ]	ermutigen
upright [ˈʌprait]	aufrecht
blessing [ˈblesiŋ]	Segen
enjoyment [inˈdʒɔimənt]	Freude, Vergnügen

Exercises

2. letter of application [ˌæpliˈkeiʃən]	Bewerbungsschreiben
yours faithfully [ˈfeiθfuli]	hochachtungsvoll
5. curtain [ˈkə:tn]	Vorhang
to tick [tik]	ticken
to handle [ˈhændl]	behandeln

Vocabulary Revision: Slavery

to make s.o. a slave	jemanden zum Sklaven machen
to offer slaves for sale	Sklaven zum Verkauf anbieten
to be against slavery	gegen die Sklaverei eingestellt sein
to preserve slavery	die Sklaverei beibehalten
to escape to the free northern states	in die freien Nordstaaten entkommen
to abolish slavery	die Sklaverei abschaffen
to proclaim the freedom of all slaves	die Freiheit aller Sklaven verkünden
to set the slaves free	die Sklaven freilassen
slave trade	Sklavenhandel
slave trader	Sklavenhändler
slave market	Sklavenmarkt
a runaway slave	ein fortgelaufener Sklave
slave-catcher	Sklavenfänger
coloured people	Farbige
an anti-slavery president	ein Präsident, der gegen die Sklaverei eingestellt ist
a quarrel about the holding of slaves	ein Streit über das Halten von Sklaven
the abolition of slavery	die Abschaffung der Sklaverei
the negroes' long road to liberty and equality	der lange Weg der Neger zu Freiheit und Gleichheit

11 A. The Suez Canal—Waterway of the World

canal [kəˈnæl]	Kanal
Suez Canal [ˈsu:iz]	Suezkanal
waterway	Wasserstraße, Schifffahrtsweg
1. Lionel Rothschild [ˈlaiənl ˈrɔθtʃaild]	*(Inhaber des Londoner Bankhauses Rothschild, 1808–1879)*
banker [ˈbæŋkə]	Bankier
to entertain [ˌentəˈtein]	zu Gast haben, bewirten
messenger [ˈmesindʒə]	Kurier, Beauftragter
study [ˈstʌdi]	Studier-, Arbeitszimmer
to disturb [disˈtə:b]	stören
Prime Minister [ˈpraiˈministə]	Premierminister
to ask	*hier:* beauftragen
to enquire [inˈkwaiə]	sich erkundigen, fragen
immediate [iˈmi:djət]	sofortig
loan [ləun]	Anleihe
amount [əˈmaunt]	Betrag
Benjamin Disraeli [ˈbendʒəmin dizˈreili]	*(brit. konservativer Staatsmann und Premierminister, 1804 bis 1881)*
bankrupt [ˈbæŋkrəpt]	bankrott
Egypt [ˈi:dʒipt]	Ägypten
share [ʃɛə]	Anteil
2. to register [ˈredʒistə]	eintragen
Egyptian [iˈdʒipʃən]	ägyptisch
strictly speaking	streng genommen
project [ˈprɔdʒekt]	Unternehmen
Ferdinand de Lesseps [ˈfə:dinənd leˈseps]	*(franz. Diplomat und Ingenieur, Erbauer des Suezkanals, 1805–94)*
Red Sea	Rotes Meer
to take	*hier:* vornehmen
consent [kənˈsent]	Zustimmung
to control [kənˈtrəul]	kontrollieren
to face	gegenübertreten, entgegensehen
criticism [ˈkritisizəm]	Kritik
MP = Member of Parliament	*(Abgeordnete(r) des Unterhauses)*

ditch [ditʃ]	Graben
to dig, dug, dug [i, ʌ]	graben
to rule [ru:l]	herrschen
vital [ˈvaitl]	lebenswichtig
importance	Bedeutung
Cape of Good Hope	Kap der Guten Hoffnung *(Südspitze Afrikas)*
to shorten (by)	verkürzen (um)
influence [ˈinfluəns]	Einfluß
to sign	unterzeichnen
to gather	*hier:* sich zusammenziehen, zusammenballen
protectorate [prəˈtektərit]	Protektorat
Turk [tə:k]	Türke
ally [ˈælai]	Verbündeter
Palestine [ˈpælistain]	Palästina
3. concept [ˈkɔnsept]	Vorstellung, Gedanke
colonial [kəˈləunjəl]	Kolonial-
especially [isˈpeʃəli]	besonders
Egyptian	Ägypter
to retain [riˈtein]	behalten
military [ˈmilitəri]	militärisch
objective [əbˈdʒektiv]	Objekt
Italian [iˈtæljən]	Italiener
Field Marshal [ˈmɑ:ʃəl]	(General)Feldmarschall
Erwin Rommel	*(dt. Generalfeldmarschall, Führer des dt. Afrikakorps im 2. Weltkrieg, 1891 bis 1944)*
headline	Schlagzeile
Alexandria [ˌæligˈzɑ:ndriə]	*(Hafenstadt im nördlichen Ägypten)*
retreat [riˈtri:t]	Rückzug
forces	Truppen, Streitkräfte
4. ruins [ruinz]	Trümmer
to shift [ʃift]	(sich) verlagern
Soviet Union [ˈsəuviet]	Sowjetunion
place	Stelle
demand (for) [diˈmɑ:nd]	Forderung (nach)

to ignore [ig'nɔ:]	übersehen, ignorieren
share-holder	Aktionär
stroke [strəuk]	Schlag
to regain [ri'gein]	zurückgewinnen, -erlangen
control [kən'trəul]	Kontrolle
Israeli [iz'reili]	israelisch
opinion [ə'pinjən]	Meinung
United Nations	Vereinte Nationen
to condemn [kən'dem]	verurteilen
to withdraw	(sich) zurückziehen
Israel ['izreil]	Israel
to and from ['tu:ən'frɔm]	nach und von
United Arab Republic ['ærəb ri'pʌblik]	Vereinigte Arabische Republik

Picture Text

artery ['ɑ:təri]	*hier:* Hauptwasserstraße
Sweden ['swi:dn]	Schweden
Denmark ['denmɑ:k]	Dänemark
Holland ['hɔlənd]	Holland
Belgium ['beldʒəm]	Belgien
USSR	UdSSR
Portugal ['pɔ:tjugəl]	Portugal
Turkey ['tə:ki]	Türkei
Cairo ['kaiərəu]	Kairo
Nile [nail]	Nil

<B. Passengers on an Ocean Liner>

ocean liner	Passagier-, Ozeandampfer
I couldn't touch a thing	ich konnte nichts anrühren
to lie flat	lang liegen
berth [bə:θ]	Koje
to pitch [pitʃ]	stampfen
meaning ['mi:niŋ]	Bedeutung
pill [pil]	Pille
to do the trick	zum Ziele führen
passage ['pæsidʒ]	Überfahrt
rough	rauh
smooth [smu:ð]	ruhig
portion ['pɔ:ʃən]	Portion
to get one's money's worth	etwas für sein Geld bekommen
fighting spirit ['spirit]	Kampfgeist
drink	(alkoholisches) Getränk
bar [bɑ:]	Bar
bridge [bridʒ]	*hier:* Kommandobrücke
pleasure ['pleʒə]	Vergnügen
bow [bau]	Bug
stern [stə:n]	Heck
see you later	bis nachher

<Gunboat Diplomacy>

gunboat ['gʌnbəut]	Kanonenboot
diplomacy [di'pləuməsi]	Diplomatie
unrest ['ʌn'rest]	Unruhe
gun [ʌ]	Kanone
to present [pri'zent]	überbringen
Sultan ['sʌltən]	Sultan
to refuse [ri'fju:z]	zurückweisen
unthinkable [ʌn'θiŋkəbl]	undenkbar
to consider [kən'sidə]	erwägen
Grand Vizier [grænvi'ziə]	Großwesir
negotiation [ni,gəuʃi'eiʃən]	Verhandlung
solemn ['sɔləm]	ernst, feierlich
no choice but [tʃɔis]	keine (andere) Wahl als
within [wi'ðin]	innerhalb

Exercises

3. Eugénie [öʒe'ni:]	*(franz. Kaiserin, 1826–1920)*
rock [rɔk]	Felsen
to remove [ri'mu:v]	entfernen
4. meaning ['mi:niŋ]	Bedeutung
5. to block [blɔk]	blockieren, versperren
6. to mention ['menʃən]	erwähnen
7. considering [kən'sidəriŋ]	in Anbetracht
generally speaking	im allgemeinen
judging from	nach ... zu urteilen; wenn man nach ... geht

12 A. Mahatma Gandhi

Mahatma Gandhi [məˈhɑːtmə]	*(Führer der ind. Unabhängigkeitsbewegung, 1869–1948)*
1. firm	fest
past	vergangen
of	*hier:* über
domination [ˌdɔmiˈneiʃən]	(Vor)Herrschaft
rebellion [riˈbeljən]	Rebellion, Aufstand
to crush [krʌʃ]	niederwerfen
empress [ˈempris]	Kaiserin
outward [ˈautwəd]	äußerlich
unrest [ˈʌnˈrest]	Unruhe
steady	beständig
Porbandar [ˌpɔːbænˈdɑː]	*(Stadt an der Westküste Indiens)*
shy [ʃai]	scheu, schüchtern
Mohandas [mɔˈhændəs]	*(Eigenname)*
intelligent [inˈtelidʒənt]	intelligent, klug
... on reaching ...	als er ...
to study law	Jura studieren
to qualify [ˈkwɔlifai]	(sich) qualifizieren, ein Abschlußexamen ablegen
after qualifying ...	nachdem er ...
lawyer [ˈlɔːjə]	Rechtsanwalt
to take up	*hier:* vertreten
cause [kɔːz]	Sache
court [kɔːt]	Gericht(shof)
to organize [ˈɔːgənaiz]	organisieren, aufbauen
stretcher-bearer [ˈstretʃə]	Krankenträger
praise [preiz]	Lob
to publish [ˈpʌbliʃ]	herausgeben
strike	Streik
racial discrimination [disˌkrimiˈneiʃən]	Rassendiskriminierung
to imprison [imˈprizn]	einsperren, ins Gefängnis werfen
this led to his ...	dies führte dazu, daß er ...
2. rapid [ˈræpid]	schnell, rasch
to limit (to) [ˈlimit]	beschränken (auf)
politician [ˌpɔliˈtiʃən]	Politiker
that the success ... depended on his ...	daß der Erfolg ... davon abhing, daß er ...
support [səˈpɔːt]	Unterstützung
comfortable [ˈkʌmfətəbl]	behaglich, bequem
to go	*hier:* umhergehen
barefoot [ˈbɛəfut]	barfuß
violence [ˈvaiələns]	Gewalt(tätigkeit)
by	*hier:* mit
to introduce	einführen
to call	aufrufen
salt [sɔːlt]	Salz
monopoly [məˈnɔpəli]	Monopol, Alleinherstellungsrecht
to make	*hier:* gewinnen
3. to represent [ˌrepriˈzent]	darstellen, verkörpern
insoluble [inˈsɔljubl]	unlösbar
to deal with	sich auseinandersetzen mit
method [ˈmeθəd]	Methode
to break	übertreten
to regard (as) [riˈgɑːd]	betrachten (als)
martyr [ˈmɑːtə]	Märtyrer
to appeal to [əˈpiːl]	sich wenden an, dringend bitten
to oppose	entgegenarbeiten
to delay [diˈlei]	auf-, hinausschieben
step by step	Schritt für Schritt
transfer [ˈtrænsfəː]	Übertragung
to solve [sɔlv]	lösen
to insist on [inˈsist]	bestehen auf
4. was	*hier:* bestand
riot [ˈraiət]	Aufruhr, Krawall
Calcutta [kælˈkʌtə]	*(Stadt an der Mündung des Ganges im NO Indiens)*
massacre [ˈmæsəkə]	Blutbad
... by going ...	... indem er ...
fearless	furchtlos
to avoid [əˈvɔid]	vermeiden
brotherhood [ˈbrʌðəhud]	Brüderlichkeit
extremist [iksˈtriːmist]	Extremist

threatening letter	Drohbrief
bomb [bɔm]	Bombe
to explode [iks'pləud]	explodieren
follower ['fɔləuə]	Anhänger
. . . warned him against . . .	. . . warnten ihn davor . . .
prayer meeting [prɛə]	Gebetsversammlung
fanatic [fə'nætik]	Fanatiker
to step out of	hervortreten aus
unfinished	unvollendet
unsolved	ungelöst
successor [sək'sesə]	Nachfolger
Nehru ['neru:]	*(1. ind. Ministerpräsident, Nachfolger Gandhis, 1889–1963)*
within	innerhalb

<B. Perfect Control>

control	(Selbst)Beherrschung
naturalist ['nætʃrəlist]	Naturforscher
marble ['mɑ:bl]	Marmor
to open on to	gehen nach *(Tür)*
veranda [və'rændə]	Veranda
to outgrow	entwachsen
sight	Anblick
era ['iərə]	Ära, Zeitalter
hostess ['həustis]	Gastgeberin
straight ahead	geradeaus
gesture ['dʒestʃə]	Geste, Gebärde
to summon ['sʌmən]	herbeiwinken
to widen ['waidn]	(sich) weiten
bowl [bəul]	Schüssel, Schale
bait [beit]	Köder
snake [sneik]	Schlange
cobra ['kəubrə]	Kobra
impulse ['impʌls]	Impuls, Drang
tumult ['tju:mʌlt]	Tumult
to frighten s.o. into doing a thing	jemanden durch Schrecken zu etwas treiben
image ['imidʒ]	Bild, Statue
corner	Winkel
to ring out	ertönen
to slam [slæm]	zuschlagen *(Tür)*
host [həust]	Gastgeber
Wynnes [wins]	*(Familienname)*
to light up	erhellen

<The Blind Men and the Elephant>

Hindostan [ˌhindɔ'stɑ:n]	*(hier: alte Bezeichnung für Indien)*
to be inclined to [in'klaind]	aufgelegt sein zu
observation [ˌɔbzə'veiʃən]	Beobachtung
to satisfy ['sætisfai]	befriedigen
mind [ai]	Verlangen, Lust
sturdy [ə:]	stark, massiv
to bawl [bɔ:l]	brüllen
bless me! [e]	du meine Güte!
tusk [ʌ]	Stoßzahn
smooth [smu:ð]	glatt
sharp [ɑ:]	scharf
'tis = it is	
mighty ['maiti]	überaus
wonder ['wʌndə]	Wunder
spear [spiə]	Speer
to squirm [skwə:m]	sich winden
bold [əu]	kühn, beherzt
spake [ei] = spoke	sprach *(veraltet)*
quoth [kwɔθ]	sprach *(veraltet)*
snake [ei]	Schlange
to stretch [e]	strecken
eager ['i:gə]	eifrig
like [ai]	ähnlich
plain [ei]	klar
he chanced to touch ['tʃɑ:nst tə 'tʌtʃ]	zufällig berührte er
to resemble [ri'zembl]	ähnlich sein, gleichen
marvel ['mɑ:vəl]	Wunder(ding)
fan [æ]	Fächer
to grope [əu]	(herum)tasten
tail [ei]	Schwanz
scope [əu]	*hier:* Reichweite
to dispute [dis'pju:t]	streiten, zanken
to exceed in [ik'si:d]	zu weit gehen in
stiff [i]	steif
to be in the right	im Recht sein, recht haben
partly [ɑ:]	teilweise
to be in the wrong	im Irrtum sein, unrecht haben
John Godfrey Saxe ['dʒɔn 'gɔdfri 'sæks]	*(am. Dichter, 1816–1887)*

Exercises

2. subordinate clause [səˈbɔːdnit]	Nebensatz
4. guard	*hier:* Schaffner
5. rice [rais]	Reis
pot [pɔt]	Topf
to play a trick on s.o.	jemandem einen (üblen) Streich spielen

Vocabulary Revision: Idioms

to set the ball rolling	den Stein ins Rollen bringen
to be born lucky	als Glückspilz geboren sein
to be broke	„pleite" sein
to turn the tables	den Spieß umdrehen
to place importance on s.th.	Wert auf etwas legen
to play a trick on s.o.	jemandem einen Streich spielen
to be popular with s.o.	bei jemandem beliebt sein
to be in full swing	in vollem Gange sein
to rain cats and dogs	in Strömen gießen
to carry s.th. in one's mind	an etwas denken
to be well ahead of s.o.	jemandem weit voraus sein
to call for s.o.	jemanden abholen
to take s.o. by surprise	jemanden überrumpeln
to lie in wait	auf der Lauer liegen
to corner s.o.	jemanden stellen
to catch sight of s.th.	etwas erblicken
to run a course	einen Kursus veranstalten
in the nick of time	gerade im rechten Augenblick
we are running short of money	das Geld wird uns knapp

<The Commonwealth and its Peoples>

What is the Commonwealth?

association [əˈsəusiˈeiʃən]	Bündnis
dependency [diˈpendənsi]	abhängiges Gebiet, Kolonie
to administer [ədˈministə]	verwalten
to occupy [ˈɔkjupai]	einnehmen

The Queen and the Commonwealth

from	von ... aus
monarchy [ˈmɔnəki]	Monarchie
to acknowledge [əkˈnɔlidʒ]	anerkennen

A Multi-racial Association

to contain [kənˈtein]	umfassen
character [ˈkæriktə]	Charakter
to be based on [beist]	beruhen auf
predominantly Negro [priˈdɔminəntli]	überwiegend von Negern bevölkert
to rule [uː]	regieren
minority [maiˈnɔriti]	Minderheit
Burma [ˈbəːmə]	*(Republik in Hinterindien)*
religion [riˈlidʒən]	Religion
politics [ˈpɔlitiks]	Politik
to choose [tʃuːz]	vorziehen

Some Commonwealth Countries

Christian [ˈkristjən]	christlich
Hindi [ˈhinˈdiː]	*(wichtigste indische Sprache)*

official [ə'fiʃəl]	offiziell
Sinhalese [ˌsiŋhə'li:z]	*(indische Sprache)*
Tamil ['tæmil]	*(drawidische Sprache)*
dialect ['daiəlekt]	Dialekt
belief [bi'li:f]	Glaube, Religion
Maori ['mauri]	*(neuseel. Sprache)*

Common Ties

ties [taiz]	Bande
apart from [ə'pɑ:t]	abgesehen von
a good deal [i:]	ziemlich viel
aid [eid]	Hilfe

Important People

important [im'pɔ:tənt]	bedeutend
discoverer [dis'kʌvərə]	Entdecker
such [ʌ]	so, solcherart
Jomo Kenyatta ['jəumou ken'jætə]	*(Präsident d. Republik Kenia, geb. ca. 1893)*

Sir Walter Raleigh

Sir Walter Raleigh ['wɔltə 'rɔ:li]	*(engl. Seefahrer und Schriftsteller, 1552–1618)*
court [ɔ:]	Hof
Elizabeth I [i'lizəbəθ]	*(Königin von England, 1533–1603)*
Netherlands ['neðələndz]	Niederlande
to fail [ei]	fehlschlagen
interest in ['intrist]	Interesse an
future ['fju:tʃə]	(zu)künftig
vain [ei]	vergeblich
El Dorado [ˌeldɔ'rɑ:dəu]	*(sagenhaftes Goldland in Südamerika)*
downfall	Sturz
for	denn
James I [dʒeimz]	*(König von England, 1566–1625)*
to succeed s.o. [sək'si:d]	jdm. (nach)folgen
to distrust [dis'trʌst]	mißtrauen
bold [əu]	kühn
unfair ['ʌn'fɛə]	ungerecht

Captain Cook

to be apprenticed to [ə'prentist]	in die Lehre kommen zu
navigator ['nævigeitə]	Seefahrer
to rise to [ai]	aufsteigen zu
rank [æ]	Rang
to name [ei]	nennen
to take possession of s.th. [pə'zeʃən]	von etwas Besitz ergreifen, etwas in Besitz nehmen
kindness ['kaindnis]	Güte, Freundlichkeit
at	von

Robert Clive

Robert Clive [klaiv]	*(Begründer der engl. Herrschaft in Ostindien, 1725–74)*
ill-mannered ['ilmænəd]	ungehobelt
behaviour [bi'heivjə]	Benehmen, Betragen
to earn one's living ['liviŋ]	seinen Lebensunterhalt verdienen
East India Company ['i:st 'indjə 'kʌmpəni]	Ostindische Kompanie *(bekannteste Handelskompanie)*
foundation [faun'deiʃən]	Grund, Fundament
series ['siəri:z]	Reihe
to overthrow [ˌəuvə'θrəu]	stürzen
cruel ['kru:əl]	grausam
Nawab [nə'wɑ:b]	*(Fürstentitel in Indien)*
Bengal [beŋ'gɔ:l]	Bengalen *(Landschaft im nordöstlichen Indien)*
hungry for power ['pauə]	machthungrig
dishonesty [dis'ɔnisti]	Betrug, Unehrlichkeit
dealing ['di:liŋ]	Geschäft
disgrace [dis'greis]	Ungnade
just [ʌ]	gerecht
administrator [əd'ministreitə]	Verwalter

Cecil Rhodes

Cecil Rhodes ['sesl 'rəudz]	*(brit.-südafrikanischer Wirtschaftsführer und Staatsmann, 1853–1902)*

to be in control of s.th. [kən'trəul]	etwas unter sich haben, *hier:* besitzen
gold-mining interests ['intrists]	(Geschäfts)Anteile am Goldbergbau
to enter politics ['pɔlitiks]	in die Politik gehen
Cape [ei]	Kapkolonie
passionate ['pæʃənit]	leidenschaftlich
Bechuanaland [ˌbetʃu'ɑ:nəlænd]	*(ehem. brit. Protektorat in Südafrika, jetzt Botswana)*
Rhodesia [rəu'di:zjə]	Rhodesien
to extend [iks'tend]	ausdehnen
he did not live to see it	er hat dies nicht mehr erlebt
Matoppo Hills [mə'tɔpəu]	*(Gebirgskette in Rhodesien)*
scholarship ['skɔləʃip]	Stipendium
student ['stju:dənt]	Student

Rudyard Kipling

Rudyard Kipling ['rʌdjəd 'kipliŋ]	*(engl. Dichter und Schriftsteller, 1865–1936)*
age [eidʒ]	Zeitalter
at peace [i:]	in Frieden, ruhig
immense [i'mens]	ungeheuer
journalist ['dʒə:nəlist]	Journalist
official [ə'fiʃəl]	Beamter
literature ['litəritʃə]	Literatur
imperialism [im'piəriəlizəm]	Imperialismus
burden [ə:]	Bürde, Verantwortung
heroic [hi'rəuik]	heroisch
duty ['dju:ti]	Pflicht
culture ['kʌltʃə]	Kultur
out of date	überholt
ballad ['bæləd]	Ballade
literary ['litərəri]	literarisch
classic ['klæsik]	Klassiker

Jan Smuts

Jan Smuts ['dʒæn 'smʌts]	*(Südafrikanischer Staatsmann, 1870–1950)*
descent [di'sent]	Abstammung
policy ['pɔlisi]	Politik
tirelessly ['taiəlisli]	unermüdlich
Nationalist Party ['næʃnəlist]	Nationalistenpartei
anti-British ['ænti 'britiʃ]	gegen Großbritannien eingestellt
outbreak ['autbreik]	Ausbruch
to be returned to power [ri'tə:n]	wieder an die Macht gebracht werden
to hold [əu]	innehaben
charter ['tʃɑ:tə]	Charta
delegation [ˌdeli'geiʃən]	Delegation
opposition [ˌɔpə'ziʃən]	Opposition *(polit.)*
racial segregation ['reiʃəl ˌsegri'geiʃən]	Rassentrennung
in vain [ei]	vergeblich
to declare [di'klɛə]	erklären (zu)

Important Dates

defeat [di'fi:t]	Niederlage
Malta ['mɔ:ltə]	*(Insel im Mittelmeer)*
Cyprus ['saiprəs]	Cypern *(Insel im Mittelmeer)*
Aden ['eidn]	*(Hafenstadt im Süden Arabiens)*
to pass into [pɑ:s]	übergehen auf
Union of South Africa ['ju:njən]	Südafrikanische Union
self-government ['gʌvənmənt]	Selbstverwaltung, -regierung
Imperial Conference [im'piəriəl 'kɔnfərəns]	Empirekonferenz
to include [in'klu:d]	einschließen
statute ['stætju:t]	Statut, (Satzung)
recognition [ˌrekəg'niʃən]	Anerkennung

Opinions about the Commonwealth

misleading [mis'li:diŋ]	irreführend
community [kə'mju:niti]	Gemeinschaft
Sir Robert Menzies ['menziz]	*(austral. Politiker, Ministerpräsident, geb. 1894)*
error ['erə]	Irrtum
sentiment ['sentimənt]	Gesinnung

attachment [ə'tætʃmənt]	Bindung
newly independent [ˌindi'pendənt]	kürzlich unabhängig geworden
eagerness ['i:gənis]	Begierde, Verlangen
as if	als ob
Duncan Sandys ['dʌŋkən 'sænz]	*(Eigenname)*
Secretary of State ['sekrətri]	Minister *(in Großbritannien)*
relation [ri'leiʃən]	Beziehung
political [pə'litikəl]	politisch
to involve in [in'vɔlv]	hineinbeziehen in
unwelcome [ʌn'welkəm]	unwillkommen
controversy ['kɔntrəvə:si]	Streit
outside ['aut'said]	*hier:* außerhalb des Commonwealth liegend
economical [ˌi:kə'nɔmikəl]	wirtschaftlich
profit ['prɔfit]	Gewinn
to press [e]	drängen
to discharge [dis'tʃɑ:dʒ]	nachkommen *(einer Verpflichtung)*
to involve [in'vɔlv]	mit sich bringen

13 A. Lindbergh's Flight

Charles Lindbergh ['lindbə:g]	*(am. Flieger, dem die erste Atlantiküberquerung gelang, geb. 1902)*
1. to compete for [kəm'pi:t]	sich bewerben um
as early as	schon
Paris ['pæris]	Paris
Newfoundland	Neufundland *(kanadische Insel im Atlantik*
airship	Luftschiff
to fly	fliegen lassen
to lose sight of	aus den Augen verlieren
pilot ['pailət]	Pilot
to start on	starten zu
Air Force	Luftwaffe
St. Louis ['lu:is]	*(Stadt im Staate Missouri, USA)*
single-engined	einmotorig
spirit ['spirit]	Geist
Spirit of St. Louis	*(Name des Flugzeugs)*
2. to think about	überlegen, nachdenken über
airfield	Flugplatz
to make to	vornehmen an
there were	es waren
detail ['di:teil]	Einzelheit
safety-belt	Sicherheitsgurt
goggles ['gɔglz]	Schutzbrille
boxing-match	Boxkampf
to pray [prei]	beten
stiff [stif]	steif
cramped ['kræmpt]	verkrampft
stomach ['stʌmək]	Magen
awake [ə'weik]	wach
to keep awake	wach bleiben
Nova Scotia ['nəuvə 'skəuʃə]	Neuschottland *(Halbinsel im südöstlichen Kanada)*
province ['prɔvins]	Provinz
to pass	dahinziehen, vorbeigleiten
underneath [ˌʌndə'ni:θ]	unter(halb)
take-off	Start *(Flugzeug)*
to catch sight of	erblicken
St. John's	*(Hauptstadt von Neufundland, Kanada)*
weary ['wiəri]	ermüdend, anstrengend
Irish	irisch
iceberg ['aisbə:g]	Eisberg
to toss about [tɔs]	hin- und herschleudern
flashlight	Taschenlampe
to inspect [in'spekt]	untersuchen, inspizieren
wing	Flügel *(Flugzeug, Vogel)*
to light up	er-, beleuchten
to be tricked	genarrt werden

vision [ˈviʒən]	Erscheinung, Trugbild
to change	(sich) verwandeln
dragon [ˈdrægən]	Drache
monster [ˈmɔnstə]	Ungeheuer
to swallow (up) [ˈswɔləu]	verschlingen
eyelid [ˈailid]	Augenlid
to ache [eik]	schmerzen
to fall asleep	einschlafen
certain	sicher
to pinch [pintʃ]	zwicken, kneifen
controls	Steuerungs- und Kontrollvorrichtungen
to trouble [ˈtrʌbl]	verwirren
so	*hier:* das
seemingly	scheinbar
fishing-boat	Fischerboot
there were	*hier:* waren
ahead of him	*hier:* vor ihm
were they . . . ?	waren es . . . ?
distance	Ferne
to graze [greiz]	weiden
600 miles away	600 Meilen weit entfernt
course [kɔ:s]	Kurs
Devon [ˈdevn]	*(Grafschaft im südwestlichen England)*
3. overwhelming [ˌəuvəˈwelmiŋ]	überwältigend
reception [riˈsepʃən]	Empfang
to greet [gri:t]	(be)grüßen, empfangen
aviator [ˈeivieitə]	Flieger
to lie in store for s.o.	harren *(+ Gen.)*, auf jemanden warten
welcome [ˈwelkəm]	Willkommen, *hier:* begeisterter Empfang

<B. Machines in Daily Life>

use	Verwendung
1. Praed Street [preid]	*(Straße in London)*
Paddington [ˈpædiŋtən]	*(Stadtteil von London)*
lit [lit]	erleuchtet
attendant [əˈtendənt]	*hier:* Bedienung
soap powder [ˈpaudə]	Seifenpulver
clean [kli:n]	sauber
2. underground garage	Tiefgarage
Hyde Park [haid]	*(Park in London)*
to hold out	hinhalten
automatic [ˌɔ:təˈmætik]	automatisch
none [nʌn]	keine(r, s), niemand
bay	Parklücke
sight	Anblick
employee [ˌemplɔiˈi:]	Angestellter
to park	parken
3. landing system	Landesystem
to apply the brakes	bremsen
to assure [əˈʃuə]	garantieren, sichern
automation [ˌɔ:təˈmeiʃən]	Automation
word	Parole
in case of emergency [iˈmə:dʒənsi]	im Notfall
automated [ˌɔ:təˈmeitid]	vollautomatisiert

<The Young Dead Soldiers>

nevertheless [ˌ- - -ˈ-]	nichtsdestoweniger
silence [ˈsailəns]	Schweigen
at night [ai]	nachts
to count [au]	*hier:* die Stunden zählen
to end [e]	beenden
Archibald Macleish [ˈɑ:tʃibəld məˈkli:ʃ]	*(am. Dichter, geb. 1892)*

14 A. We, too, are America

1. bundle [ˈbʌndl]	Bündel, Haufen
resentment [riˈzentmənt]	Ressentiment, Groll, Haß
to explode [iksˈpləud]	sich entladen
Mississippi [ˌmisiˈsipi]	*(Staat im Süden der USA)*
explosion [iksˈpləuʒən]	Ausbruch, Explosion
Rosa Parks [ˈrəuzə]	*(Eigenname)*
Montgomery [məntˈgʌməri]	*(Hauptstadt des Staates Alabama)*
Alabama [ˌæləˈbɑ:mə]	*(Staat im Süden der USA)*
in one's fifties	in den „Fünfzigern" *(zwischen 50 und 60 Jahre alt)*

familiar [fəˈmiljə]	(alt)vertraut, (wohl)bekannt
practice [ˈpræktis]	Brauch, Verfahren
that is to say	das heißt
to move	aufstehen, Platz machen
disturbance [disˈtə:bəns]	Störung
to murmur [ˈmə:mə]	murmeln
damn [dæm]	verdammt
nigger [ˈnigə]	*(Schimpfwort für „Neger")*
to giggle [ˈgigl]	kichern
entire [inˈtaiə]	ganz
incident [ˈinsidənt]	Vorfall, (zufälliges) Ereignis
2. arrest	Festnahme, Verhaftung
gathering	Versammlung
local [ˈləukəl]	ortsansässig
to hold	abhalten
to discuss [disˈkʌs]	besprechen, diskutieren
plan of action	Schlachtplan
to call	*hier:* ausrufen
boycott [ˈbɔikət]	Boykott
Baptist [ˈbæptist]	Baptist(in), Baptisten-
minister [ˈministə]	Pfarrer, Geistlicher
Dr. Martin Luther King [ˈmɑ:tin ˈlu:θə]	*(farbiger am. Pfarrer, führende Persönlichkeit im gewaltlosen Widerstand gegen die Rassentrennung, 1929—68)*
to distribute [disˈtribju:t]	verteilen
pamphlet [ˈpæmflit]	Flugblatt
citizen [ˈsitizn]	Einwohner
packed [pækt]	zum Bersten voll
call of action	Zeichen zum Handeln
rostrum [ˈrɔstrəm]	Kanzel
to mistreat [ˈmisˈtri:t]	schlecht behandeln, mißhandeln
to segregate [ˈsegrigeit]	absondern, isolieren
to humiliate [hju:ˈmilieit]	demütigen
to kick about [kik]	herumstoßen
brutal [ˈbru:tl]	brutal, roh
oppression [əˈpreʃən]	Unterdrückung
alternative [ɔ:lˈtə:nətiv]	(andere) Wahl
patient	geduldig, zufrieden
by then	inzwischen
non-violent [ˈnɔnˈvaiələnt]	gegen Gewaltanwendung eingestellt
to preach [pri:tʃ]	predigen
to keep from	abhalten von
3. reaction [ri:ˈækʃən]	Reaktion
to jail [dʒeil]	ins Gefängnis bringen
despite [disˈpait]	trotz
act	Tat, Maßnahme
protest [ˈprəutest]	Protest
to take to	bringen vor
Supreme Court [sju:ˈpri:m]	*(Oberstes Bundesgericht in den USA)*
to rule	entscheiden
municipal [mju:ˈnisipəl]	städtisch
segregation [ˌsegriˈgeiʃən]	Rassentrennung
effect [iˈfekt]	(Aus)Wirkung
Christian [ˈkristjən]	christlich
leadership [ˈli:dəʃip]	Führung, Führerschaft
disciple [diˈsaipl]	Anhänger, Jünger
non-violence [ˈvaiələns]	Gewaltlosigkeit
to involve [inˈvɔlv]	einbeziehen, hineinziehen
to turn	*hier:* hinhalten, darbieten
cheek [tʃi:k]	Wange
preacher [ˈpri:tʃə]	Prediger
champion [ˈtʃæmpjən]	(Vor)Kämpfer, Verfechter
to award [əˈwɔ:d]	zuerkennen, verleihen
Nobel Peace Prize [ˈnəubel]	Friedensnobelpreis

<Picture Text>

civil rights [ˈsivl]	Bürgerrechte

B. At the Doctor's

particulars [pəˈtikjuləz]	Personalien, Angaben
what's the trouble?	wo fehlt's denn?
a sore throat	eine Halsentzündung
to take one's temperature	Fieber messen

100 = 100° Fahrenheit	
pulse [pʌls]	Puls
inflamed [inˈfleimd]	entzündet
to gargle [ˈgɑ:gl]	gurgeln
prescription [prisˈkripʃən]	Rezept *(Arzt)*
chemist [ˈkemist]	Apotheker
gargle	Mittel zum Gurgeln, Mundwasser
foreigner [ˈfɔrinə]	Ausländer
to be entitled to [inˈtaitld]	Anspruch haben auf
surgery [ˈsə:dʒəri]	Sprechstunde, Sprechzimmer

<Boyhood on a Missouri Farm>

aversion to [əˈvə:ʃən]	Abscheu vor, Abneigung gegen
to be aware [əˈwɛə]	wissen
to arraign [əˈrein]	anklagen
in s.o.'s hearing [ˈhiəriŋ]	in jemandes Gegenwart
pulpit [ˈpulpit]	Kanzel
to approve [əˈpru:v]	billigen
holy [ˈhəuli]	heilig
doubter [ˈdautə]	Zweifler
Bible [ˈbaibl]	Bibel
to settle one's mind [ˈsetl]	sich beruhigen
to read [i:]	vorlesen
to make s.th. sure [ʃuə]	etwas klarstellen
Hannibal [ˈhænibəl]	*(Stadt am Mississippi, USA)*
to misuse [ˈmisˈju:z]	mißhandeln
a good deal [i:]	eine ganze Menge
sharp [ɑ:]	scharf
vivid [ˈvivid]	lebhaft, lebendig
shadowless [ˈʃædəulis]	schattenlos, *hier:* klar
slowdrifting [ˈsləudriftiŋ]	langsam dahintreibend
to hire [ˈhaiə]	mieten
halfway [ˈhɑ:fˈwei]	halb
cheery [ˈtʃiəri]	heiter
innocent [ˈinəsnt]	unschuldig
gentle [ˈdʒentl]	sanft
noisy [ˈnɔisi]	lärmend
creature [ˈkri:tʃə]	Geschöpf
to yell [e]	kreischen
to whoop [hu:p]	schreien, brüllen
maddening [ˈmædəniŋ]	zum Verrücktwerden
to devastate [ˈdevəsteit]	verheeren
unendurable [ˈʌninˈdjuərəbl]	unerträglich
to lose one's temper [ˈtempə]	die Geduld verlieren
Sandy [ˈsændi]	*(Kurzform für Alexander)*
to shut s.o. up	jemanden zum Schweigen bringen
tear [ˈtiə]	Träne
to tremble [ˈtrembl]	zittern
to comfort [ˈkʌmfət]	trösten
to bear [bɛə]	ertragen
thankful [ˈθæŋkful]	dankbar
friendless [ˈfrendlis]	verlassen
Mark Twain [ˈmɑ:k ˈtwein]	*(am. Schriftsteller, 1835–1910)*

<I, too, am America>

to sing [siŋ]	besingen, *(im Lied)* verherrlichen
besides [biˈsaidz]	außerdem
to be ashamed [əˈʃeimd]	sich schämen
Langston Hughes [ˈlæŋstən ˈhju:z]	*(am. Schriftsteller, 1902—67)*

Exercises

4. to break	zerreißen
5. context [ˈkɔntekst]	Zusammenhang
7. Atlanta [ətˈlæntə]	*(Hauptstadt des Staates Georgia, USA)*
Georgia [ˈdʒɔ:dʒiə]	*(Staat im Süden der USA)*
summary [ˈsʌməri]	Zusammenfassung

Vocabulary Revision: Fighting for Liberty and Independence

to be firmly under British rule	fest unter britischer Herrschaft sein
to gain control of a country	Macht über ein Land erlangen
to defeat a rival	einen Rivalen besiegen
to crush a rebellion	einen Aufstand niederwerfen
to organize strikes	Streiks organisieren
to protest against racial discrimination	gegen die Rassendiskriminierung protestieren
to devote oneself to the Independence Movement	sich der Unabhängigkeitsbewegung widmen
to fight by peaceful means	mit friedlichen Mitteln kämpfen
to avoid violence	Gewalt vermeiden
to support the struggle for freedom	den Kampf für die Freiheit unterstützen
to transfer power to a state	einem Staat Macht übertragen
to achieve an aim	ein Ziel erreichen
to discuss a plan of action	einen „Schlachtplan" diskutieren
to wait for the call of action	auf das Zeichen zum Aufbruch warten
to start a riot	einen Aufruhr starten
to jail s.o.	jemanden ins Gefängnis werfen
to break s.o.'s resistance	jemandes Widerstand brechen
to warn s.o. against s.th.	jemanden vor etwas warnen
to be on the alert	auf der Hut sein
The desire for freedom was steadily growing.	Der Wunsch nach Freiheit wuchs ständig.

15 A. The Space Race

space	Weltraum
1. baseball [ˈbeisbɔːl]	*(besonders in den USA verbreitetes Schlagballspiel)*
to take place	stattfinden
Milwaukee [milˈwɔːkiː]	*(Industrie- und Handelsstadt am Michigansee im N der USA)*
Yankee [ˈjæŋki]	*(Spitzname für „Amerikaner", besonders für Bewohner der Nordstaaten)*
topic [ˈtɔpik]	Thema
subway [ˈsʌbwei]	Untergrundbahn
embassy [ˈembəsi]	Botschaft
official	Beamter
announcement [əˈnaunsmənt]	Bekanntmachung, Ankündigung
satellite [ˈsætəlait]	(künstl.) (Erd)Satellit
outer space	Weltraum
man-made	vom Menschen gemacht
Sputnik [ˈsputnik]	*(Name des ersten künstlichen Erdsatelliten)*
inch [intʃ]	Zoll *(= 2,54 cm)*
diameter [daiˈæmitə]	Durchmesser
age	Zeitalter
front	Vorder-
2. challenge [ˈtʃælindʒ]	Herausforderung
to take up	*hier:* annehmen
Cape Canaveral [kəˈnævərəl]	*(Raketenversuchszentrum an der Ostküste Floridas, USA)*
Wernher v. Braun	*(in den USA lebender dt. Raketenspezialist, geb. 1912)*

to be ahead	voraus sein
Lunik [ˈlunik]	*(Name der Raumsonde)*
far side	andere Seite, *hier:* Rückseite
capsule [ˈkæpsju:l]	Kapsel
to recover	*hier:* bergen
to launch [lɔ:ntʃ]	(ab)schießen
3. exploration [ˌeksplɔ:ˈreiʃən]	(Er)Forschung
Columbus [kəˈlʌmbəs]	Kolumbus
far	bei weitem, wesentlich
to leave to chance	dem Zufall überlassen
to experience [iksˈpiəriəns]	kennenlernen
to withstand	widerstehen, aushalten
acceleration [ækˌseləˈreiʃən]	Beschleunigung
to read	ablesen
instrument [ˈinstrumənt]	Meßgerät, -instrument
weightlessness [ˈweitlisnis]	Schwerelosigkeit
gravity [ˈgræviti]	Schwerkraft
hold	Halt, *hier:* Gewalt
weightless	schwerelos
up and down	Oben und Unten
to overcome	überwinden
magnetic [mægˈnetik]	Magnet-, magnetisch
object	Gegenstand
guide-rope	Leitseil
liquid [ˈlikwid]	Flüssigkeit
food	Essen, Speise
pudding [ˈpudiŋ]	Pudding
to float [fləut]	schweben, treiben
nor [nɔ:]	auch nicht *(Satzanfang)*
lid [lid]	Deckel
to squeeze [skwi:z]	pressen, drücken
shortage (of) [ˈʃɔ:tidʒ]	Mangel (an)
field	(Fach)Gebiet
highly trained people	hochspezialisierte Fachkräfte
4. Yuri Gagarin [ˈjuəri gəˈgɑ:rin]	*(erster Astronaut; Sowjetunion)*
altitude [ˈæltitju:d]	Höhe
Moscow [ˈmɔskau]	Moskau
to witness [ˈwitnis]	Zeuge sein von
no sooner	kaum
astronaut [ˈæstrənɔ:t]	Astronaut
Alan B. Shepard [ˈælən ˈʃepəd]	*(erster am. Astronaut)*
Mercury [ˈmə:kjuri]	Merkur *(hier: Name der Raumkapsel)*
orbit [ˈɔ:bit]	Umlaufbahn, *hier:* Erdumkreisung
Soviet	sowjetisch
material [məˈtiəriəl]	Material
Conrad [ˈkɔnræd]	*(am. Astronaut)*
Cooper [ˈku:pə]	*(am. Astronaut)*
spacecraft [ˈspeiskrɑ:ft]	Raumfahrzeug
to detatch [diˈtætʃ]	sich loslösen
spaceman	Raumfahrer
to rejoin [riˈdʒɔin]	sich wieder vereinen

<Picture Text>

spacecraft [ˈspeiskrɑ:ft]	Raumschiff

<B. Walk in Space—A Dialogue>

Gemini 4 [ˈdʒemini]	*(Name der Raumkapsel)*
McDivitt [məkˈdivit]	*(am. Astronaut)*
White	*(am. Astronaut)*
communication	Verbindung
to look like	aussehen als ob
rotation [rəuˈteiʃən]	Drehbewegung
to get to work	sich an die Arbeit machen
get out in front	mach, daß du nach vorn kommst
to recontact [ˈri:kənˈtækt]	wieder Verbindung herstellen
spacecraft [krɑ:ft]	Raumschiff
thankful [ˈθʌŋkful]	dankbar
Ed	*(Kurzform für Edward)*
we're pointing ... to the ground ...	wir stehen nahezu Kopf

to blind [blaind]	blenden
to get back in	wieder hereinkommen
Bermuda [bəːˈmjuːdə]	Bermuda-Inseln *(im nördlichen Atlantischen Ozean)*
to get in	hineinbringen
second [ˈsekənd]	Sekunde

A Fight with a Shark

fight [ai]	Kampf
shark [ɑː]	Hai(fisch)
giant [ˈdʒaiənt]	Riesen-, riesig
terrific [təˈrifik]	schrecklich, fürchterlich
to fight [ai]	kämpfen gegen
harpoon [hɑːˈpuːn]	Harpune
fast [ɑː]	fest
to come on	herankommen
to close astern [əsˈtəːn]	sich von achtern nähern
to drive forward	*hier:* vorstoßen, sich hineinfressen
tail [ei]	Schwanz
blood-mushed [ˈblʌdˈmʌʃt]	blutig zermantscht
to drive [ai]	hineinstoßen
resolution [ˌrezəˈluːʃən]	Entschlußkraft
malignancy [məˈlignənsi]	Feindseligkeit
to swing over [swiŋ]	sich herumrollen
loop [uː]	Schlaufe, Schlinge
to come taut [tɔːt]	straff werden, sich straffen
to shiver [ˈʃivə]	erbeben
to snap [æ]	reißen
defeat [diˈfiːt]	Niederlage
though [ðəu]	trotzdem, aber doch *(am Satzende)*
cruel [kruəl]	grausam
Ernest Hemingway [ˈəːnist ˈhemiŋwei]	*(am. Schriftsteller, 1898–1961)*
abridged [əˈbridʒd]	gekürzt

Exercises

1. inversion [inˈvəːʃən]	Inversion *(sprachlich)*

16 A. UNO Fights Sickness and Starvation

UNO = United Nations Organization	
to fight	bekämpfen
1. destructive [disˈtrʌktiv]	zerstörend
tuberculosis (TB) [tjuːˌbəːkjuˈləusis]	Tuberkulose
quiet	*hier:* lautlos
Sachakhera [ˈsætʃəˈkɛərə]	*(Name eines Dorfes in Indien)*
tiny [ˈtaini]	winzig
near	nahe
nevertheless	nichtsdestoweniger
to listen to	zuhören, lauschen
attentive [əˈtentiv]	aufmerksam
blue-turbaned [ˈtəːbənd]	einen blauen Turban tragend
spread	Ausbreitung
to shade [ʃeid]	beschatten
to inoculate [iˈnɔkjuleit]	impfen
village leader	Dorfältester
youngsters [ˈjʌŋstəz]	Jungen; Kinder
to line up	sich in einer Reihe aufstellen
needle [niːdl]	Nadel
to test for	untersuchen (auf)
Asia [ˈeiʃə]	Asien
2. soil [sɔil]	Ackerland
completely	völlig
worthless	wertlos
to strike down	niederwerfen
malaria-carrying	Malaria übertragend
mosquito [məsˈkiːtəu]	Moskito
absolute [ˈæbsəluːt]	unumschränkt
acre [ˈeikə]	*(engl. Flächenmaß, 4047 qm)*
to envelop [inˈveləp]	einhüllen
headquarters [ˈhedˈkwɔːtəz]	Hauptquartier
deadly	tödlich
sting [stiŋ]	Stich, Stachel

to lay low	niederwerfen
to declare war on s.o.	jemandem den Krieg erklären
insect [ˈinsekt]	Insekt
to wipe out	vertilgen, ausrotten
operation [ˌɔpəˈreiʃən]	Unternehmen *(milit.)*
top priority [praiˈɔriti]	absoluter Vorrang
to set up	gründen, bauen
to affect [əˈfekt]	befallen
productive [prəˈdʌktiv]	ertragreich
to feed [fi:d]	ernähren
Himalayas [ˌhiməˈleiəz]	Himalaja
fertile [ˈfə:tail]	fruchtbar
swamp [swɔmp]	Sumpf
victim [ˈviktim]	Opfer
helicopter [ˈhelikɔptə]	Hubschrauber
ton [tʌn]	Tonne
fund [fʌnd]	Fond
underdeveloped	unterentwickelt
supplies	*hier:* Unterstützung
3. to industrialize [inˈdʌstriəlaiz]	industrialisieren
to till [til]	bestellen, pflügen
plough [plau]	Pflug
underfed [ˈʌndəˈfed]	unterernährt
to clothe [kləuð]	(be)kleiden
on an average	im Durchschnitt
life expectation	Lebenserwartung
in the long run	auf die Dauer
this is where	hier; an diesem Punkt
educational [ˌedju:ˈkeiʃənl]	Bildungs-
cultural [ˈkʌltʃərəl]	kulturell, Kultur-
to step in	eingreifen
adequate [ˈædikwit]	aus-, hinreichend
to finance [faiˈnæns]	finanzieren
foundation [faunˈdeiʃən]	Gründung
process [ˈprəuses]	Prozeß, Entwicklung
ignorance [ˈignərəns]	Unwissenheit

<Picture Text p. 91 and 93>

Thailand [ˈtailænd]	*(Königreich in Hinterindien)*
to provide [prəˈvaid]	besorgen

<Research Unlimited>

unlimited [ʌnˈlimitid]	uneingeschränkt, unbegrenzt
Dr. Peter Marshall [ˈmɑ:ʃəl]	*(Eigenname)*
chaplain [ˈtʃæplin]	Geistlicher
sermon [ˈsə:mən]	Predigt
invention [inˈvenʃən]	Erfindung
strides [ai]	*hier:* Fortschritte
to remember [riˈmembə]	sich erinnern an
mood [u:]	Stimmung
optimism [ˈɔptimizəm]	Optimismus
to mark [ɑ:]	kennzeichnen
decade [ˈdekeid]	Jahrzehnt
to perfect [pəˈfekt]	vervollkommnen
use [ju:s]	Verwendung(szweck), Gebrauch
electricity [ilekˈtrisiti]	Elektrizität
internal combustion engine [inˈtə:nl kəmˈbʌstʃən ˈendʒin]	Verbrennungsmotor
in prospect [ˈprɔspekt]	in Aussicht
lighting [ˈlaitiŋ]	Beleuchtung
home [əu]	Haushalts-
commonplace [ˈkɔmənpleis]	alltäglich
drama [ˈdrɑ:mə]	Schauspiel
advertising [ˈædvətaiziŋ]	Werbung
to take for granted [ˈgrɑ:ntid]	als selbstverständlich betrachten
to amaze [əˈmeiz]	in (Er)Staunen setzen
to whisk [wisk]	*hier:* im Nu bringen
motion picture [ˈməuʃən ˈpiktʃə]	Film
weekly [ˈwi:kli]	wöchentlich
diet [ˈdaiət]	Nahrung, Speise
electric eyes [iˈlektrik]	Photozellen
approach [əˈprəutʃ]	(Heran)Nahen
radar [ˈreidə]	Radar
to enable [iˈneibl]	es möglich machen
in the dark	im Dunkeln
penicillin [ˌpeniˈsilin]	Penicillin
sulfa drugs [ˈsʌlfədrʌgz]	Sulfonamide
to conquer [ˈkɔŋkə]	besiegen
many a	manch ein

germ [dʒə:m]	Krankheitserreger
vast [vɑ:st]	weit, ausgedehnt
all of this	all dies
convenience [kən'vi:njəns]	Annehmlichkeit
comfort ['kʌmfət]	Bequemlichkeit
complicated ['kɔmplikeitid]	kompliziert
troubled ['trʌbld]	beunruhigt
human ['hju:mən]	menschlich
spiritually ['spiritjuəli]	geistig
realm [relm]	Bereich
religion [ri'lidʒən]	Religion
to discard [dis'kɑ:d]	beiseite legen
high [ai]	hochfliegend
gift [i]	Gabe
to crash to the ground [kræʃ]	zusammenbrechen
realistic [riə'listik]	realistisch
insane ['in'sein]	wahnsinnig
corrupt [kə'rʌpt]	gewissenlos
widely ['waidli]	umfassend
to delve into [delv]	sich hineingraben
nuclear energy ['nju:kliə 'enədʒi]	Kernenergie
conscience-stricken ['kɔnʃəns 'strikən]	von Gewissensbissen geplagt
morals ['mɔrəlz]	Moral
ethics ['eθiks]	Ethik
character ['kæriktə]	Charakter
civilisation [,sivilai'zeiʃən]	Zivilisation
lying ['laiiŋ]	(das) Lügen
propaganda [,prɔpə'gændə]	Propaganda
selfishness ['selfiʃnis]	Selbstsucht
nationalism ['næʃnəlizəm]	Nationalismus
self-interest ['self'intrist]	Eigennutz
greed [i:]	Habgier
profit ['prɔfit]	Gewinn
licence ['laisəns]	Zügellosigkeit
to disguise [dis'gaiz]	verkleiden
materialism [mə'tiəriəlizəm]	Materialismus
hook [u]	Angelhaken
baited with security ['beitid wið si'kjuəriti]	mit dem Köder „Sicherheit" versehen
to confront [kən'frʌnt]	gegenüberstehen
to match [æ]	entsprechen, passen zu
researcher [ri'sə:tʃə]	Forscher
housed [hauzd]	untergebracht *(Haus, Wohnung)*
gadget ['gædʒit]	Gerät, Vorrichtung
undernourished ['ʌndə'nʌriʃt]	unterernährt
to neglect [ni'glekt]	hintansetzen
flabby ['flæbi]	matt, schlapp

<A Story for Discussion>

The Cigarette Lighter

to see s.o. off	jemanden *(der abreist)* begleiten *(zum Bahnhof usw.)*
Southampton platform [sauθ'æmptən]	Bahnsteig für den Zug nach Southampton
Waterloo Station ['wɔtəlu: 'steiʃən]	*(Bahnhof in London)*
for good	für immer
something for you to remember me by	etwas, um dich an mich zu erinnern
handsome ['hænsəm]	hübsch
generous ['dʒenərəs]	großzügig
on the high seas [si:z]	auf hoher See
store [ɔ:]	Kaufhaus
old chap [tʃæp]	„alter Knabe"
to finger ['fiŋgə]	berühren, befingern
price tag [tæg]	Preisschild
to come up	herbeikommen
detective [di'tektiv]	Detektiv
shoplifting ['ʃɔpliftiŋ]	Ladendiebstahl
to deal with a situation [di:l, ,sitju'eiʃən]	sich in einer Lage verhalten
to suggest [sə'dʒest]	vorschlagen
satisfaction [,sætis'fækʃən]	Zufriedenheit
to charge s.o. with s.th. [tʃɑ:dʒ]	jemanden einer Sache beschuldigen

Magistrates' Court [ˈmædʒistrits ˈkɔːt]	Friedensgericht	charge	Anklage
clerk [ɑː]	Gerichtsbeamter	on one's behalf [biˈhɑːf]	für jemanden

Vocabulary Revision: Fighting Disease

to be medically examined	ärztlich untersucht werden
to stop the spread of a disease	die Verbreitung einer Krankheit aufhalten
to have one's children inoculated	seine Kinder impfen lassen
to test s.o. for TB	jemanden auf Tbc untersuchen
to catch a disease	eine Krankheit bekommen
to be struck down by a disease	von einer Krankheit befallen sein
to be a victim of a disease	einer Krankheit zum Opfer fallen
to be protected against a disease	gegen eine Krankheit geschützt sein
to die of a disease	an einer Krankheit sterben
to recover from a disease	sich von einer Krankheit erholen
to fight sickness	gegen Krankheit kämpfen
to fight for better living conditions	für bessere Lebensbedingungen kämpfen
to be trained as a nurse	als Krankenschwester ausgebildet werden
to study medicine	Medizin studieren
a doctor's waiting-room	Wartezimmer
The next please.	Der Nächste bitte.
What's the trouble?	Wo fehlt's?
to have a bad cold	eine Erkältung haben
to take s.o.'s temperature	Fieber messen
to feel s.o.'s pulse	jemandem den Puls fühlen
to have an inflamed throat	eine Halsentzündung haben
to diagnose flu	Grippe feststellen
to write a prescription	ein Rezept schreiben
to gargle three times a day	dreimal täglich gurgeln
to be entitled to free treatment	Anspruch auf freie Behandlung haben
National Health Service	staatlicher Gesundheitsdienst
National Insurance	staatliche Sozialversicherung
Welfare State	Wohlfahrtsstaat

North America
Canada
USA
Hawaii
British Honduras
Jamaica
Guyana
South America
Pacific Ocean
Atlantic Ocean
Gambia
Sierra Leone

D1849577